Edexcel GCSE

advancing learning, changing lives

Spanish

Teacher's Guide

Tracy Traynor

Foundation

A PEARSON COMPANY

Published by Pearson Education Limited, a company incorporated in England and Wales, having its registered office at Edinburgh Gate, Harlow, Essex, CM20 2JE. Registered company number: 872828

www.pearsonschoolsandfecolleges.co.uk

Edexcel is a registered trade mark of Edexcel Limited

Text © Pearson Education Limited 2009

First published 2009

12 11 10 09 08

10 9 8 7 6 5 4 3 2 1

British Library Cataloguing in Publication Data
A catalogue record for this book is available from the British Library.

ISBN: 978 1 846903 94 6

Edited by Sara McKenna
Designed by Ken Vail Graphic Design
Typeset by Ken Vail Graphic Design
Original illustrations © Pearson Education Limited, 2009
Cover design by Wooden Ark studio
Cover illustration © Pearson Education Limited, 2009
Printed in the United Kingdom by Ashford Colour Press.

Acknowledgements
Every effort has been made to contact copyright holders of material reproduced in this book. Any omissions will be rectified in subsequent printings if notice is given to the publishers.

Websites
The websites used in this book were correct and up-to-date at the time of publication. It is essential for tutors to preview each website before using it in class so as to ensure that the URL is still accurate, relevant and appropriate. We suggest that tutors bookmark useful websites and consider enabling students to access them through the school/college intranet.

Disclaimer
This material has been published on behalf of Edexcel and offers high quality support for the delivery of Edexcel qualifications.

This does not mean that the material is essential to achieve any Edexcel qualification, nor does it mean that it is the only suitable material available to support any Edexcel qualification. No Edexcel material will be used verbatim in setting any Edexcel examination or assessment. Any resource lists produced by Edexcel shall include this and other appropriate resources.

Copies of official specifications for all Edexcel qualifications may be found on the Edexcel website – www.edexcel.com

Important notice
This software is suitable for use on PCs only. It will not run on a Mac.

If the CD is loaded into a CD drive on a PC it should autorun automatically. If it does not, please click on RB.exe (D:product_name_here/RB.exe).

Active content
Your browser security may initially try to block elements of this product. If this problem occurs, please refer to the Troubleshooting document which can be found in the root of this CD
(D: product_name_here /Troubleshooting.doc).

Installation instructions
This product may be installed to your local hard drive or to the network. Further instructions on how to do this are available from the main menu.

VLE Pack
The root of this CD contains the content from this product as a zipped SCORM 1.2 Content Pack to allow for convenient uploading to your VLE.

Please follow the usual instructions specific to your VLE system to upload this content pack.

For Mac users
This CD does not run on a Mac.

Contents

Introduction

Edexcel GCSE Spanish provides complete preparation for the new GCSE specification.

The course offers a lively, communicative approach, underpinned by a clear grammatical progression. It consists of differentiated materials to meet the needs of a wide ability range. It is designed to continue from either *Mira 1, 2* and *3* or *Mira Express 1* and *2* but it is also suitable for students who have followed a different course at Key Stage 3.

Edexcel GCSE Spanish exists in two different versions, each of which is differentiated to match the requirements and provide complete coverage of the new GCSE specification as follows:

Edexcel GCSE Spanish Higher (GCSE Grades A*–C)
Edexcel GCSE Spanish Foundation (GCSE Grades C–G)

Edexcel GCSE Spanish: components

Student Book	1 Higher 1 Foundation
Audio CDs (× 5)	1 set of CDs for Higher 1 set of CDs for Foundation
Workbook	1 Workbook for Higher 1 Workbook for Foundation
Teacher's Guide and Teacher's Guide CD-Rom (included at the back)	1 Higher 1 Foundation
Assessment Pack	1 pack covering both Higher and Foundation
ActiveTeach	The whiteboard resource, covering both Higher and Foundation

Student Book

The Student Book is designed to last for two years and contains all the language required for the preparation of the GCSE examination.

There are nine modules. It is expected that Modules 1–5 will be completed in the first year of the course and Modules 6–9 in the second.

Audio CDs

There are five CDs. They contain listening material for both presentation and practice. The material includes texts, dialogues and interviews, all recorded using native speakers.

Workbook (*Cuaderno Verde*)

The Workbook provides self-access reading and writing tasks, which are ideal for homework, reinforcement, self-study or for cover lessons. There is one page or one double-page spread in the Workbook for each spread of the Student Book.

At the end of each module there is a page of grammar revision and a two-page *Palabras* section (as given in the Student Book), to be used for reference and revision. All Workbook pages are referred to at the end of the appropriate unit in the Teacher's Guide, with solutions to the activities.

Teacher's Guide

The Teacher's Guide contains:

- overview grids for each module
- clear teaching notes for all activities
- full transcripts of the recorded material
- solutions for Student Book and Workbook activities
- suggestions for reinforcement and extension activities
- suggestions for ICT activities.

The Teacher's Guide CD-Rom accompanying the Teacher's Guide provides:

- separate, customisable Schemes of Work for the specification
- matching grids showing the links between the specification and the Student Book. This information is presented in two different ways: first by topic/theme/context and then unit by unit for each module of the book.

Assessment Pack

The Assessment Pack covers both Higher and Foundation Student Books and has been written by an experienced examiner. The types of questions follow the examination board papers and give much-needed practice in developing examination skills.

There are three short tests which are designed to be used in the middle of each year of the course. The long test is designed to be used towards the end of the first year of the course. Depending on when Module 5 is covered, the mini-test can be used during the second year of the course, or can be combined with the long test to create a comprehensive end-of-first-year test.

The Assessment Pack includes the following important features:

- Listening and Reading tests have clear and concise mark schemes
- extra Speaking and Writing assessment tasks are provided to use or adapt
- Speaking assessments have pages for students and for teachers
- Rubrics reflect the language used by the examining bodies, familiarising students with GCSE-style questions throughout Years 10 and 11.

ActiveTeach

ActiveTeach is an interactive whiteboard resource that allows you to flick through the pages of the Student Book and access support resources, making front-of-class teaching more engaging.

With ActiveTeach you can

- display any page of the Student Book on the whiteboard
- zoom in on key texts, pictures and boxes
- open ready-made grids to record answers
- play the audio for the activities and see the audioscripts.

You can also

- access *Edexcel GCSE Spanish* videos
- download the audio files of the *Palabras* lists
- access additional interactive grammar activities
- look at graded examples of the writing assessment in the style of the exam board
- access tips and advice on preparing for exams in the Exam Zone.

How the course works

Progression

The first one or two double-page spreads of each module (*Repaso*) are devoted to language that should already be familiar to students from Key Stage 3. In later modules they also contain a small number of items and grammatical structures that have been taught in earlier modules in *Edexcel GCSE Spanish*. The rest of the units continue to revise earlier material and introduce new grammar and structures. The level increases from the beginning to the end of each module ensuring a steady progression.

As well as clear progression within each module, language is constantly recycled throughout the book in a systematic spiral of revision and extension. What is covered is clearly shown in the Teacher's Guide, in the planning summary at the beginning of each module, to help teachers plan sequences of lessons appropriate for the ability group they teach.

Core units

In each module, the *Repaso* unit is followed by three, four or five core units.

The objectives for these units are clearly listed at the top of the page in the Student Book. They consist of two objectives, usually covering the topic **content** and the **grammar** in the unit.

Grammar boxes

The key structures introduced in a unit and reminders of grammar points previously introduced are presented in grammar boxes, providing support for speaking and writing activities. Grammar boxes contain page references

to the *Gramática* section at the back of the Student Book, where the structures are explained and practised more fully.

Lesson starters and plenaries

For all of the units in the Student Book there are two lesson starters (the first at the beginning and the second approximately half-way through, where a second lesson is likely to begin) and a plenary suggested in the Teacher's Guide.

- The starters are simple activities that allow students to review previous knowledge and prepare for new language to be learnt in the unit. They are designed to get the lesson off to a brisk start, focusing students' attention and promoting engagement and challenge.
- The plenaries aim to draw out the learning points and actively involve students. They encourage them to explain and demonstrate what they have learnt in the lesson and to identify links between what they have learnt so far and what they will learn later.

Skills and strategies

Tip boxes appear throughout *Edexcel GCSE Spanish* to help students improve their language-learning skills and to equip them with strategies that will enhance their performance in the examination. These are easily recognised by the tip box symbol ✪. This symbol is also used in the *Prueba oral* and *Prueba escrita* units to identify targeted activities which will help improve exam performance.

Further support

Te toca a ti

At the back of the Student Book is the *Te toca a ti* section. This provides a double-page spread of further reading and writing practice for each module, supplying a variety of types of 'authentic' texts to work on. These pages are ideal for independent work or for cover lessons.

Reference material

The Student Book also contains essential reference material:

- *Palabras:* at the end of each module there is a summary of the vocabulary and phrases covered, arranged by topic. This will serve as a valuable revision tool and is also replicated in the Workbook.
- *Gramática:* at the end of the Student Book, the grammar section explains the grammar points introduced in the Student Book in more detail and includes exercises to give active practice in some of the more important points.
- Also at the end of the Student Book is the *Vocabulario*, a comprehensive Spanish–English wordlist, and a shorter English–Spanish wordlist.

Incorporating ICT

Appropriate use of Information and Communication Technology (ICT) to support modern foreign language learning is a requirement of the National Curriculum.

Suggestions of ICT activities (word-processing, using email, video-conferencing, researching on the internet, etc.) have been included in the Teacher's Guide and are indicated by ⌦.

Grammar coverage

Grammar is fully integrated into the teaching sequence in *Edexcel GCSE Spanish,* to ensure that the students have the opportunity to learn thoroughly the underlying structures of the Spanish language. Most units have a grammar objective so that students can clearly see which grammar structures they are learning. The key grammar points are presented in the grammar boxes on the Student Book pages, and fuller explanations and practice activities are provided in the *Gramática* section at the end of the Student Book.

In addition, there are pages at the end of each chapter in the Foundation Workbook which focus on grammar.

All the grammar necessary for the GCSE is covered in the Student Book:

1 Nouns and pronouns
Gender
Singular/Plural
Definite and indefinite article
lo plus adjective
Subject pronouns
Object pronouns
Relative pronouns: *que, donde, cuando*
Disjunctive pronouns: *conmigo, para mí*
Indefinite pronouns: *algo*
Interrogative pronouns: *cuál, qué, quién, cómo, dónde*

2 Adjectives and adverbs
Position of adjectives
Agreement of adjectives
Comparatives and superlatives
Demonstrative adjectives: *este, esta, estos, estas*
Possessive adjectives
Adverbs

3 Verbs
The infinitive
Present tense
Present continuous tense
Preterite
Imperfect tense
Near future tense
Future tense
Perfect tense
Conditional
Negatives
Questions forms
Reflexive verbs

4 Structural features
Prepositions
Question words
Qualifiers
Connectives
desde hace

5 Extras
Numbers
Days
Dates
Times

Controlled assessments and exam preparation

Every module in the Student Book includes *Prueba oral* and *Prueba escrita* units to help prepare students for the Speaking and Writing controlled assessment sections of the exam. They take the students step-by-step through the process of preparing for controlled assessments, with clear tips and advice from examiners on how they can build up skills and improve their grades.

Leer y escuchar are units dedicated to listening and reading, to help prepare students for the exams. The activities are designed to enable them to become familiar with and to practise answering questions in the style of the final examination, with tips to improve their skills and aim for higher grades.

Coverage of Edexcel themes and topic areas in *Prueba oral, Prueba escrita* and *Leer y escuchar* units

Module 1 De vacaciones	Edexcel themes (Speaking/Writing)	Edexcel topic area (Listening/Reading)
Prueba oral – discussion (pp. 16–17)	**Travel and tourism** Holidays Accommodation	**Out and about** Basic weather Accommodation
Prueba escrita (pp. 18–19)	**Travel and tourism** Holidays Accommodation	**Out and about** Basic weather Accommodation
Module 2 De paseo por Sevilla	**Edexcel themes (Speaking/Writing)**	**Edexcel topic area (Listening/Reading)**
Prueba oral – interaction (pp. 36–37)	**Travel and tourism** Holidays Eating, food, drink	**Out and about** Visitor information Local amenities Accommodation Public transport Directions
Prueba escrita (pp. 38–39)	**Travel and tourism** Holidays	**Out and about** Visitor information
Leer y escuchar (Modules 1–2) (pp. 40–41)	**Travel and tourism** Holidays	**Out and about** Visitor information Basic weather Local amenities
Module 3 A clase	**Edexcel themes (Speaking/Writing)**	**Edexcel topic area (Listening/Reading)**
Prueba oral – presentation (pp. 56–57)		**Future plans, education and work** School and college
Prueba escrita (pp. 58–59)		**Future plans, education and work** School and college
Module 4 ¡Perdidos!	**Edexcel themes (Speaking/Writing)**	**Edexcel topic area (Listening/Reading)**
Prueba oral – discussion (pp. 74–75)	**Travel and tourism** Holidays	**Out and about** Visitor information **Personal information** Family and friends
Prueba escrita (pp. 76–77)		**Personal information** Family and friends
Leer y escuchar (Modules 3–4) (pp. 78–79)	**Sport and leisure** Lifestyle choices	**Personal information** Family and friends **Future plans, education and work** School and college
Module 5 Los trabajos	**Edexcel themes (Speaking/Writing)**	**Edexcel topic area (Listening/Reading)**
Prueba oral – interaction (pp. 94–95)	**Sport and leisure** Hobbies/interests Sporting events **Business, work and employment** Work experience/part-time jobs	**Personal information** General interests Leisure activities **Future plans, education and work** Simple job applications and CV Work and work experience
Prueba escrita (pp. 96–97)	**Business, work and employment** Work experience/part-time jobs	**Future plans, education and work** Work and work experience

continued

Module 6 Mi tiempo libre	Edexcel themes (Speaking/Writing)	Edexcel topic area (Listening/Reading)
Prueba oral – presentation (pp. 114–115)	**Sport and leisure** Hobbies/interests	**Personal information** Leisure activities
Prueba escrita (pp. 116–117)	**Media and culture** Music/film/reading Fashion/celebrities/religion Blogs/internet	**Personal information** General interests Leisure activities
Leer y escuchar (Modules 5–6) (pp. 118–119)	**Media and culture** Music/film/reading **Sport and leisure** Hobbies/interests Lifestyle choices **Business, work and employment** Work experience/part-time jobs	**Personal information** General interests Leisure activities
Module 7 ¡Viva mi barrio!	**Edexcel themes (Speaking/Writing)**	**Edexcel topic area (Listening/Reading)**
Prueba oral – interaction (pp. 132–133)	**Media and culture** Fashion/celebrities/religion	**Out and about** Local amenities Accommodation
Prueba escrita (pp. 134–135)	**Media and culture** Fashion/celebrities/religion	**Out and about** Local amenities Accommodation
Module 8 La salud	**Edexcel themes (Speaking/Writing)**	**Edexcel topic area (Listening/Reading)**
Prueba oral – discussion (pp. 148–149)	**Sport and leisure** Lifestyle choices	**Personal information** Lifestyle (healthy eating and exercise)
Prueba escrita (pp. 150–151)	**Sport and leisure** Lifestyle choices	**Personal information** Lifestyle (healthy eating and exercise)
Leer y escuchar (Modules 7–8) (pp. 152–153)	**Sport and leisure** Lifestyle choices	**Out and about** Local amenities Accommodation **Personal information** Lifestyle (healthy eating and exercise)
Module 9 Nuestro planeta	**Edexcel themes (Speaking/Writing)**	**Edexcel topic area (Listening/Reading)**
Prueba oral – presentation (pp. 164–165)	**Sport and leisure** Lifestyle choices	
Prueba escrita (pp. 166–167)	**Sport and leisure** Lifestyle choices	
Leer y escuchar (Module 9) (pp. 168–169)	**Sport and leisure** Lifestyle choices	

Coverage of themes and topic areas by Edexcel GCSE Spanish

R = *Repaso*; U = Unit ; PO = *Prueba oral*; PE = *Prueba escrita*; LE = *Leer y escuchar*

EDEXCEL THEMES (Speaking/Writing)

Edexcel theme	Module and unit	Pages
Media and culture		
Music/film/reading	M6 R1, M6 R2, M6 U4, M6 PE, M6 LE	100–103, 110–111, 116–119
Fashion/celebrities/religion	M6 PE M7 U3, M7 U4, M7 PO, M7 PE	116–117 128–135
Blogs/internet	M6 U5, M6 PE	112–113, 116–117
Sport and leisure		
Hobbies/interests	M2 R1 M5 PO M6 R1, M6 R2, M6 U1, M6 U3, M6 PO, M6 LE	22–23 94–95 100–105, 108–109, 114–115, 118–119
Sporting events	M5 PO M6 U2	94–95 106–107
Lifestyle choices	M4 U1, M4 LE M6 LE M8 U1, M8 U2, M8 U3, M8 PO, M8 PE, M8 LE M9 R, M9 U1, M9 U2, M9 PO, M9 PE, M9 LE	64–65, 78–79 118–119 142–153 156–161, 164–169
Travel and tourism		
Holidays	M1 R, M1 U1, M1 U2, M1 PO, M1 PE M2 R1, M2 R2, M2 U1, M2 U2, M2 U4, M2 U5, M2 PO, M2 PE, M2 LE M4 PO	6–11, 16–19 22–29, 32–41 74–75
Accommodation	M1 U2, M1 U3, M1 U4, M1 PO, M1 PE	10–19
Eating, food, drink	M2 U3, M2 U4, M2 PO	30–33, 36–37
Business, work and employment		
Work experience/part-time jobs	M5 whole module M6 LE	82–97 118–119
Product or service information	M8 R2	140–141

continued

EDEXCEL TOPIC AREAS (Listening/Reading)

Edexcel topic area	Module and unit	Pages
Out and about		
Visitor information	M2 U1, M2 U4, M2 U5, M2 PO, M2 PE, M2 LE	26–27, 32–41
	M4 PO	74–75
Basic weather	M1 U1, M1 PO, M1 PE	8–9, 16–19
	M2 R1, M2 LE	22–23, 40–41
Local amenities	M2 PO, M2 LE	36–37, 40–41
	M7 U2, M7 PO, M7 PE	126–127, 132–135
	M8 LE	152–153
Accommodation	M1 U1, M1 U2, M1 U3, M1 U4, M1 PO, M1 PE	8–19
	M2 PO	36–37
	M7 R, M7 U1, M7 PO, M7 PE	122–125, 132–135
	M8 LE	152–153
Public transport	M2 R2, M2 PO	24–25, 36–37
	M3 R2	46–47
Directions	M2 U2, M2 PO	28–29, 36–37
Customer service and transactions		
Cafés and restaurants	M2 U3	30–31
Shops	M2 U2	28–29
	M7 U3, M7 U4	128–131
	M8 R2	140–141
Dealing with problems	M1 U4	14–15
	M7 U4	130–131
Personal information		
General interests	M2 R1	22–23
	M5 PO	94–95
	M6 R1, M6 R2, M6 U1, M6 U3, M6 U4, M6 PE, M6 LE	100–105, 108–111, 116–119
Leisure activities	M1 R, M1 U1, M1 U2	6–11
	M2 R1	22–23
	M5 PO	94–95
	M6 R1, M6 R2, M6 U1, M6 U3, M6 PO, M6 PE, M6 LE	100–105, 108–109, 114–119
Family and friends	M4 R, M4 U1, M4 U4, M4 U5, M4 PO, M4 PE, M4 LE	62–65, 70–79
	M6 U3	108–109
Lifestyle (healthy eating and exercise)	M8 U1, M8 U2, M8 U3, M8 PO, M8 PE, M8 LE	142–153
Future plans, education and work		
Basic language of the internet	M6 U5	112–113
Simple job advertisements	M5 U4	90–91
Simple job applications and CV	M5 U4, M5 U5, M5 PO	90–95
School and college	M3 whole module	44–59
	M4 LE	78–79
Work and work experience	M4 U1, M4 U5	64–65, 72–73
	M5 whole module	82–97
	M9 U2	160–161

Personal Learning and Thinking Skills

The activities and contexts provided throughout the course offer a range of opportunities for students to apply skills from the six groups of the Personal Learning and Thinking Skills framework.

Examples of activities to help students achieve the outcomes associated with these generic skills are identified in the customisable Scheme of Work.

Personal Learning and Thinking skills	Examples in Edexcel GCSE Spanish
1 Independent enquirers	Student Book activities throughout the course (e.g. M8 U3 ex. 5); ICT-based activities (e.g. M3 Repaso 1 ICT suggestion after ex. 6, Teacher's Guide page 61)
2 Creative thinkers	Regular activities developing skills strategies (how to improve listening/speaking, etc.) (e.g. M1 Repaso ex. 3 + tip box); Starters requiring students to apply logic and make connections (e.g. M8 U3 Starter 2, Teacher's Guide page 185); Prueba activities to develop anticipation skills in exam contexts (e.g. M2 Prueba oral ex. 2)
3 Reflective learners	Ongoing opportunities to assess work and identify areas for improvement (M1 U2 ex. 6 + tip box), including all Pruebas and Plenaries (e.g. M9 U3 Plenary, Teacher's Guide page 205)
4 Team workers	Regular pair work activities (M6 U1 ex. 2), including many Starters; regular peer assessment, including controlled assessment peer work (e.g. M1 Prueba oral ex. 4); links with partner schools (M2 Repaso 1 ICT suggestion after ex. 6, Teacher's Guide page 33)
5 Self-managers	Ongoing advice on managing learning (e.g. M9 U1 Plenary, Teacher's Guide page 199), including strategies to improve learning (e.g. M4 U4 ex. 1 + tip box) and exam performance (e.g. M5 Prueba oral)
6 Effective participators	Opportunities throughout the course for students to contribute (e.g. M9 U2 ex. 7 and ICT suggestion which follows, Teacher's Guide page 202), including presentations (e.g. M6 U2 ex. 3) and all Plenaries (e.g. M3 U3 Plenary, Teacher's Guide page 72)

Module 1 De vacaciones (Student Book pages 6–21)

Unit	Main topics and objectives	Grammar	Skills
Repaso ¿Adónde fuiste? (pp. 6–7)	• Talking about where you went on holiday • Using the preterite	The preterite (regular verbs, **ir/ser**)	Extending sentences with sequencers **(primero... luego...)**
1 ¿Qué tal tus vacaciones? (pp. 8–9)	• Talking about holidays and weather • Using irregular verbs in the preterite	The preterite (irregular verbs)	Learning phrases meaning the same thing Listening out for negatives Improving writing
2 Vacaciones para todos (pp. 10–11)	• Describing accommodation • Using the imperfect tense for description	The imperfect tense	Identifying positive and negative opinions Including opinions and justifications Adapting model texts
3 En el hotel (pp. 12–13)	• Booking a hotel room • Using verbs with **usted**	Using verbs with **usted**	Using **usted** appropriately
4 Reclamaciones (pp. 14–15)	• Making complaints in a hotel • Using **me hace falta**	Using **me hace(n) falta**	Using reading strategies: cognates and context
Prueba oral: Holidays (pp. 16–17)	Exam speaking practice	Revision	
Prueba escrita (pp. 18–19)	Exam writing practice	Revision	
Te toca a ti (pp. 172–173)	Self-access reading and writing		

1 Repaso *¿Adónde fuiste?* (Student Book pages 6–7)

Main topics and objectives

- Talking about where you went on holiday
- Using the preterite

Grammar

- Using the preterite

Key language

¿Cuándo fuiste de vacaciones?
el año/verano/invierno pasado
hace (dos) años

¿Adónde fuiste de vacaciones?
Fui a…

Grecia
Estados Unidos
Francia
la República Dominicana
la India
Argentina
España

¿Con quién fuiste?
Fui con mi familia/mis padres/
* mis amigos.*
solo/a

¿Qué hiciste?
Escuché música.
Tomé el sol.
Fui de excursión.

Visité monumentos.
Mandé mensajes.
Esquié.
Bailé.
Jugué al voleibol.
Monté en bicicleta.
Saqué fotos.

¿Qué tal lo pasaste?
Lo pasé mal/fenomenal/genial/
* bien/regular.*

Resources

CD 1, track 2
Cuaderno Verde, page 3
Gramática 196

Starter 1

To revise the preterite

Write up the following, jumbling the order of the second column. Give students three minutes to match the sentence halves.

Escucho	*música.*
Mandé	*mensajes.*
Jugué	*al voleibol.*
Tomo	*el sol.*
Visito	*monumentos.*
Fui	*de excursión.*

Check answers, asking students to translate the completed sentences into English and to identify the tense used in each one.

1 Escucha y escribe las letras correctas. (1–5)

Listening. Students listen to five conversations about holidays and identify the correct five answers for each one (from the phrases/labelled pictures **a–y**). For every speaker there is one correct answer from each column.

Audioscript *Track 2*

1 – *¿Cuándo fuiste de vacaciones?*
  – *Fui de vacaciones el verano pasado.*
  – *¿Adónde fuiste de vacaciones?*
  – *A la República Dominicana.*
  – *¿Con quién fuiste?*
  – *Fui sola.*
  – *¿Qué hiciste?*
  – *Escuché música y tomé el sol.*
  – *¿Qué tal lo pasaste?*
  – *Lo pasé genial.*
2 – *A ver… hace dos años fui a Grecia con mis amigos. Bailé y jugué al voleibol en la playa. Lo pasé mal. Fue un poco aburrido.*

3 – *El invierno pasado fui a Francia con mis padres. Mandé mensajes y esquié en las montañas. Lo pasé fenomenal.*
4 – *¿Cuándo fuiste de vacaciones?*
  – *El año pasado fui a la India.*
  – *¿Con quién fuiste?*
  – *Fui solo.*
  – *¿Qué hiciste?*
  – *A ver… monté en bicicleta y saqué muchas fotos.*
  – *¿Qué tal lo pasaste?*
  – *Lo pasé regular.*
5 – *Hace cinco años fui de vacaciones a Estados Unidos con mi familia. Fui de excursión y visité monumentos. Lo pasé bien.*

Answers

1 *b, i,* o, p, w
2 d, f, k, s, u
3 c, h, l, r, v
4 a, j, n, t, y
5 e, g, m, q, x

G Grammar

Use the Grammar box to review the preterite. It gives the endings for regular verbs (using **escuchar**, **comer** and **salir**) and the irregular verbs **ir** and **ser**. It also shows the spelling changes in verbs ending in **-gar** and **-car**.

Ask students if they can identify any patterns that will help them remember preterite forms (**-er/-ir** verbs have the same endings; the 'we' form of **-ar** verbs is the same in the present and the preterite). Also ask how they would know whether **ir** or **ser** was intended, giving examples as necessary to show that they should use the context to work it out.

R Students write out the preterite singular forms of **tomar, beber** and **compartir**.

✚ Students work in pairs, taking it in turn to prompt in English using one of the verbs in the Grammar box (e.g. *she ate*) and to respond with the preterite form in Spanish.

Starter 2

To distinguish between present and preterite verb forms (singular)

Write up the following blank grid and list of verbs, jumbling the order of the verbs (shown here under the appropriate column for reference). Give students 2 minutes to group the verbs in the correct column.

Present	Preterite

vas	*pasaste*
bailas	*navegué*
habla	*escuchó*
escucho	*bailé*
escucha	*chateó*
estás	*escribiste*
	fui

Check answers, asking students to translate each verb.

2 What did David do on holiday? Write down the four correct letters.

Reading. Students read the text and identify the four things David did on holiday (from **a–h**).

Answers
b, h, e, d

3 Look at the photos below and imagine one of the holidays in detail. Then have a conversation about it with your partner.

Speaking. In pairs: students choose and discuss one of the holidays pictured. They take it in turn to ask and answer questions. The questions and answer openings are supplied.

⭐ **ResultsPlus**

Tip box on adding detail using sequencers.

Results Plus tip boxes are included throughout the Student Book to give advice on improving speaking and writing performance in the exam.

4 Escribe un correo sobre tus vacaciones. Utiliza las frases siguientes.

Writing. Students write an email about their own holidays, using the expressions supplied.

⭐ **ResultsPlus**

🖱 If your pupils have regular access to a computer, they could create their own vocabulary notebook on computer using Word or Excel or a DTP package. Again, encourage them to think about different ways of organising vocabulary (topic, gender, type of word, etc.) to help them remember it. Suggest using colours as a way of identifying gender (e.g. always using blue for masculine words and pink for feminine, etc.); they may be able to picture the colour when they are trying to remember the gender of a word.

They could also save and print out edited lists of vocabulary, with either the English or Spanish missing, to test themselves/each other.

Plenary

Review how the preterite is formed. Either challenge the class to come up with 12 verbs used in the unit in the 'I' and 'he/she' forms, or write up the stems for three regular verbs and have students in turn supply the ending for each form ('I', 'you', 'he/she').

Cuaderno Verde, page 3

1

Answers

f	u	x	m	s	j	a	i	c
u	o	e	s	c	u	c	h	é
i	t	q	e	r	g	f	s	n
p	c	s	a	q	u	é	l	m
v	b	a	i	l	é	o	m	a
b	n	l	m	t	l	c	b	n
e	u	í	a	t	e	v	f	d
t	q	ó	r	c	o	m	í	é

1 *I listened – escuché*   **2** I sent – mandé
3 I went out – salí   **4** I ate – comí
5 I went – fui   **6** I played – jugué
7 I took (photos) – saqué   **8** I danced – bailé

2

Answers

(e) *El verano pasado fui a* **(c)** Granada de vacaciones. Fui **(g)** sola. Primero fui a la ciudad por la **(d)** mañana y visité muchos **(a)** monumentos y también saqué **(f)** fotos. Luego fui a la montaña. Esquié **(b)** por la tarde. ¡Lo pasé genial!

1 ¿Qué tal tus vacaciones? (Student Book pages 8–9)

Main topics and objectives

- Talking about holidays and weather
- Using irregular verbs in the preterite

Grammar

- The preterite (irregular verbs)

Key language

Descansé.
Nadé.
Hice yoga.
Di una vuelta en bicicleta.
Vi lugares de interés.
Monté a caballo.
Patiné.
Esquié.
Hice alpinismo.
¡No tuve miedo!
Hice vela.

¡Lo pasé genial!
¡Lo pasé bien!
¡Lo pasé bastante bien!
¡Fue regular!
¡Fue un poco aburrido!
¡No me gustó nada!

¿Qué tiempo hizo?
Hizo buen tiempo.
Hizo mal tiempo.
Hizo calor.
Hizo frío.
Hizo sol.
Hizo viento.
Hubo niebla.
Hubo tormenta.
Llovió.
Nevó.

Resources

CD 1, tracks 3–5
Cuaderno Verde, pages 4–5
Gramática 196

Starter 1

To review the preterite (regular verbs)

Write up the following. Give students 3 minutes to work out what goes in the blank boxes.

pagar	comer	abrir	nadar	beber	escribir
pagué	comí				escribí
		abriste	nadaste	bebiste	
pagó		abrió		bebió	

Check answers, asking students to summarise the preterite endings in the singular for each verb group.

1 Escucha y escribe la letra correcta. (1–10)

Listening. Students listen to two people talking about what they did on holiday. For each statement, they note the letter of the correct picture: the first speaker's activities are from pictures **a–e** and the second speaker's from **f–j**.

Audioscript *Track 3*

1 Descansé en la playa. ¡Fue regular!
2 Hice yoga. Fue un poco aburrido.
3 Di una vuelta en bicicleta. ¡Lo pasé bastante bien!
4 Nadé en el mar. ¡No me gustó nada!
5 Vi lugares de interés. ¡Lo pasé genial!
6 Hice alpinismo. ¡Lo pasé genial y no tuve miedo!
7 Esquié. ¡Fue regular!
8 Patiné en la pista de hielo. ¡No me gustó nada!
9 Hice vela en el mar. ¡Lo pasé bastante bien!
10 Monté a caballo. ¡Fue un poco aburrido!

Answers

1 *a* **2** c **3** d **4** b **5** e **6** i **7** h **8** g **9** j **10** f

⭐ ResultsPlus

Tip box on expressions which aren't translated word for word.

2 Escucha otra vez y escribe la letra correcta. (1–10)

Listening. Students listen to the exercise 1 recording again and note the opinion given on each activity (from **a–f**).

Audioscript *Track 4*

As exercise 1.

Answers

1 *d* **2** e **3** c **4** f **5** a **6** a **7** d **8** f **9** c **10** e

G Grammar

Use the Grammar box to review/introduce the preterite forms of the irregular verbs **hacer, tener, ver** and **dar** in the singular.

R Students work in pairs to identify patterns in the verbs which will help them remember them.

⭐ ResultsPlus

Tip box on recognising and noting paraphrases.

3 Match up the sentences which mean the same thing.

Reading. Students read the tip box on paraphrases, then match each of sentences **1–4** with a sentence from **a–d** that has the same meaning.

Answers

1 b **2** c **3** a **4** d

Starter 2

To review weather vocabulary and time expressions.

Write up the following. Give students 3 minutes to translate into English.

1 *Ayer hizo… buen tiempo/frío/sol/viento/mal tiempo/calor.*
2 *El invierno pasado… llovió/nevó.*
3 *Hace dos meses hubo… niebla/tormenta.*

Check answers. If students have struggled to remember the vocabulary, remind them of strategies for working out unknown words, e.g. context, cognates, educated guesses.

4 Escucha. Copia y completa la tabla en inglés. (1–6)

Listening. Students copy out the table. They then listen to five people talking about their holidays and complete the table with the details in English. You could play the recording twice to allow the students to focus on different aspects: the weather and activities the first time and opinions the second time.

Audioscript *Track 5*

1 *Hizo calor e hicimos alpinismo todos los días. Lo pasamos genial. Fue estupendo.*
2 *Hizo buen tiempo e hice equitación. Lo pasé bien – fue interesante.*
3 *No llovió, pero hizo frío. Monté en bicicleta y lo pasé mal.*
4 *Hizo sol y mucho calor también. Hice natación y lo pasé muy bien – fue estupendo.*
5 *No hizo viento y di una vuelta en bicicleta. ¡Lo pasé genial – fue divertido!*
6 *Hubo una tormenta gigantesca. Fui a la piscina a nadar y fue un poco aburrido.*

Answers

	weather	activity	opinion
1	*hot*	*climbing*	*brilliant*
2	nice weather	horse-riding	good
3	no rain but cold	cycling	rubbish
4	hot and sunny	swimming	very good
5	no wind	cycling	brilliant
6	big storm	swimming	boring

✪ ResultsPlus

Tip box on listening out for negatives.

5 Lee los textos y contesta a las preguntas.

Reading. Students read the two texts, then answer each of the *Who…?* questions (**1–8**).

Answers

1 Alicia   2 Alicia   3 José   4 José   5 Alicia
6 José   7 Alicia   8 José

6 Escribe un texto sobre tus vacaciones. Contesta a las preguntas en español.

Writing. Students write a short text on their holidays. Questions are supplied to help them identify what to include. Sample openings are supplied for support.

✪ ResultsPlus

Tip box on improving writing: including time expressions, sequencers, connectives and opinions.

Plenary

Ask the class to summarise how the preterite is used.

Use ActiveTeach to display the texts in exercise 5 on p. 9. Ask students to identify and translate into English each preterite form. Alternatively, ask students to look at the texts in their books.

Cuaderno Verde, pages 4–5

1

Answers

1 Hizo sol.
2 Hizo calor.
3 No nevó.
4 No hizo buen tiempo.
5 Llovió.
6 Hizo viento.
7 Hubo niebla.
8 No hubo tormenta.
9 Hizo frío.
10 No hizo mal tiempo.

2

Answers

1 *En el centro llovió.* ✓
2 En el norte hizo mucho frío. ✓
3 En la capital hizo mucho calor.
4 Hubo niebla en el oeste. ✓
5 En el sur hizo sol. ✓
6 En el este no hizo buen tiempo.
7 En Barcelona hubo tormenta. ✓
8 Hizo buen tiempo en Cáceres.

3

Answers

1 Marta **2** Ramón **3** Ramón **4** Marta
5 Marta **6** Ramón **7** Marta

4

Answers

1 Un día que hizo mucho frío…
2 El primer día hizo sol y calor.
3 Después fui a la pista de patinaje.
4 Otro día hizo muy mal tiempo.
5 Lo pasé bastante bien.

2 Vacaciones para todos (Student Book pages 10–11)

Main topics and objectives

- Describing accommodation
- Using the imperfect tense for description

Grammar

- The imperfect tense

Key language

¿Dónde te quedaste?
Me quedé en...
¿Dónde te alojaste?
Me alojé en...
un camping

un hotel de lujo
un parador
una pensión
un albergue juvenil

Estaba...
en la costa/montaña/ciudad
en el campo
(No) Era (nada)...
animado/a
antiguo/a
barato/a
bonito/a
caro/a
cómodo/a

feo/a
moderno/a
ruidoso/a
tranquilo/a
(No) Tenía (ni... ni...)
(un) bar/gimnasio/restaurante
(una) cafetería/discoteca/piscina
climatizada/sauna

Resources

CD 1, tracks 6–8
Cuaderno Verde, pages 6–7
Gramática 198

Starter 1

To practise recognising tenses; to review vocabulary for talking about holidays

Write up the following. Give students 3 minutes working in pairs to translate the sentences into English.

Me quedé en un camping en Escocia. Era muy tranquilo. Tenía una piscina.

Me alojé en un hotel en España. Estaba en el campo. Tenía un restaurante. También había un gimnasio.

Check answers. Ask students to identify each verb and say what tense it is. Check that students remember when the imperfect tense is used.

1 Escucha y escribe la letra correcta. (1–5)

Listening. Students listen to five people talking about a recent holiday. They identify where each person stayed by writing down the letter of the correct picture (from **a**–**e**).

Before playing the recording, check students know what a parador is.

Audioscript *Track 6*

1 – *¿Dónde te alojaste, Mónica?*
 – *Me alojé en una pensión en Portugal. La pensión estaba en el centro de la ciudad. Era antigua, pero muy cómoda. Tenía un bar, pero no tenía restaurante.*
2 – *¿Dónde te quedaste, Adrián?*
 – *Pues, me quedé en un albergue juvenil en Gales con unos amigos. Estaba en la montaña. El albergue era un poco feo, pero barato. No tenía ni piscina, ni gimnasio.*
3 – *¿Dónde te quedaste, Laura?*
 – *Me quedé en un camping muy bonito en Escocia con vistas a las montañas. Era muy tranquilo. Tenía una piscina.*
4 – *¿Dónde te alojaste, Ibrahim?*

 – *Me alojé en un parador en España. Estaba en el campo. ¡Qué cómodo era! Había de todo: tenía un restaurante, una sauna y una piscina climatizada. También había un gimnasio.*
5 – *Y tú, Jorge, ¿dónde te quedaste?*
 – *Me quedé en un hotel de lujo en Francia. El hotel estaba en la costa. Era moderno y había una piscina, un bar y una discoteca. ¡Era muy ruidoso!*

Answers

1 d **2** e **3** a **4** c **5** b

2 Escucha otra vez y completa la tabla en inglés. (1–5)

Listening. Students copy out the table. They then listen to the recording in exercise 1 again and complete the table with the details in English. A language box is supplied.

Audioscript *Track 7*

As exercise 1.

Answers

	location	description	facilities
Mónica	Portugal, in town	old but very comfortable	bar, no restaurant
Adrián	Wales, in mountains	ugly but cheap	no swimming pool, no gym
Laura	Scotland, in mountains	very beautiful, quiet	swimming pool
Ibrahim	Spain, country(side)	comfortable	restaurant, sauna, (heated) swimming pool, gym
Jorge	France, on coast	modern but very noisy	swimming pool, bar, disco

G Grammar

Use the Grammar box to review the imperfect tense.

R Students look at the language box on p. 10 for 1 minute. Then they close their books and try to come up with as many descriptions of a hotel and a B&B as they can, using *estaba* + a location and *era* + an adjective.

Starter 2

To review question words

Write up the following, without distinguishing the letters in bold. Explain to students that each wordline has a question word hidden in it. Which pair can be first to identify all the question words?

(Any random letters surrounding the text in bold – shown here for reference only – will do.)

1 h**cómo**soró
2 quo**qué**atrzo
3 **cuándo**erael
4 cuán**chit**dónde
5 es**quién**sonl

When checking answers, ask students to translate the question words into English. Can they think of any other question words in Spanish? (e.g. *adónde, cuánto*, etc.)

3 Escucha y lee las preguntas. Escribe la letra correcta.

Listening. Students listen to a series of questions (**1–8**) and note the appropriate English version of each (from **a–h**).

Audioscript *Track 8*

1 *¿Cuándo fuiste de vacaciones?*
2 *¿Adónde fuiste?*
3 *¿Con quién fuiste?*
4 *¿Dónde te alojaste?*
5 *¿Cómo era el hotel?*
6 *¿Qué tiempo hizo?*
7 *¿Qué hiciste durante tus vacaciones?*
8 *¿Qué tal lo pasaste?*

Answers

1 f **2** e **3** h **4** b **5** c **6** d **7** a **8** g

4 Using the questions from exercise 3 and these notes, have a conversation with your partner about a holiday. Remember to answer each question with a full sentence.

Speaking. In pairs: students use the questions from exercise 3 to have a conversation about a holiday. They take it in turn to ask and answer questions and must remember to answer in complete sentences. The details to include are supplied.

5 Lee el texto y contesta a las preguntas en inglés.

Reading. Students read the text and answer the comprehension questions in English.

Answers

1 in February
2 one week
3 *any four of:* on the coast, very modern, lively, expensive, luxury hotel, had a great restaurant and a gym
4 cold and rainy on first day, then sunny
5 basketball, tennis, windsurfing and sailing
6 went for bike ride, then went dancing and to a party; finally saw a firework competition
7 hopes to go back

6 Describe tus vacaciones.

Writing. Students write a description of their own holidays.

★ ResultsPlus

Tip box on reusing the features of model texts to improve students' own writing.

Students could prepare exercise 6 on computer. Once they have produced a first draft, they should look at a partner's text on screen and highlight (using underline or a different colour) any words where they spot an error, without saying what the error is or correcting it. Students then correct their own texts and produce a second draft.

Plenary

Ask students to tell you when the imperfect tense is used and to give you examples from the unit.

Give students a random mixture of preterite, present and imperfect sentences in Spanish from the unit. Students identify the tense.

Cuaderno Verde, pages 6–7

1

Answers

1 El hotel estaba en la montaña.
2 La discoteca era ruidosa.
3 La piscina era grande.
4 El restaurante era bonito.
5 Había un gimnasio moderno.
6 No había playa.

2

Answers

1 El hotel **estaba** en la costa.
2 **Era** ruidoso.
3 **Tenía** una sauna y un gimnasio.
4 La discoteca **era** barata.
5 **Había** un restaurante fantástico.
6 El bar no **era** caro.
7 La piscina **estaba** en el jardín.
8 **Había** una cafetería moderna.

3

Answers

1 Gustavo **went to Valencia** with his friends.
2 His hotel was **in the centre**.
3 On the first day it **was cold** and it **rained**.
4 He visited the **cathedral** and **museums**.
5 At night there **were** lots of **fireworks**.
6 Gustavo hopes **to return** again next **year**.

4a

Answers

1 ¿Cuándo fuiste de vacaciones? *b*
2 ¿Adónde fuiste? **e**
3 ¿Dónde te quedaste? **a**
4 ¿Cómo era el hotel? **f**
5 ¿Qué tiempo hizo? **c**
6 ¿Qué hiciste durante las vacaciones? **d**

3 En el hotel (Student Book pages 12–13)

Main topics and objectives

- Booking a hotel room
- Using verbs with **usted**

Grammar

- Using verbs with **usted**

Key language

Quiero reservar…
una habitación individual/doble
sin/con baño

con balcón/vistas al mar/cama de
*   matrimonio*
para (cuatro) noches
del (16) al (20) de agosto
¿Cuánto es, por favor?
Son (200€).

¿Hay…?
servicio de habitaciones
conexión a Internet
¿Hasta qué hora se sirve el
*   desayuno/la comida/la cena?*

¿A qué hora cierra la recepción?
¿Hasta qué hora está abierto el
*   restaurante?*
¿Se admiten perros?
Tengo una reserva para esta noche.

Resources

CD 1, tracks 9–11
Cuaderno Verde, page 8

Starter 1

To review dates

Write up the following. Give students 3 minutes working in pairs to write out the dates in full, using the model supplied.

*14 February - **el catorce de febrero***

19 December	*17 July*
9 September	*25 January*
2 April	*30 November*

Check answers. Ask students to give you the months of the year in sequence. Review how to say 'the 1st of…' (*el primero de…*).

1 Match the booking forms to the hotel guests. Then read the booking forms and note down…

Reading. Students read the three hotel booking forms and identify the correct person for each form (from **a–d**). They then note down for each person the date of arrival, the number of nights and details of the room required. There is one distractor.

Answers

1 d
Date of arrival: 9th December
Number of nights: 2
Details of room requested: single, balcony, sea view

2 c
Date of arrival: 21st June
Number of nights: 5
Details of room requested: double, balcony, sea view, double bed

3 b
Date of arrival: 2nd May
Number of nights: 9
Details of room requested: 1 double, 1 single, balcony, sea view, double bed

---

2 Listen and read the conversation and fill in the grid. Then listen and fill in the grid for the other conversations. (1–4)

Listening. Students copy out the table. They listen and read the first conversation and complete the table with the details in English. They then listen to three more conversations and complete the table with the details in English.

Audioscript *Track 9*

1 – *¿En qué puedo ayudarle?*
– *Quiero reservar una habitación doble.*
– *¿Quiere una habitación con baño o sin baño?*
– *Con baño y con balcón, y con vistas al mar, por favor.*
– *¿Para cuántas noches?*
– *Para cuatro noches, del 16 al 20 de agosto. ¿Cuánto es, por favor?*
– *Son 200 euros.*

2 – *¿En qué puedo ayudarle?*
– *Quiero reservar una habitación individual.*
– *¿Con baño o sin baño?*
– *Con baño y con balcón, por favor.*
– *¿Para cuántas noches?*
– *Para tres noches, del 4 al 7 de julio. ¿Cuánto es, por favor?*
– *Son 120 euros.*

3 – *¿En qué puedo ayudarle?*
– *Quiero reservar una habitación doble, por favor.*
– *A ver… ¿quiere una habitación con baño o sin baño?*
– *Con baño y con cama de matrimonio.*
– *¿Para cuántas noches?*
– *Para dos noches, del 15 al 17 de septiembre. ¿Cuánto es, por favor?*
– *Son 190 euros.*

4 – *¿En qué puedo ayudarle?*
– *Quiero reservar dos habitaciones dobles.*
– *¿Con baño o sin baño?*
– *Con baño, con balcón y con vistas al mar.*
– *¿Para cuántas noches?*
– *Para siete noches, del 13 al 20 de mayo. ¿Cuánto es, por favor?*
– *Son 490 euros.*

Answers

type of room	with	nights	cost
double	bath, balcony, sea view	4 16th–20th August	200€
single	bath, balcony	3 4th–7th July	120€
double	bath, double bed	2 15th–17th September	190€
2 doubles	bath, balcony, sea view	7 13th–20th May	490€

⭐ ResultsPlus

Tip box on using **usted** in formal contexts.

Starter 2

To review the alphabet in Spanish

Spell out the names of a few celebrities in Spanish for students to write down.

Check answers and review the pronunciation of all the letters of the alphabet.

3 Con tu compañero/a, haz dos diálogos utilizando el diálogo del ejercicio 2 como modelo.

Speaking. In pairs: students practise the dialogue in exercise 2, taking it in turn to ask and answer questions. They then make up dialogues of their own using the two sets of picture prompts supplied (**a** and **b**).

4 Escucha y escribe los nombres. (1–6)

Listening. Students listen to six conversations and note the names spelled out in each one.

Audioscript *Track 10*

1 – ¿Su apellido, por favor?
– Rodríguez.
– ¿Cómo se deletrea?
– R-O-D-R-Í-G-U-E-Z.
2 – ¿Su apellido, por favor?
– Alegre.
– ¿Cómo se deletrea, por favor?
– A-L-E-G-R-E.
3 – ¿Su apellido, por favor?
– Peinador.
– ¿Cómo se deletrea?
– P-E-I-N-A-D-O-R.
4 – ¿Su apellido, por favor?
– Mallol.
– ¿Cómo se deletrea?
– M-A-L-L-O-L.

5 – ¿Su apellido, por favor?
– Yanez.
– ¿Cómo se deletrea?
– Y-A-N-E-Z.
6 – ¿Su apellido, por favor?
– McKay.
– ¿Cómo se deletrea?
– M-C-K-A-Y.

Answers

1 Rodríguez **2** Alegre **3** Peinador **4** Mallol
5 Yanez **6** McKay

5 Lee y empareja las preguntas con los dibujos correctos.

Reading. Students read the questions and match each of them to the correct picture (from **a–f**).

Answers

1 c **2** f **3** d **4** e **5** b **6** a

6 Escucha. Copia y completa la tabla en inglés. (1–6)

Listening. Students copy out the table. They listen to six conversations and complete the table with the details in English.

Audioscript *Track 11*

1 – ¿Su apellido, por favor?
– Watson.
– ¿Cómo se deletrea?
– W-A-T-S-O-N.
– Vale.
– ¿Hasta qué hora está abierto el restaurante, por favor?
– El restaurante está abierto hasta las 23:00 horas.
2 – ¿Su apellido, por favor?
– Khan.
– ¿Cómo se deletrea?
– K-H-A-N.
– Vale.
– ¿Hasta qué hora se sirve el desayuno, por favor?
– El desayuno se sirve hasta las 10:00, señor.
3 – ¿Su apellido, por favor?
– Me llamo Davies.
– ¿Cómo se deletrea?
– D-A-V-I-E-S.
– Vale.
– ¿Hay conexión a Internet?
– Por desgracia no, señor.
4 – ¿Su apellido por favor, señora?
– Carter.
– ¿Cómo se deletrea?
– C-A-R-T-E-R.
– Vale.
– ¿A qué hora cierra la recepción?
– La recepción cierra a las tres de la madrugada.
5 – ¿Su apellido, por favor?
– Patel.
– ¿Cómo se deletrea?

– P-A-T-E-L.
– *Vale.*
– *¿Hay servicio de habitaciones?*
– *Claro, claro… por supuesto.*
6 – *¿Dígame?*
– *Tengo una reserva para esta noche.*
– *¿Su apellido por favor, señora?*
– *Yang.*
– *¿Cómo se deletrea?*
– *Y-A-N-G.*
– *Vale.*
– *Una habitación doble con vistas la mar. Aquí está su llave.*
– *Gracias. ¿Se admiten perros?*
– *Sí, señora. Se admiten perros.*

Answers

	name	question	answer
1	Watson	Until what time is restaurant open?	11:00 pm
2	Khan	Until what time is breakfast served?	10:00 am
3	Davies	Is there internet access?	Unfortunately not
4	Carter	What time does reception close?	3:00 am
5	Patel	Is there room service?	Yes, of course
6	Yang	Are dogs allowed?	Yes

7 Con tu compañero/a, haz el diálogo. Luego haz otros diálogos cambiando las palabras subrayadas.

Speaking. In pairs: students practise the dialogue shown, taking it in turn to ask and answer the questions. They then put together their own dialogues, using the details shown in the three sets of picture prompts (1–3) to replace the underlined text. A language box is supplied.

Plenary

Prepare dialogues of the type shown in exercise 7 round the class, with you asking the questions and students taking it in turn to give the answers. They must give different details from one another in their responses.

Cuaderno Verde, page 8

1

Answers

1 Habitaciones con o sin baño. *Rooms with or without a bathroom.*
2 Todas las habitaciones con vistas al mar y balcón. *All rooms with sea view and balcony.*
3 Se sirve el desayuno hasta las diez. *Breakfast is served until 10:00 am.*
4 Hay servicio de habitaciones. *There is room service.*
5 No hay conexión a Internet. *There is no internet access.*
6 La recepción no cierra por la noche. *24-hour reception.*

4 Reclamaciones (Student Book pages 14–15)

Main topics and objectives

- Making complaints in a hotel
- Using **me hace falta**

Grammar

- Using **me hace falta**

Key language

¿Qué le pasa, señor/señorita?
Quiero quejarme...

El baño no está limpio.
El aseo está sucio.
La habitación no está limpia.
Hay mucho ruido.
El ascensor/El aseo/La luz/La ducha... no funciona.
Me hace falta... papel higiénico/ jabón/un secador.
Me hacen falta... toallas.

Quiero un descuento.
Quiero cambiar de habitación.
Quiero hablar con el director.

Resources

CD 1, tracks 12–14
Cuaderno Verde, pages 9–10

Starter 1

To review hotel language; to review adjectives

Write up the following, omitting the words in brackets. Give students 3 minutes to complete each sentence with the correct opposite and translate it into English. If necessary for support, you could supply the missing adjectives in the masculine singular form, in random order.

1 *La habitación no está limpia - está (sucia).*
2 *La luz no funciona - está (rota).*
3 *Hay mucho ruido - no es (tranquilo).*

1 Escucha y lee la canción. Escribe las letras en el orden correcto.

Listening. Students listen to the song, reading the text at the same time. They then identify the correct picture (from **a–e**) for each verse of the song (**1–5**).

Audioscript *Track 12*

¡Ay, este hotel!
Este hotel me vuelve loca.
Quiero quejarme ahora.
¡Quiero un descuento ya!

1 *La habitación no está limpia.*
Hay insectos en la cama.
El aire acondicionado está roto.
Y la luz no funciona.
[Estribillo]
2 *El aseo no está limpio.*
No hay papel higiénico.
El baño está sucio.
Y también hay mucho ruido.
[Estribillo]
3 *Me hace falta una pastilla de jabón.*
¿Qué vamos a hacer Ramón?
Quiero cambiar de habitación.
Esa es mi intención.
[Estribillo]
4 *En el suelo hay cucarachas.*
En el baño no hay toallas.
El mar, ¿dónde está?

Aquí no hay buenas vistas.
[Estribillo]
5 *Necesito un secador.*
No funciona el ascensor.
Quiero hablar con el director.
¡Ay! ¡Qué horror! ¡Qué horror!
[Estribillo]

Answers

1 a **2** c **3** b **4** e **5** d

2 Busca estas frases en español en la canción.

Reading. Students reread the text of the song in exercise 1 and identify the Spanish version of the English sentences listed.

Answers

a Quiero quejarme ahora.
b ¡Quiero un descuento ya!
c El aire acondicionado está roto.
d El aseo no está limpio.
e Y también hay mucho ruido.
f Quiero cambiar de habitación.
g En el suelo hay cucarachas.
h No funciona el ascensor.

★ ResultsPlus

Tip box on reading strategies.

R In pairs, students take it in turn to point to one of the pictures in exercise 1 and to say what is wrong.

3 Escucha y escribe los problemas en inglés. (1–3)

Listening. Students listen to three conversations and note in English the problems mentioned.

Audioscript *Track 13*

1 – ¿Qué le pasa, señor?
  – Quiero quejarme. El aseo está sucio y no hay papel higiénico. Me hace falta jabón también.
2 – ¿Qué le pasa, señora?
  – Quiero quejarme. El baño no está limpio. La ducha no funciona.

– *Lo siento mucho, señora.*
– *También me hacen falta toallas y hay mucho ruido.*
3 – *¿Qué le pasa, señor?*
– *Quiero quejarme. Mi habitación está sucia. Me hace falta un secador y la luz no funciona.*

Answers

1 *dirty toilet*, no toilet paper, no soap
2 dirty bath, shower doesn't work, no towels, lots of noise
3 dirty room, no hairdryer, light doesn't work

Starter 2

To review *me gusta(n)/me encanta(n)* **in preparation for using** *me hace(n) falta*

Write up the following. Give students 3 minutes to write four sentences, each featuring one of the phrases and an appropriate noun.

me gusta   me gustan   me encanta
me encantan

Check answers, asking students to summarise how expressions like *me gusta* work.

4 Listen to these longer conversations. What does each customer ask for and how does the receptionist react? (1–3)

Listening. Students copy out the table. They then listen to three people complaining about their accommodation and complete the table with the details in English. A language box is supplied.

Audioscript *Track 14*

1 – *¿Qué le pasa, señor?*
– *Quiero quejarme. El aseo está sucio y no hay papel higiénico. Me hace falta jabón también. Quiero un descuento.*
– *Lo siento mucho. Vamos a limpiar la habitación y también le vamos a dar un descuento.*
2 – *¿Qué le pasa, señora?*
– *Quiero quejarme. El baño no está limpio. La ducha no funciona.*
– *Lo siento mucho, señora.*
– *También me hacen falta toallas y hay mucho ruido. Quiero hablar con el director.*
– *Un momento… El director no está. Pero tengo una habitación libre con vistas al mar.*
3 – *¿Qué le pasa?*
– *Quiero quejarme. Mi habitación está sucia y la luz no funciona. Quiero cambiar de habitación.*
– *Lo siento mucho. El hotel está casi completo, pero vamos a limpiar la habitación y voy a llamar al ingeniero.*

Answers

	customer's request	receptionist's reaction
1	*discount*	*will clean room and give discount*
2	talk to manager	manager not there; will move customer to a room with a sea view
3	change room	can't move (hotel almost full), but will clean the room and call an engineer

G Grammar

Use the Grammar box to present **me hace falta** and **me hacen falta**.

R Give students a range of prompts (e.g. the items in the unit, *un tenedor, unas cucharas, unas reglas, un bolígrafo,* etc.) for them to produce sentences (e.g. *Me hace falta un tenedor,* etc.).

5 Con tu compañero/a, haz diálogos.

Speaking. In pairs: students put together three dialogues, taking it in turn to ask and answer. Prompts are supplied in English.

6 Lee el texto y completa las frases en inglés.

Reading. Students read Rafa's text and then complete the sentences summarising it in English.

Answers

1 Rafa's holidays in Barcelona were **terrible**.
2 He stayed **in a B&B near the Plaza Real**.
3 There was no **soap**, no **towels** and a lot of **noise** at night.
4 There were also enormous **cockroaches**.
5 Next year Rafa is going to **go camping**.
6 At least there won't be any **cockroaches**.

+ Students write down all the verbs in the text, identify the tense and translate them into English.

7 Describe unas vacaciones horrorosas. Utiliza las palabras en azul del ejercicio 6.

Writing. Students write a description of a terrible holiday. They include the words in blue in Rafa's text.

Students could prepare exercise 7 on computer. Encourage them to check their texts for accuracy and to produce a second draft.

Plenary

Ask students to summarise how **me hace falta** and **me hacen falta** are used.

Challenge the class to use these expressions to come up with ten different things that are missing.

Cuaderno Verde, page 9

1

Answers

1 El baño no está limpio./No está limpio el baño.
2 El ascensor no funciona./No funciona el ascensor.
3 El aire acondicionado está roto./Está roto el aire acondicionado.
4 Me hace falta una pastilla de jabón.
5 La habitación está sucia./Está sucia la habitación.
6 No hay papel higiénico.
7 Me hacen falta toallas.
8 Hay insectos en el suelo./En el suelo hay insectos.

2

Answers

1 Lo siento, le **voy a hacer un descuento**.
2 Lo siento, ¿quiere **cambiar de habitación**?
3 Voy a llamar **al ingeniero**.
4 Vamos a **limpiar el cuarto de baño**.
5 Vamos a limpiar **la habitación**.
6 Voy a llamar al servicio **de limpieza**.
7 Le voy **a dar toallas**.
8 Le voy a dar **papel higiénico**.

3

Answers

1 No funciona el aire acondicionado./El aire acondicionado no funciona.
2 Me hace falta papel higiénico.
3 El ascensor está roto./Está roto el ascensor.
4 Hay insectos en el baño./En el baño hay insectos.
5 El suelo está sucio./Está sucio el suelo.

2

Answers

1 me quedé
2 descansó
3 había
4 tenía
5 hice
6 esquié
7 nevó
8 fui
9 saqué
10 llovió
11 estaba
12 patiné
13 visité
14 hizo
15 era
16 hablé
17 bailé
18 mandé
19 pasé

Cuaderno Verde, page 10

1

Answers

	Infinitive	Preterite	
1	comprar	*compraste*	you (*tú*) bought
2	dar	**dio** un paseo en bicicleta	he/she went for a bike ride
3	hacer	**hice** vela	I went sailing
4	llover	**llovió**	it rained
5	alojarse	me **alojé**	I stayed
6	montar	**montaste** a caballo	you (*tú*) went horseriding

Prueba oral: Holidays (Student Book pp. 16–17)

Topics revised	Resources
● Talking about holidays	CD 5, tracks 2–4

Overview

Read through the task box at the top of the page and outline for students how this section works. They will hear a Speaking controlled assessment model discussion in three parts and do exercises focused on the language used. These exercises, along with the advice/activities on how to improve speaking performance in Results Plus, will help them prepare to take part in a discussion of their own on the topic.

1 Listen to the first part of Tom's discussion and choose the correct answers.

Listening. Explain to the students that they will hear a sample of the kind of discussion they are expected to have in the Speaking controlled assessment.

They listen to the first part of the discussion, then complete the multiple-choice sentences.

Audioscript *Track 2*

Part 1

– *¿Dónde estás en esta foto?*
– *Estoy en Estepona en Andalucía. Andalucía está en el sur de España. Fui de vacaciones a Estepona el verano pasado en agosto y lo pasé fenomenal.*
– *¿Quién es la chica de la foto?*
– *Es mi amiga española, Elena. Tiene quince años y es muy simpática. En esta foto estoy en la playa. Fui a la playa todos los días porque hizo sol e hizo mucho calor. Me encanta el calor. Como ves en la foto, soy muy deportivo. Me gusta jugar al voleibol. Durante las vacaciones jugué mucho al voleibol con Elena y jugué al baloncesto con mis padres y mi hermano. ¡Qué divertido! Me gusta hacer natación también y nadé en el mar.*

Answers

1 Andalucía   2 verano   3 mi amiga española   4 a la playa   5 voleibol   6 natación

✚ Students listen again and note the various ways in which Tom expresses an opinion (*lo pasé fenomenal, es muy simpática, me encanta, ¡Qué divertido!*).

2 Listen to the second part of Tom's discussion and fill in the blanks.

Listening. Students now listen to the second part of Tom's discussion and complete the gap-fill version of the transcript.

With a confident class you could ask students first to read the text and try to work out plausible answers, then use the recording to check.

Audioscript *Track 3*

– *¿Qué más hiciste durante tus vacaciones?*
– ***Hice** muchas cosas, por ejemplo monté a caballo. **Fue** muy divertido y me gustó mucho. Un día **fui** de excursión con mis padres. **Primero** visité monumentos y saqué muchas fotos, **luego** fui a un museo y **después** fui de compras. Por lo general, lo pasé **genial**, pero el último día fui a una corrida de toros en Ronda y fue un desastre. ¡Qué horror! No me gustó nada.*
– *¿Dónde te quedaste?*
– ***Me quedé** en un hotel de lujo. **Pasé** dos semanas allí. El hotel **tenía** una piscina y una discoteca – ¡qué guay! Me gustó mucho, porque me encanta bailar.*

Answers

Also in bold in the audioscript.
1 Hice   2 Fue   3 fui   4 Primero   5 luego
6 después   7 genial   8 Me quedé   9 Pasé   10 tenía

3 Here are the final questions Tom is asked. Which question does each answer go with? Listen and check your answers.

Listening. Students first match each of the sentences (1–6) to the questions asked (a and b). They then listen to check their answers

Audioscript *Track 4*

Part 3

– *¿Te gusta pasar tus vacaciones en España?*
– *Me gusta mucho ir de vacaciones a España porque hace mucho sol. Normalmente vamos a España, pero a veces vamos a Grecia porque también hace buen tiempo en Grecia.*
– *¿Qué vas a hacer el año que viene?*
– *Pues, en invierno voy a ir a Alemania porque voy a hacer esquí. En verano creo que voy a volver a España. Voy a ir a la Alhambra en Granada. También voy a visitar los museos y ver los monumentos antiguos en Córdoba y en Sevilla. Voy a montar a caballo otra vez. Va a ser muy divertido.*

Answers

1 a   2 b   3 b   4 a   5 b   6 a

⊛ ResultsPlus

The Results Plus support for speaking activities is differentiated, allowing students to identify and work towards their target level: covering the basics, Grade C, increasing their marks. Encourage students to adopt the techniques in these sections in all extended speaking activities.

Read through and discuss the Results Plus section together.

4 Now it's your turn! Choose your own photo and then prepare to talk about it.

Speaking. Students participate in a discussion on their own holidays in the style of a controlled assessment task. They should use all the support supplied, here and elsewhere on the spread:

- the Results Plus advice on the language to include
- Tom's responses, adapted to talk about themselves
- the English notes in the task box, p. 16
- their answers to exercises 1–3.

Each student takes part in a discussion as the person answering the questions. If they are working with a partner, they will take turns asking and answering.

If possible, record the discussions or have the students record themselves. They can then swap recordings with a partner, listen to each other's version and offer comments on how it might be improved. A simple marking system is suggested (one/two/three stars for listed categories). Students should then identify two or three areas which they would like to improve next time they do an extended speaking task.

Prueba escrita (Student Book pp. 18–19)

Topics revised
● Writing about holidays

1 Read the text and put these headings into the order of the text.

Reading. Students read the text on holidays and reorder the captions (**a–f**) as they are mentioned.

> **Answers**
>
> c, a, f, e, b, d

2 Find the equivalent of these expressions in Spanish in the text. Copy them out.

Reading. Students reread the text in exercise 1 and write out the Spanish versions of the ten English phrases listed.

> **Answers**
>
> **1** Primero desayuno, luego hago natación…
> **2** …y después hago vela o voy de excursión.
> **3** El verano pasado fui de vacaciones a Francia con mi familia.
> **4** ¡Fue un desastre!
> **5** También había una piscina climatizada.
> **6** Hice muchas cosas, por ejemplo…
> **7** Saqué unas fotos buenas.
> **8** Al final lo pasé bien…
> **9** …el año que viene creo que no voy a ir de camping.
> **10** ¡Lo voy a pasar bomba!

3 Look at the sentences you found in exercise 2. Make a note of which tense they are in: present, preterite, imperfect or near future.

Reading. Students note which tense is used in each of the Spanish sentences they wrote in exercise 2.

> **Answers**
>
> **Present:** 1, 2
> **Preterite:** 3, 4, 6, 7, 8
> **Imperfect:** 5
> **Near future:** 9, 10

4 Answer the following questions in English.

Reading. Students reread the text and answer the comprehension questions in English.

> **Answers**
>
> **1** very ugly, had no pool
> **2** cold every day, one day windy, another day it rained
> **3** went swimming
> **4** went on a trip with his parents, saw some very interesting monuments, took some good photos
> **5** Spain, Italy, Germany and France
> **6** youth hostels

5 You might be asked to write about your holidays as a controlled assessment task. Use the Results Plus to help you prepare your account.

Students read through the language support material supplied in preparation for doing their own extended writing task in exercise 6.

⭐ ResultsPlus

The Results Plus section gives students the support they need to structure and improve their writing. The support is differentiated, allowing students to identify and work towards their target level: covering the basics, Grade C, increasing their marks. Encourage students to adopt the kind of approach taken in this section in all extended writing activities.

6 Now write a full account of your holidays.

Writing. Students write their own text on their holidays in the style of a controlled assessment task (at least 100 words). As well as the Results Plus guidelines on the language to include, they should use all the support supplied here:

● Carlos's text, adapted to refer to themselves
● relevant language from throughout the module
● the sample structure for the text.

Students may find it helpful if you can create model answers together for this first module.

7 Check carefully what you have written.

Writing. Students check their own work using the list of features supplied.

Te toca a ti (Student Book pages 172–173)

De vacaciones

• Self-access reading and writing

A Reinforcement

1 Match up the texts to the correct hotel.

Reading. Students read the three profiles and match each person to the appropriate holiday.

Answers

1 c **2** b **3** a

2 Write out these dialogues in the correct order. Start with the green sentence each time.

Reading. Students write out the two dialogues in the correct order. The starting sentence is given in green each time for support.

Answers

1 **a** *¿En qué puedo ayudarle?*
   g Quiero reservar una habitación doble.
   b ¿Quiere una habitación con baño o sin baño?
   d Con baño, con balcón y con vistas al mar, por favor.
   e ¿Para cuántas noches?
   c Para cinco noches, del 21 al 26 de junio. ¿Cuánto es, por favor?
   f Son 280€.
2 **h** *Dígame.*
   g Tengo una reserva para esta noche.
   c ¿Su apellido, por favor?
   a Williams.
   e ¿Cómo se deletrea?
   f W-I-L-L-I-A-M-S.
   d Vale. Una habitación doble con balcón. Aquí está su llave.
   i Gracias. ¿Hasta qué hora está abierto el restaurante, por favor?
   b El restaurante está abierto hasta las 22:00 horas.

B Extension

1 Match the descriptions to the holidays. There is one holiday too many.

Reading. Students read four people's descriptions of their holidays, then match each person to the correct holiday advert. There is one distractor.

Answers

1 b **2** c **3** a

2 Write down the letters of the four sentences that are true about the texts in exercise 1.

Reading. Students reread the three descriptions in exercise 1 and the eight sentences in English about them. They identify which four of the sentences are true.

Answers

b, d, f, g

3 Write an account of this holiday.

Writing. Students write a description of a recent holiday using the notes in English. A language box is supplied.

Module 2 De paseo por Sevilla (Student Book pages 22–43)

Unit	Main topics and objectives	Grammar	Skills
Repaso 1 Mi vida (pp. 22–23)	• Giving personal information • Using the present tense	The present tense (regular verbs, **jugar**, irregular verbs **hacer**, **ser**, **tener**)	Using adverbs of frequency Extending sentences with **cuando**...
Repaso 2 En ruta (pp. 24–25)	• Talking about means of transport • Using adjectives to give opinions on travel	Adjectives	Using **en** to talk about means of transport Listening for the 24-hour clock
1 ¿Qué vas a hacer? (pp. 26–27)	• Planning a day out • Using the near future	The near future tense	Thinking about the sound of place names before listening; picking out key phrases as they listen
2 Comprando recuerdos (pp. 28–29)	• Asking for and understanding directions to shops • Using **al/a la**... (to the...)	Using **al/a la**	Practising pronunciation
3 Tomando tapas (pp. 30–31)	• Ordering in a restaurant • Using **me gusta** + definite article	Using **me gusta** + definite article	Practising pronunciation Practising adjective agreement
4 En Sevilla (pp. 32–33)	• Describing a visit to Seville • Using the preterite to describe past actions	The preterite	
5 Las fiestas (pp. 34–35)	• Talking about festivals • Using the present tense ('we' form)	Using the present tense: 'we' form	Using a variety of adjectives Improving writing skills (using questions to help structure text; extending sentences with connectives; using adjectives)
Prueba oral: Tourist information (pp. 36–37)	Exam speaking practice	Revision	
Prueba escrita (pp. 38–39)	Exam writing practice	Revision	
Leer y escuchar (Modules 1–2) (pp. 40–41)	Listening and reading skills	Revision	
Te toca a ti (pp. 174–175)	Self-access reading and writing		

2 Repaso 1 *Mi vida* (Student Book pages 22–23)

Main topics and objectives

- Giving personal information
- Using the present tense

Grammar

- The present tense (regular verbs, **jugar**, irregular verbs **hacer, ser, tener**)

Key language

siempre
todos los días
a menudo
a veces
de vez en cuando
los fines de semana
los sábados
una vez a la semana
nunca

Me llamo...
¿Cuántos años tienes?
Tengo... años.
¿De dónde eres?
Soy de...
¿Dónde vives?
Vivo en...
¿Qué haces en tu tiempo libre?

Chateo con mis amigos.
Escribo un blog.
Descargo música.
Juego con el ordenador.
Juego al fútbol.
Voy de compras.
Voy al cine.
Veo películas.
Leo libros y revistas.
Hago esquí.
Voy a la piscina.

¿Qué tiempo hace?
Hace buen tiempo/mal tiempo/
    calor/frío/sol/viento.
Hay niebla/tormenta.

Llueve.
Nieva.

Cuando...

Resources

CD 1, tracks 15–17
Cuaderno Verde, page 13
Gramática 192

Starter 1

To review vocabulary for activities; to review key verbs

Write up the following, leaving a gap for each word in brackets. Supply the words in brackets separately, in random order. (With a confident class, you could let them try the activity without supplying answer options.) Give students 3 minutes to complete the expressions with the correct verb.

Me gusta...
1 (descargar) música.
2 (jugar) con el ordenador.
3 (ir) de compras.
4 (chatear) con mis amigos.
5 (leer) revistas.
6 (escribir) un blog.

Check answers, asking students to translate them into English.

1 Escucha y lee los textos. Escribe las letras correctas para Antonio y Julieta.

Listening. Students listen to two people talking about what they do and follow the texts in their books. They note the activities each person mentions (from pictures **a–h**).

Audioscript *Track 15*

1 Me llamo Antonio y soy de España. Vivo en Salamanca. Tengo diecisiete años. Me encanta la informática. Todos los días chateo con mis amigos. También descargo música y los fines de semana escribo un blog de música rock. Siempre voy de vacaciones a la playa. Me encanta tomar el sol.

2 ¡Hola! ¿Qué tal estás? Me llamo Julieta. Vivo en Sevilla con mi familia, pero soy de Guatemala. Tengo quince años. A veces salgo con mis amigos y vamos de compras. También voy al cine una vez a la semana, pero nunca veo películas de terror. Los fines de semana me gusta leer. Leo libros y revistas. A menudo voy de vacaciones a Nueva York.

> ### Answers
> **Antonio:** *d*, g, e, c
> **Julieta:** a, f, b, h

2 Read the texts again. What do the phrases in blue mean? Use them to help you answer the questions below.

Reading. Students reread the texts in exercise 1 and translate the words in blue (adverbs of frequency) into English. They then answer the comprehension questions.

> ### Answers
> todos los días – *every day*
> los fines de semana – *at weekends*
> siempre – *always*
> a veces – *sometimes*
> una vez a la semana – *once a week*
> nunca – *never*
> a menudo – *often*
>
> 1 He writes a music blog.
> 2 He always goes to the beach; he loves sunbathing.
> 3 He chats to his friends (on the net) and downloads music.
> 4 She goes to the cinema.
> 5 She goes shopping with her friends.
> 6 She never watches horror films.

G Grammar

Use the Grammar box to review the present tense singular of the three regular verb groups, plus the stem-changing verb **jugar** and the irregular verbs **hacer**, **ser** and **tener**.

R Play a chain game round the class to practise the verb paradigms. Each student gives the next verb in the conjugation.

Starter 2

To review weather vocabulary

Use ActiveTeach to display the pictures and text in exercise 5 on p. 23. Alternatively, ask students to look at the activity in their books.

Ask students to identify the correct caption for each weather picture. They can write their answers or this can be done orally as a class.

3 Escucha y apunta la pregunta y la respuesta en inglés. (1–5)

Listening. Students listen and note down the questions and responses in English.

Audioscript *Track 16*

1 – ¿Cuántos años tienes?
  – Tengo quince años.
2 – ¿Qué haces en tu tiempo libre?
  – Generalmente voy de compras o voy al cine.
3 – ¿De dónde eres?
  – Soy de Argentina.
4 – ¿Adónde vas de vacaciones?
  – Siempre voy de vacaciones a Perú.
5 – ¿Dónde vives?
  – Vivo en Buenos Aires.

> **Answers**
> **1** *How old are you? – 15*
> **2** What do you do in your free time? – Usually I go shopping or to the cinema.
> **3** Where are you from? – I'm from Argentina.
> **4** Where do you go on holiday? – I always go to Peru.
> **5** Where do you live? – I live in Buenos Aires.

4 With a partner, ask these questions and answer them for Antonio or Julieta. Then answer them for yourself.

Speaking. In pairs: students take it in turn to ask and answer questions as though they were Antonio or Julieta from exercise 1. They should use the adverbs of frequency covered in exercises 1 and 2 in their responses. A dialogue framework and a language box are supplied for support.

Students then take it in turn to answer the questions as themselves.

★ ResultsPlus

Tip box on including adverbs of frequency in speaking and writing.

5 Escucha. ¿Qué tiempo hace? Escribe las letras correctas. (1–7)

Listening. Students listen to seven weather descriptions and note the weather types mentioned in each, using pictures **a–j**.

Audioscript *Track 17*

1 *De vez en cuando hace mal tiempo. Hace viento y llueve mucho.*
2 *Hace sol, pero nunca hace calor. Generalmente hace buen tiempo.*
3 *Hace sol todos los días, pero llueve mucho.*
4 *A veces hay tormenta. La temperatura es de 25 grados casi todo el año.*
5 *Aquí siempre hay mucha niebla. Los inviernos son largos y nieva.*
6 *En el norte de este país llueve mucho y a menudo hace frío.*
7 *En el sur hace calor y hace sol. Siempre hay muchos turistas aquí.*

> **Answers**
> **1** *j*, b, d **2** c, f **3** c, d **4** a, h
> **5** e, i **6** d, g **7** h, c

R Students listen again and note down the adverbs of frequency.

6 Describe la rutina de Pepe.

Writing. Using the picture prompts, students complete the sentences describing Pepe's routine in different types of weather.

★ ResultsPlus

Tip box on extending sentences by using connectives like **cuando**.

> **Answers**
> **1** Cuando hace viento, juego con el ordenador.
> **2** En invierno, cuando nieva, esquío.
> **3** Cuando hace buen tiempo, juego al fútbol; pero cuando llueve, leo.
> **4** Cuando hace sol, voy de compras; pero cuando hace frío, voy al cine.
> **5** Si hace buen tiempo, salgo con mis amigos; pero si hace mal tiempo, voy a la piscina.

✎ If you have links with a school in Spain, use the activities in this module as a cue for students to make contact with Spanish students in their year. They can introduce themselves and talk about their experiences of school. This could be done as a videoconference (if you have the technology in place) or as an exchange of emails, with students

asking and answering questions in Spanish
(and then reciprocating by doing the activity in
English).

Plenary

Ask students to summarise the endings for the
present tense, either focusing just on regular
verbs or also including the irregular verbs **ser**
and **tener**.

Prompt using the pictures in exercise 5 (from
a–j) for students to give you the correct Spanish
weather expression as quickly as they can.

Cuaderno Verde, page 13

1

Answers
1 *todos los sábados*
2 a veces
3 a menudo compro
4 también me encanta
5 nunca leo
6 siempre voy
7 los fines de semana
8 los domingos leo
9 de vez en cuando escribo
10 todos los días juego

2

Answers
1 0 2 V 3 0 4 0 5 V 6 V

2 Repaso 2 *En ruta* (Student Book pages 24–25)

Main topics and objectives
- Talking about means of transport
- Using adjectives to give opinions on travel

Grammar
- Adjectives

Key language
el autobús
el avión
el tren
el monopatín

el barco
el autocar
el coche
el metro
la bicicleta
la moto
el tranvía
a pie/andando

Voy en (tren)...
Cojo (el autobús/un taxi/la bici)...
Prefiero ir (en tren)...
porque (no) es...
*barato/caro/cómodo/ecológico/
   lento/limpio/rápido/sano*

*Quiero (cuatro) billetes para
   (Madrid).*
de ida/de ida y vuelta
¿A qué hora sale el tren?
¿De qué andén sale?
¿A qué hora llega?
¿Es directo?
No, hay que cambiar.

Resources
CD 1, tracks 18–20
Cuaderno Verde, page 14

Starter 1

To review vocabulary for the unit; to practise classifying words

Write up the following, supplying the words in random order underneath the table (shown here under the appropriate columns for reference). Give students 3 minutes to copy and complete the table by writing the words in the correct column.

frequency expression	noun	adjective

normalmente	*monopatín*	*baratos*
siempre	*avión*	*caro*
a veces	*barco*	*limpia*
generalmente	*moto*	*cómodas*

Check answers, asking students to translate the words into English and to give you the definite article for each noun, and also the gender and number of each adjective.

1 Lee y empareja las fotos con los medios de transporte.

Reading. Students read the captions and find the correct one for each picture.

> **Answers**
> 1 f 2 c 3 g 4 d 5 h 6 a
> 7 k 8 j 9 b 10 i 11 e

2 Escucha y lee. Copia y completa la tabla en inglés. (1–10)

Listening. Students copy out the table. They then listen to ten people talking about modes of transport and complete the table by noting the details in English.

Audioscript *Track 18*

1 *Normalmente cojo el autobús porque no es caro.*
2 *Prefiero ir a pie porque es sano.*
3 *Normalmente cojo un taxi porque es rápido.*
4 *Generalmente voy en monopatín porque es barato.*
5 *No me gusta nada viajar en autobús porque no es cómodo.*
6 *Generalmente voy en moto porque es rápido.*
7 *Normalmente cojo la bici porque es ecológico.*
8 *Prefiero ir en tren porque es limpio.*
9 *Para distancias largas prefiero ir en avión, pero es caro.*
10 *Para distancias largas no voy en autocar porque es muy lento.*

Answers

	mode of transport	reason/opinion
1	bus	not expensive
2	walk	healthy
3	taxi	quick
4	skateboard	cheap
5	bus	not comfortable
6	motorbike	quick
7	bike	good for the environment
8	train	clean
9	plane	expensive
10	coach	very slow

⭐ ResultsPlus
Tip box on **Voy en (tren)** – no article used.

Starter 2

To review adjectives used to give opinions on travel

Write up the following. Give students 3 minutes to complete the sentence openings with a reason including an adjective.

1 *Prefiero ir en bici...*
2 *Normalmente voy a pie...*
3 *Me gusta viajar en avión...*
4 *Nunca voy en autocar...*

Hear answers, asking students to translate their sentences into English.

3 ¿Cómo prefieres viajar? Escribe estas frases.

Writing. Students complete the gap-fill sentences using the pictures. A language box is supplied.

Point out to students that the sentences shown here illustrate three useful ways in which you can extend sentences: reasons with **porque**, using **cuando** and adverbs of frequency.

Answers

1 Normalmente prefiero ir en autocar porque es barato.
2 Generalmente voy en tren porque es cómodo.
3 Cuando llueve, prefiero ir en taxi porque es rápido.
4 Cuando hace sol, prefiero ir a pie porque es sano.
5 Todos los días voy en bici porque es ecológico.
6 Nunca voy en coche porque es caro.

➕ Students complete the following writing about themselves:

Generalmente... porque es... Pero cuando... porque... De vez en cuando..., a menudo..., nunca... porque...

4 Escucha y escribe la hora correcta. (1–8)

Listening. Students listen to eight exchanges featuring times and note the time mentioned in each. The answers are given in random order for support.

Audioscript *Track 19*

1 – ¿A qué hora sale el tren, por favor?
   – A las diez veinticinco.
2 – ¿A qué hora sale el autocar?
   – Sale a las doce cuarenta.
3 – ¿A qué hora sale el autobús?
   – Pues... sale a las nueve diez.
4 – ¿A qué hora llega el avión?
   – Llega a las trece cincuenta.
5 – ¿A qué hora llega el tren?
   – Llega a las diecinueve tres.
6 – ¿A qué hora llega el autocar?
   – El autocar llega a las veintidós treinta y dos.
7 – ¿A qué hora sale el avión?
   – Sale tarde, a las veinte cincuenta y siete.
8 – ¿A qué hora llega el autobús?
   – Llega temprano, a las seis catorce.

Answers

1	10:25	2	12:40	3	09:10	4	13:50	5	19:03
6	22:32	7	20:57	8	6:14						

➕ Play the recording again. Students note whether the people are talking about arrivals or departures and also which form of transport is mentioned.

⭐ ResultsPlus

Tip box on the 24-hour clock.

5 Listen and read the conversation. Copy and fill in the grid. Then listen to two more conversations and fill in the grid for those. (1–3)

Listening. Students copy out the grid. They listen to a conversation in a train station and complete the details in the grid. They then repeat the task for two more conversations.

Audioscript *Track 20*

1 – Buenos días. ¿Qué quiere?
   – Quiero dos billetes para Madrid, por favor.
   – ¿De ida o de ida y vuelta?
   – De ida y vuelta. ¿A qué hora sale el tren?
   – Sale a las ocho diez.
   – ¿De qué andén sale?
   – Sale del andén 7.
   – ¿A qué hora llega?
   – Llega a las trece veinte.
   – ¿Es directo?
   – No, hay que cambiar.
2 – Buenos días. ¿Qué quiere?
   – Quiero cuatro billetes para Barcelona, por favor.
   – ¿De ida o de ida y vuelta?
   – Solamente de ida. ¿A qué hora sale el tren?
   – Sale a las dieciséis cuarenta.
   – ¿De qué andén sale?
   – Sale del andén 2.
   – ¿A qué hora llega?
   – Llega a las veintidós quince.
   – ¿Es directo?
   – Sí, es directo, señor.
3 – Buenos días. ¿Qué quiere?
   – Quiero un billete para Londres, por favor.
   – ¿De ida o de ida y vuelta?
   – Pues... De ida y vuelta, por favor. ¿A qué hora sale el tren?
   – Sale a las once treinta y siete.
   – ¿De qué andén sale?
   – Sale del andén 3.
   – ¿A qué hora llega?
   – Pues... es un viaje muy largo. Llega a las veintitrés diez.
   – ¿Es directo?
   – No, hay que cambiar en París.

Answers

	¿cuántas personas?	destino	→ →←	salida	andén	llegada	directo
1	2	Madrid	→←	8:10	7	13:20	✗
2	4	Barcelona	→	16:40	2	22:15	✓
3	1	Londres	→←	11:37	3	23:10	✗

6 Con tu compañero/a, haz tres diálogos. Cambia los datos del ejercicio 5.

Speaking. In pairs: students make up three dialogues, using the written dialogue in exercise 5 as a model. Prompts are supplied.

Plenary

Review giving opinions on travel by asking students to tell you how they usually travel/ prefer to travel/don't like to travel, etc., and why.

Cuaderno Verde, page 14

1

Answers

a pie/bicicleta/avión/limpio/metro/cómodo/moto/caro/ coche/sano/barco/lento/tren/ecológico/monopatín/ barato/autocar/rápido/autobús

3

Answers

- ■ Buenos días. ¿Qué quiere?
- ● Quiero **tres billetes** para **Alicante**, por favor.
- ■ ¿De ida?
- ● No, de **ida y vuelta**. ¿**A qué hora sale** el tren?
- ■ Sale a las nueve cinco.
- ● ¿**A qué hora llega**?
- ■ Llega a las trece quince.
- ● ¿De qué **andén sale**?
- ■ Sale del andén dieciocho.
- ● ¿Es **directo**?
- ■ Sí. No hay que cambiar.

4

Answers

1 9:05 **2** 13:15 **3** 18 **4** No

1 ¿Qué vas a hacer? (Student Book pages 26–27)

Main topics and objectives

- Planning a day out
- Using the near future

Grammar

- The near future tense

Key language

Voy a...
sacar fotos
comprar recuerdos
ver vistas espléndidas

dar un paseo
tomar unas tapas
ver una corrida

¿Qué...?
¿Cómo...?
¿Cuándo...?
¿A qué hora...?

Va a ser...
aburrido/fascinante/guay/
*   horrible/impresionante/*
*   interesante*

Resources

CD 1, tracks 21–24
Cuaderno Verde, page 15
Gramática 200

Starter 1

To revise the near future tense; to practise using reading strategies

Write up the following, jumbling the order of the words in each sentence. You can retain or omit capitals and punctuation, depending on how much support you want students to have. Give students 3 minutes to write the sentences in the correct order and to translate them into English.

1 *Voy a tomar unas tapas.*
2 *Voy a comprar recuerdos.*
3 *Voy a ver vistas espléndidas.*

Check answers. Ask students to summarise how the near future tense is formed.

1 Escucha y escribe la letra correcta. (1–6)

Listening. Students listen to six conversations in which people talk about what they are going to do in Seville. They note the picture of the place mentioned in each conversation (from **a–f**).

⊛ ResultsPlus

Tip box on thinking of the sound of each place name before listening and picking out key phrases as they listen.

Audioscript *Track 21*

1 – *¿Qué vas a hacer hoy en Sevilla?*
– *Voy a dar un paseo por el parque de María Luisa de Sevilla. Es un jardín muy grande. Lo voy a pasar bien. Va a ser guay.*
2 – *Y tú, ¿qué vas a hacer hoy en Sevilla?*
– *Hay muchas cosas que ver en Sevilla. Hoy, voy a ir a la plaza de España y luego vamos a tomar unas tapas en un restaurante cerca de la plaza. La comida va a estar muy rica.*
3 – *¿Qué vas a hacer hoy en Sevilla?*
– *Voy a visitar el Alcázar. Va a ser muy interesante. Voy a sacar muchas fotos.*

4 – *¿Qué vas a hacer hoy en Sevilla?*
– *A ver, voy a ir de compras. Quiero ir al centro comercial Plaza de Armas. Hay muchas tiendas y voy a comprar recuerdos. Va a ser guay.*
5 – *¿Qué vas a hacer hoy en Sevilla?*
– *Por la mañana, quiero ver la plaza de toros y por supuesto voy a ver una corrida. Voy a aprender muchas cosas.*
6 – *¿Qué vamos a ver hoy en Sevilla?*
– *Primero, ustedes van a visitar la catedral de Sevilla y luego van a subir a la Torre de la Giralda. Van a ver vistas espléndidas de la ciudad. Va a ser impresionante.*

Answers

1 *d* **2** c **3** a **4** f **5** e **6** b

2 Lee las frases y empareja las actividades con las fotos.

Reading. Students read the sentences and find the correct sentence for each picture.

Answers

1 a **2** f **3** e **4** c **5** d **6** b

Ⓖ Grammar

Use the Grammar box to review how the near future tense (singular) is formed.

✚ Working in pairs, students take it in turn to prompt with a subject (e.g. 'he', etc.) and the letter of one of the pictures in exercise 1. Their partner responds with a sentence using the near future tense (e.g. *Va a ir al Alcázar*).

3 Escucha a las personas del ejercicio 1 otra vez. Escribe la letra correcta del ejercicio 2.

Listening. Students listen to the recording from exercise 1 again. For each speaker they find the correct sentence from exercise 2 (from **a–f**).

Audioscript Track 22

As exercise 1.

Answers
1 *d* **2** e **3** a **4** b **5** f **6** c

4 What are you going to do in Seville? Write a short text. Make sure you use the sequencers you saw in Module 1: *primero* (first), *después* (after that), *luego* (later).

Writing. Students write a short text on what they are going to do in Seville, using the near future tense and the sequencers **primero**, **después** and **luego** to structure it. Sample sentence openings are supplied.

Starter 2

To review the near future tense; to review unit vocabulary

Write up the following. Give students 3 minutes to come up with a sentence using the near future tense in a different person for each prompt. Model the first one as an example if necessary (e.g. *Va a sacar fotos.*)

En Sevilla…
1 *fotos*
2 *recuerdos*
3 *vistas espléndidas*
4 *un paseo*

Check answers, asking students to translate them into English. Ask students to summarise how the near future tense is formed.

5 Escucha y lee la conversación. Contesta a las preguntas.

Listening. Students listen to a conversation about visiting Seville and follow the text at the same time. Then they answer the comprehension questions.

You could use ActiveTeach to display this text when checking answers.

Audioscript Track 23

– *Hola Juan. ¿Qué tal?*
– *Hola María. Fenomenal, gracias.*
– *¿Qué vas a hacer hoy?*
– *Pues… voy a visitar Sevilla. Primero voy a ir al Alcázar. Voy a sacar muchas fotos y comprar recuerdos también.*
– *¿Cómo vas a ir al Alcázar?*
– *Voy a ir a pie porque hace buen tiempo.*
– *¿A qué hora abre el Alcázar?*
– *Abre a las nueve y cierra a las seis de la tarde. Después voy a tomar unas tapas en un bar.*
– *Y luego ¿qué vas a hacer?*
– *Luego voy a ir a la plaza de toros. ¡Voy a ver una corrida! ¿Quieres venir conmigo?*
– *¡Ay! Va a ser horrible. No, gracias. Odio las corridas.*

Answers
1 visit Seville, go to the Alcazar, take lots of photos, buy souvenirs
2 on foot because it's nice weather
3 9 am to 6 pm
4 if she wants to go to the bullfight
5 it'll be horrible; she hates bullfights

6 Escucha. Copia y completa la tabla en inglés. (1–3)

Listening. Students copy out the table. They listen to three conversations about visiting Seville and complete the table with the details in English.

Audioscript Track 24

1 – *Hola Pepe. ¿Qué tal?*
– *Hola Blanca. Muy bien, gracias.*
– *¿Qué vas a hacer hoy?*
– *Pues… voy a visitar Sevilla. Primero voy a ir al parque de María Luisa de Sevilla. Voy a dar un paseo y voy a sacar fotos también.*
– *¿Cómo vas a ir al parque?*
– *Voy a coger el autobús porque no es caro. ¿Quieres venir conmigo?*
– *Sí, va a ser guay.*

2 – *¿Qué vas a hacer hoy, Martín?*
– *Pues… voy a visitar Sevilla. Primero voy a ir a la plaza de España. Voy a comprar recuerdos y también voy a tomar unas tapas en un bar.*
– *¿Cómo vas a ir a la plaza?*
– *Voy a alquilar una bicicleta porque hace buen tiempo. ¿Quieres venir conmigo?*
– *Sí, ¿cómo no? Va a ser impresionante.*

3 – *Hola Clara. ¿Qué vas a hacer hoy en Sevilla?*
– *Pues… hay muchas cosas que ver en Sevilla. Primero voy a subir a la Torre de la Giralda, voy a ver vistas preciosas.*
– *¿Cómo vas a ir a la Giralda?*
– *Voy a ir a pie porque hace sol.*
– *Y luego ¿qué vas a hacer?*
– *Luego voy a ir de compras. Va a ser interesante.*

Answers

	places to visit	activities mentioned	transport & reason	opinion
1	el parque de María Luisa	go for walk take photos	bus not expensive	cool
2	la plaza de España	buy souvenirs eat tapas	bike nice weather	impressive
3	go up the Giralda tower	take in views go shopping	walking sunny	interesting

7 Now write a conversation about a trip to Seville or another destination and perform it with your partner. Use the conversation in exercise 5 for ideas.

Writing. Students write a conversation about a trip to Seville or another city they would like to visit, using exercise 5 for ideas. They then perform the conversations in pairs.

Plenary

Ask the class to summarise how the near future tense is formed. Then challenge them to come up with as many examples as they can of things they are going to do in Seville. You could vary the subject of the verb to cover a wide range of near future forms.

Finally, ask them to give their opinion of a holiday by completing and translating into Spanish *It's going to be...* with as many different adjectives as they can (*great, terrible,* etc.).

Cuaderno Verde, page 15

1

Answers
1 Voy a comprar muchos recuerdos.
2 Voy a dar un paseo por el centro comercial.
3 Voy a ir a un bar a tomar unas tapas./Voy a ir a tomar unas tapas a un bar.
4 Voy a sacar fotos en el parque.
5 Voy a ver una corrida de toros.
6 Voy a sacar fotos de los monumentos.

2

Answers
a Walking through a square **3**
b Visiting the cathedral **1**
c Going to a bullfight **7**
d Walking because of the good weather **5**
e Taking photos **2**
f Having bar snacks **4**
g Buying souvenirs **6**

2 Comprando recuerdos (Student Book pages 28–29)

Main topics and objectives

- Asking for and understanding directions to shops
- Using **al/a la...** (to the...)

Grammar

- Using **al/a la...**

Key language

¿Dónde se puede(n) comprar...?
un collar
un chorizo
una camiseta
una taza
unos pendientes

unos caramelos
unas postales

En...
el supermercado
el quiosco
el estanco
la carnicería
la confitería
la farmacia
la joyería
la tienda de recuerdos
la tienda de ropa

¿Por dónde se va al/a la...?
Está cerca/lejos.
Sigue todo recto.

Cruza la plaza/el puente.
Pasa los semáforos.
Toma la primera/segunda calle a la derecha/izquierda.
Está al final de la calle.

Primero...
Luego...
Después...

Resources

CD 1, tracks 25–29
Cuaderno Verde, pages 16–17

Starter 1

To review shop vocabulary

Write up the shops from exercise 2. Give students 3 minutes to translate them into English.

1 Escucha y escribe la letra correcta y el precio correcto. (1–6)

Listening. Students listen to six people talking about souvenirs they are buying and note the letter of the correct picture for each (from **a–f**) and the price.

Audioscript *Track 25*

1 – *Me gusta esta camiseta. ¿Cuánto es?*
  – *Veinte euros.*
  – *No sé, es un poco cara.*
2 – *¿Cuánto cuesta este chorizo?*
  – *Cinco euros con cuarenta y cinco céntimos.*
3 – *¿Te gusta esta taza? Cuesta ocho euros con cincuenta céntimos.*
4 – *El collar y los pendientes son preciosos pero caros.*
  – *Sí, ochenta y nueve euros.*
5 – *A mi hermana tal vez le gustarían unos caramelos.*
  – *A mí me gustan... son siete euros...*
6 – *Yo voy a comprar unas postales. Sólo cuestan cincuenta céntimos.*
  – *Tienes razón, Carlos. Yo también voy a comprar postales.*

Answers

1 d 20€ **2** c 5,45€ **3** f 8,50€
4 a 89€ **5** e 7€ **6** b 50 cents

2 Escucha y escribe la letra del ejercicio 1 y la(s) tienda(s) correcta(s). (1–6)

Listening. Students listen to six conversations in which people discuss where you can buy things. For each they note the letter of the item (from **a–f** in exercise 1) and the name of the shop.

Audioscript *Track 26*

1 – *¿Dónde se pueden comprar unas postales?*
  – *En el quiosco o en el estanco.*
2 – *¿Dónde se puede comprar una taza?*
  – *Una taza ... a ver, se puede comprar en la tienda de recuerdos o en el supermercado.*
3 – *¿Dónde se puede comprar un chorizo?*
  – *Un chorizo ... a ver, se puede comprar en la carnicería.*
4 – *¿Dónde se puede comprar una camiseta?*
  – *En la tienda de ropa o en la tienda de recuerdos.*
5 – *¿Dónde se pueden comprar unos caramelos?*
  – *¿Unos caramelos? A ver... en la confitería o en el supermercado.*
6 – *¿Dónde se puede comprar un collar y unos pendientes?*
  – *En la joyería o en la tienda de recuerdos.*

Answers

1 b – el quiosco/el estanco
2 f – la tienda de recuerdos/el supermercado
3 c – la carnicería
4 d – la tienda de ropa/la tienda de recuerdos
5 e – el supermercado/la confitería
6 a – la joyería/la tienda de recuerdos

3 Con tu compañero/a, pregunta y contesta por los objetos del ejercicio 1.

Speaking. In pairs: students ask and answer questions about where you can buy the items in exercise 1. A sample exchange is given.

🗣 Pronunciation

Ask the class to read the rhyme aloud, paying particular attention to the pronunciation of the letters in bold (**ía, ll, z**).

Play the recording, and ask individual students to repeat each line, following the model on the recording as closely as possible.

Audioscript *Track 27*

A mí me gustaría
Ir contigo a Sevilla.
Allí hay una carnicería
Y también una joyería.
En Sevilla te voy a comprar
Un chorizo y un collar.

✚ Students choose three shops and write a sentence for each saying what you can buy there, using *se puede(n) comprar*.

Starter 2

To review *al/a la*

Write up the following, leaving a gap for the words in brackets. Give students 2 minutes to complete the sentence using **al** or **a la**. You could supply the answer options for support.

Cuando voy de compras, voy (al) supermercado, (a la) farmacia, (a la) tienda de ropa, (al) estanco y (al) supermercado.

Check answers, asking students to summarise the rules for using **a** + the definite article.

4 Escucha y lee. Empareja las frases con los dibujos.

Listening. Students listen to nine sentences used to give directions in the street, reading the text at the same time. They then find the correct sentence (**1–9**) for each picture (**a–i**).

Audioscript *Track 28*

1 *Está cerca.*
2 *Está lejos.*
3 *Sigue todo recto.*
4 *Cruza la plaza.*
5 *Cruza el puente.*
6 *Pasa los semáforos.*
7 *Toma la primera calle a la derecha.*
8 *Toma la segunda calle a la izquierda.*
9 *Está al final de la calle.*

Answers

1 g 2 i 3 a 4 c 5 d 6 h 7 b 8 e 9 f

🅡 Working in pairs, students take it in turn to prompt with one of the Spanish sentences in exercise 4. His/Her partner points to the correct picture.

5 Lee los mensajes y mira el mapa. ¿Adónde van? Escribe el nombre de la tienda.

Reading. Students read the two messages and look at the map. They write the name of the shop each person is going to.

Answers

1 la farmacia 2 la confitería

6 Escucha las direcciones y mira el mapa. Escribe la letra correcta del ejercicio 5. (1–9)

Listening. Students listen to the conversations and use the details given in them and the map to identify the places that are beeped out in the recording (from **a–i** in exercise 5). The key structures are given.

Audioscript *Track 29*

1 – *¿Por dónde se va al [BEEP]?*
– *Está cerca. Sigue todo recto, pasa los semáforos y está a la izquierda.*
2 – *¿Por dónde se va a la [BEEP], por favor?*
– *Primero sigue todo recto. Pasa los semáforos. Luego toma la segunda calle a la derecha. Está al final de la calle.*
3 – *¿Por dónde se va al [BEEP], por favor?*
– *Está lejos. Primero sigue todo recto. Cruza la plaza. Luego cruza el puente. Después toma la primera calle a la izquierda. Está allí.*
4 – *¿Por dónde se va a la [BEEP], por favor?*
– *A ver… sigue todo recto… toma la primera calle a la derecha. Está al final de la calle.*
5 – *¿Por dónde se va a la [BEEP]?*
– *Primero sigue todo recto, luego toma la segunda calle a la izquierda. Está al final de la calle.*
6 – *¿Por dónde se va a la [BEEP], por favor?*
– *Está lejos. Primero sigue todo recto. Cruza la plaza. Luego cruza el puente. Está a la derecha.*
7 – *¿Por dónde se va a la [BEEP], por favor?*
– *Está cerca. Primero pasa los semáforos. Luego toma la primera calle a la izquierda. Está al final de la calle.*
8 – *¿Por dónde se va a la [BEEP]?*
– *Sigue todo recto. Cruza la plaza y está a la izquierda.*
9 – *¿Por dónde se va al [BEEP], por favor?*
– *A ver… Primero pasa los semáforos. Luego toma la primera calle a la derecha. Está a la derecha.*

Answers

1 estanco 2 carnicería 3 supermercado
4 farmacia 5 tienda de recuerdos 6 confitería
7 tienda de ropa 8 joyería 9 quiosco

✚ Students work in pairs, taking it in turn to ask for and give directions using the map in exercise 5.

🅖 Grammar

Use the Grammar box to review **a** + the definite article (singular).

7 Write a question for your partner. Your partner looks at the map and writes down how to get there.

Writing. In pairs: students take it in turn to write a question asking for directions to a place on the map in exercise 5, and to respond with written instructions on how to get there.

Plenary

Ask students to summarise how **a** is used with the definite article (singular).

Students take it in turn to ask you how to get to a particular shop, using **al/a la** as appropriate. Respond each time with a single instruction, getting another student to translate this into English.

Cuaderno Verde, pages 16–17

1

Answers

a *el supermercado– supermarket*
b el quiosco – newspaper stall
c la carnicería – butcher's
d la farmacia – chemist's
e la tienda de ropa – clothes shop
f el estanco – tobacconist/stamps

2

Answers

e	s	t	á	r	t	r	c	d
a	i	p	a	s	a	e	a	e
l	g	t	o	m	a	c	l	r
p	u	e	n	t	e	t	l	e
l	e	j	o	s	n	o	e	c
c	r	u	z	a	d	e	l	h
i	z	q	u	i	e	r	d	a
s	e	m	á	f	o	r	o	s

1 **Está** cerca. *It is **near***.
2 Está **lejos**. ***It is** far*.
3 **Sigue** todo **recto**. *Go **straight on***.
4 **Cruza** la plaza. *Cross the **square***.
5 Cruza el **puente**. ***Cross** the bridge*.
6 **Pasa** los **semáforos**. *Go past the **traffic lights***.
7 **Toma** la primera calle a la **derecha**. *Take the **first** street on the right*.
8 Toma la segunda **calle** a la **izquierda**. *Take the **second** street on the left*.
9 Está **al** final de la calle. *It's at the end of the **street***.

3

Answers

1 la carnicería **2** el supermercado **3** la joyería
4 la confitería

4

Answers

1 Sigue todo recto y pasa los semáforos. Toma la segunda calle a la derecha. Está a la izquierda.
2 Pasa los semáforos y sigue todo recto. Cruza la plaza y toma la primera calle a la izquierda. Está a la derecha.
3 Pasa los semáforos y sigue todo recto. Cruza la plaza y toma la primera calle a la izquierda. Está a la izquierda.
4 Pasa los semáforos y sigue todo recto. Cruza la plaza y toma la primera calle a la derecha. Está a la izquierda.

3 Tomando tapas (Student Book pages 30–31)

Main topics and objectives

- Ordering in a restaurant
- Using **me gusta** + the definite article

Grammar

- Using **me gusta** + definite article

Key language

¿Qué (no) te gusta comer?
(No) Me gusta el/la…
(No) Me gustan los/las…
Como (paella), pero no como nunca (flan).

De primer plato/segundo plato/ postre…
voy a tomar…
me pone…

el gazpacho
las lentejas con chorizo
el jamón serrano
la tortilla de patatas
la paella
la chuleta de cerdo con verduras
el filete de ternera
los calamares
la merluza
el flan
los helados de fresa, vainilla y chocolate

la tarta de queso
el pan
la bebida

Me falta un tenedor/un cuchillo/ una cuchara.
No hay sal/aceite/vinagre.
El plato/vaso está sucio.

Resources

CD 1, tracks 30–34
Cuaderno Verde, pages 18–19
Gramática 208

Starter 1

To review *me gusta(n)*

Write up the following, supplying the singular and plural words in random order underneath the table (shown here under the appropriate columns for reference). Give students 3 minutes to put the words in the correct column.

me gusta	me gustan

la paella	*los perritos calientes*
el helado	*las hamburguesas*
la tarta	*los calamares*
el jamón	*las tapas*
el chocolate	*las tortillas*

Check answers, asking students to summarise how **me gusta** and **me gustan** are used.

1 Escucha y lee. ¿Qué significa?

Listening. Students listen to the menu on the recording, reading the text at the same time. They then translate the menu into English. Encourage them to use reading strategies, resorting to a dictionary only if stuck.

Audioscript *Track 30*

Restaurante La Alhambra
Menú del día – 15€

Primer plato
gazpacho
lentejas con chorizo
jamón serrano
tortilla de patatas

Segundo plato
paella
chuleta de cerdo con verduras

filete de ternera
calamares
merluza

Postres
flan
helados de fresa, vainilla y chocolate
tarta de queso

+ pan + bebida

Answers

Starter
1 *gazpacho – gazpacho soup*
2 lentejas con chorizo – *lentils with chorizo*
3 jamón serrano – *serrano ham*
4 tortilla de patatas – *potato omelette*

Main course
5 paella – *paella*
6 chuleta de cerdo con verduras – *pork chop with vegetables*
7 filete de ternera – *fillet of veal/beef*
8 calamares – *squid*
9 merluza – *hake*

Desserts
10 flan – *crème caramel*
11 helados de fresa, vainilla y chocolate – *ice cream: strawberry, vanilla and chocolate*
12 tarta de queso – *cheesecake*
13 pan + bebida – *bread + drink*

---

2 Escucha y escribe los platos mencionados. (1–2)

Escucha otra vez. ¿Les gusta 🖤 o no les gusta 🖤?

Listening. Students listen to two people discussing their food likes and dislikes. On first listening they note the foods mentioned. When they listen again, they note whether the speaker likes or dislikes each food, using a heart symbol or a crossed-out heart symbol.

Audioscript *Track 31*

1 – ¿Qué te gusta comer?
– A ver… me gusta mucho la tortilla de patatas.
– No me gusta nada el gazpacho. No me gusta la sopa. A mí me gusta la paella.
– A mí también.
2 – ¿Te gusta comer calamares?
– Sí, me gustan mucho.
– A mí me gusta la carne, el filete de ternera y las chuletas de cerdo por ejemplo, pero no me gustan nada las verduras.

Answers

1 tortilla de patatas
gazpacho ✗
paella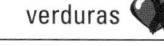
2 calamares ♥
filete de ternera + chuletas de cerdo ♥
verduras ✗

Pronunciation

Read through the words as a class to practise the pronunciation of **z**, **c**, **ll** and **j**. Then play the recording. Ask individual students to read the sentences, following the model on the recording. Challenge them to see who can sound the most authentically Spanish.

Audioscript *Track 32*

Nuestras especialidades son el gazpacho, la tortilla y las lentejas con chorizo.

3 Con tu compañero/a, pregunta y contesta.

Speaking. In pairs: students take it in turn to ask and answer questions about their food preferences. The questions and answer openings are supplied for support.

G Grammar

Use the Grammar box to review **el/la/los/las** + noun after **me gusta(n)**. Students then work out which article to use with each of the items on the menu in exercise 1.

R Students working in pairs take it in turn to prompt with a food (e.g. *gazpacho*) and to respond with a sentence (e.g. *Me gusta el gazpacho* or *No me gusta el gazpacho*).

Starter 2

To review *me gusta(n)*; to review the near future tense

Write up the following. Give students 3 minutes to complete the sentence openings using different foods.

Me gusta…, pero no me gustan…
De primer plato voy a tomar…
De segundo voy a…
De postre…

Hear some answers. Ask students to summarise how **me gusta(n)** is used and how the near future tense is formed.

4 Escucha y lee. Busca estas frases en español en el texto.

Listening. Students listen to Valeria ordering food in a restaurant, and follow the text at the same time. They then find the Spanish versions of the English sentences listed.

Audioscript *Track 33*

– ¿Qué va a tomar?
– Tengo hambre. De primer plato voy a tomar gazpacho.
– ¿Y de segundo plato?
– De segundo voy a tomar filete de ternera, y de postre tarta de queso, por favor.
– Muy bien. ¿Y para beber…?
– Ah… sí. También tengo sed. Me pone agua mineral, pero sin gas.
– Muy bien.

– ¡Que aproveche!
– El gazpacho, ¡qué rico!
– Todo está muy bueno.
– ¿Algo más?
– No, nada más. ¿Me trae la cuenta, por favor?

Answers

a ¿Qué va a tomar?
b ¿Y para beber?
c Tengo sed.
d Voy a tomar…
e ¡Que aproveche!
f ¿Algo más?
g Tengo hambre.
h De primer plato…
i De postre…

⭐ ResultsPlus

Tip box on making adjectives agree.

⊕ Zona Cultura

Culture box on tipping in Spain.

5 Con tu compañero/a, haz tres diálogos cambiando las frases subrayadas del ejercicio 4.

Speaking. In pairs: students make up three dialogues along the lines of the one in exercise 4. They take it in turn to play the part of the customer and the waiter, changing the underlined expressions each time.

6 Escucha. Copia y completa la tabla en inglés. (1–5)

Listening. Ask students to read through the picture captions first, then check comprehension. Students copy out the table. They listen to five dialogues in a restaurant and complete the table in English with the details of the food and drink ordered and the letter(s) of the problem(s) mentioned (from **a–h**). There is one distractor.

Audioscript *Track 34*

1 – *¿Qué va a tomar?*
– *Tengo mucha hambre. De primero voy a tomar lentejas con chorizo y de segundo merluza, por favor.*
– *Muy bien, ¿y para beber?*
– *Una limonada. …*
– *¡Que aproveche!*
– *Gracias… un momentito. Por favor, me falta un cuchillo.*
– *Lo siento, señora. Aquí tiene.*

2 – *Chuleta de cerdo con verduras. ¡Que aproveche, señor!*
– *Gracias.*
– *¿Algo más, señor?*
– *No gracias… Ah sí… un momento, señor… no hay aceite.*
– *¡Ay! Lo siento. Aquí tiene.*

3 – *Me gustan mucho los calamares. Voy a tomar calamares y un agua mineral.*
– *¿Y de postre?*
– *De postre me gustaría tomar tarta de queso. …*
– *¡Que aproveche!*
– *Gracias… Un momento, señora… este vaso está sucio.*
– *¡Ay! Lo siento, señor. Aquí tiene un vaso limpio.*

4 – *Hola. De primer plato vamos a tomar jamón serrano y tortilla de patatas. Y de segundo paella y filete de ternera.*
– *Muy bien. ¿Y para beber?*
– *Coca-Cola.*
– *Vale. …*
– *Aquí tiene. ¡Que aproveche!*
– *Gracias… Señor… no hay ni sal ni vinagre…*
– *Lo siento. Aquí tiene.*

5 – *Vale. Aquí tiene gazpacho con pan. ¡Que aproveche!*
– *Un momento, señor, este plato está sucio.*
– *Lo siento, señorita. Aquí tiene un plato limpio.*
– *Y me falta una cuchara.*
– *Lo siento. Aquí tiene.*

Answers

	food /drink ordered	problems
1	*lentils with sausage, hake, lemonade*	*b*
2	pork chop with vegetables	e
3	squid, mineral water, cheesecake	h
4	serrano ham, potato omelette, paella, veal/beef steak, coke	d, f
5	gazpacho soup and bread	g, c

7 Write a dialogue in the restaurant. Use exercise 4 as a model, but make sure you include two problems from exercise 6.

Writing. Students write a dialogue set in a restaurant. They use the one in exercise 4 as a model, changing the underlined details and adding two problems from exercise 6.

Plenary

Listen to a few dialogues from exercise 7. Invite constructive feedback from the rest of the class on content and delivery.

Cuaderno Verde, pages 18–19

1

Answers

Camarero:	¿Qué va a tomar?
Marta:	Tengo **(1) hambre**. De primer plato **(2) voy a tomar** tortilla.
Camarero:	¿Y de segundo plato?
Marta:	**(3) No me gusta** mucho la carne. ¿Hay pescado?
Camarero:	Sí, hay calamares y merluza.
Marta:	Pues, **(4) me gustan** los calamares y también la merluza… La merluza, por favor.
Camarero:	Muy bien. ¿Y para beber?
Marta:	**(5) Tengo sed**. ¿Me pone **(6) agua mineral** con gas?
Camarero:	Muy bien.
	…
Marta:	Por favor, **(7) no hay** sal y **(8) me falta** un tenedor.
Camarero:	Lo siento, señorita. Aquí tiene. ¡Que aproveche!
	…
Marta:	La tortilla, ¡qué rica!
	…
Camarero:	¿Qué va a tomar de postre? **(9) Hay** flan, helado y tarta de fresas.
Marta:	**(10) Me gusta el** helado. Un helado de vainilla, por favor.

2

Answers

1 No hay vinagre. **f**
2 Me falta un tenedor. **a**
3 Me falta una cuchara. **c**
4 No hay sal. **d**
5 El vaso está sucio. **h**
6 No hay aceite. **e**
7 Me falta un cuchillo. **b**
8 El plato está sucio. **g**

3

Answers

1 Me gustan las lentejas.
2 ¿Te gustan los calamares?
3 No me gustan las fresas.
4 Me gusta la tortilla.
5 No me gusta el pescado.

4 En Sevilla (Student Book pages 32–33)

Main topics and objectives

- Describing a visit to Seville
- Using the preterite to describe past actions

Grammar

- The preterite

Key language

Revision of unit vocabulary so far

Resources

CD 1, track 35
Cuaderno Verde, page 20
Gramática 196

Starter 1

To review the present tense and the preterite of common verbs

Write up the following. Give students 3 minutes to complete the table.

Todos los días		El año pasado	
		visité	I visited
compro	I buy		
			I went
		me gustó	

Check answers.

1 Escucha y escribe las letras correctas. (1–6)

Listening. Students listen to someone talking about a trip to Seville and answer the multiple-choice questions. You may want to point out that more than one answer is sometimes required.

Audioscript *Track 35*

1 – ¿Adónde fuiste de vacaciones el año pasado?
– Fui a Sevilla, en España.
– ¿A Sevilla? ¡Qué guay! ¿Cuánto tiempo pasaste allí?
– Pasé una semana en Sevilla con mis padres.

2 – ¿Qué hiciste en Sevilla?
– Hice mucho. Primero fui de excursión y visité muchos monumentos. También vi vistas espléndidas y saqué muchas fotos. Un día subí a la Giralda y fui de compras.

3 – ¿Qué tal lo pasaste?
– Lo pasé fenomenal. La ciudad me gustó mucho, especialmente la Giralda y las tiendas.

4 – ¿Qué compraste?
– Pues… fui a una tienda de recuerdos y compré unas postales y una camiseta. Los recuerdos de Sevilla son muy bonitos, pero también caros.

5 – ¿Cómo visitaste la ciudad?
– Un día cogí un autobús turístico, pero también visité la ciudad a pie. No monté en bicicleta porque hay mucho tráfico en la ciudad.

6 – ¿Qué comiste durante tu visita?
– Comí platos típicos de España: calamares y gazpacho. ¡Qué ricos! Mi plato favorito es los calamares.

Answers

1 d **2** f, h, e **3** i **4** o, m **5** r, q **6** w, t

G Grammar

Use the Grammar box to review the preterite (regular 'I' forms, plus some irregular).

2 With your partner, imagine a visit to Seville and have a conversation about it.

Speaking. In pairs: students imagine they have been to Seville recently and discuss their trips, taking it in turn to ask and answer questions. The questions and answer openings are supplied.

Starter 2

To practise using the preterite

Write up the following. Give students 3 minutes to complete each sentence with the correct preterite form of each infinitive shown.

Fui a Sevilla y…
1 (ver) vistas espléndidas.
2 (visitar) la ciudad a pie.
3 lo (pasar) fenomenal.
4 (comer) jamón.
5 no (comprar) nada.

(*Answers:* **1** vi **2** visité **3** pasé **4** comí **5** compré)

Check answers.

3 Lee los textos y contesta a las preguntas en inglés.

Reading. Students read the three texts and identify which person is being described in each of the questions. Some vocabulary is glossed for support.

Answers

1 Carlos **2** Isabel **3** Pablo
4 Carlos **5** Pablo **6** Isabel

4 Lee los textos otra vez. Busca estas frases en español.

Reading. Students reread the texts in exercise 4 and identify the Spanish versions of the English sentences listed.

Answers

1 hay muchos sitios fascinantes
2 fue un rollo
3 fue una experiencia inolvidable
4 todo era muy caro
5 vi unos monumentos increíbles
6 me encantó

5 Write a paragraph about your holiday in Seville (or another city). Use the questions from exercise 2 to help you structure your writing.

Writing. Students write a text about a holiday in Seville or another city of their choice. They should use the questions in exercise 2 to structure their writing and aim to include language from the text in exercise 1.

💰➕ Students could choose and research a Spanish city on-line using Spanish-language tourist sites. You could set them the challenge of working out an itinerary for a weekend there, either with their family or with a group of friends.

Plenary

Challenge the class to come up with all the verbs used in the preterite in this unit.

Have the class choose a city. Then go round the class with students taking it in turn to say something positive or negative about it, using either **me gustó…** or **no me gustó…**

Cuaderno Verde, page 20

1

Answers

1 Pasé unos días…
2 Otro día fui de compras.
3 Después fui en autobús al puerto.
4 Me gustó mucho.
5 Lo que más me gustó fue…

2

Answers

1 The weather was good. **T**
2 On the second day Raúl took photos.
3 Raúl visited the market. **T**
4 He bought postcards at the museum.
5 Raúl walked to the beach.
6 He liked his meal in the restaurant. **T**
7 He went to a music concert. **T**
8 He saw a bullfight.

5 Las fiestas (Student Book pages 34–35)

Main topics and objectives
- Talking about festivals
- Using the present tense ('we' form)

Grammar
- Using the present tense ('we' form)

Key language
el Eid al Fitr
San Fermín/San Fermines
El día de los Muertos
el Ramadán

la Nochevieja
el Diwali
la Navidad
la Feria de Abril
una fiesta religiosa
celebrar
decorar
preparar
cocinar
cenar
bailar
cantar
venir
llevar
traer regalos

importante
especial
divertido/a
fascinante
impresionante
emocionante
increíble

Resources
CD 1, tracks 36–38
Cuaderno Verde, pages 21–22
Gramática 190

Starter 1

To review the 'we' form of present tense -ar verbs; to review language for talking about festivals

Write up the following. Give students 3 minutes to translate the sentences into English.

1 *Preparamos una cena deliciosa.*
2 *Compramos dulces para la familia y los amigos.*
3 *Decoramos las casas con lámparas de colores.*
4 *Celebramos el veinticuatro de diciembre.*

Check answers.

1 Escucha y lee la entrevista. Contesta a las preguntas en inglés.

Listening. Students listen to Samir being interviewed about a special celebration, following the text at the same time. They then answer the comprehension questions in English.

Audioscript *Track 36*

– ¿Cuál es la mejor fiesta, en tu opinión?
– Me gusta mucho Eid al Fitr. Es una fiesta muy importante para nosotros los musulmanes.
– ¿Cuándo tiene lugar?
– Al final del mes lunar del Ramadán.
– ¿Qué pasa durante el Ramadán?
– No comemos ni bebemos durante el día.
– ¿Cómo es la fiesta del Eid al Fitr?
– Preparamos una cena deliciosa. Es el día más feliz del año. Compramos dulces para la familia y los amigos y traemos regalos para los niños. Hay un ambiente muy especial y emocionante y lo pasamos fenomenal.

Answers
1 Eid al Fitr.
2 At the end of Ramadan.
3 Muslims drink and eat nothing during the day.
4 It is the happiest day of the year.
5 Sweets or presents.

Cultural note
During Ramadan, millions of Muslims fast from sunrise to sunset in order to achieve spiritual purification. Ramadan takes place during the ninth month of the Islamic calendar. Ramadan concludes with three days of feasting: Eid al Fitr is the name of the feast. It means 'the fast is broken'.

G Grammar

Use the Grammar box to review the present tense (singular and 'we' form) of regular verbs. Students then identify all the verbs in the 'we' form in the text in exercise 1.

2 Escucha y escribe la letra de la festividad correcta. (1–3)

Listening. Students listen to three people talking about their favourite festivals and identify the festival being described each time (from **a–c**).

Audioscript *Track 37*

1 – ¿Cuál es la mejor festividad?
  – Me gusta mucho la celebración de la Nochevieja. Es una fiesta importante.
  – ¿Cuándo tiene lugar?
  – La última noche del año, el treinta y uno de diciembre.
  – ¿Qué pasa durante la fiesta?
  – Comemos doce uvas de la suerte mientras suenan las doce campanadas.
  – ¿Cómo es?
  – Es difícil, pero es divertido y hay un ambiente muy emocionante.
2 – ¿Cuál es la mejor festividad?
  – Me encanta la fiesta de San Fermín en Pamplona. Es una fiesta impresionante.

– ¿Cuándo tiene lugar?
– Tiene lugar el siete de julio.
– ¿Qué pasa?
– La gente lleva una camiseta y unos pantalones blancos y un pañuelo rojo y todos corren por la calle para escapar de los toros.
– ¿Cómo es?
– Me encanta esta celebración. Hay un ambiente muy especial. ¡Es increíble!

3 – ¿Cuál es la mejor festividad?
– Me gusta mucho la celebración del día de los Muertos. Es una fiesta fascinante.
– ¿Cuándo tiene lugar?
– En noviembre.
– ¿Qué pasa?
– Las familias hacen altares para sus muertos.
– ¿Cómo es?
– Es interesante. Es un ritual que celebra la vida. Hay un ambiente único.

Answers
1 c 2 a 3 b

3 Listen again and answer the questions for each of the three festivals.

Listening. Students listen to the recording in exercise 2 again and answer the comprehension questions for each of the three festivals.

Audioscript *Track 38*

As exercise 2.

Answers
1 ● New Year's Eve – 31st December
  ● eat 12 grapes as the bells ring
  ● importante – *important*; difícil – *difficult*; divertido – *fun*; emocionante – *exciting*
2 ● San Fermines – *7th July*
  ● bull running – people wear white with a red handkerchief
  ● impresionante – *impressive*; especial – *special*; increíble – *incredible*
3 ● el día de los Muertos – November
  ● people make shrines for their dead relatives
  ● fascinante – *fascinating*; interesante – *interesting*; único – *unique*

Starter 2

To practise distinguishing tenses

Write up the following. Give students 3 minutes to correct the sentences by replacing the verbs with appropriate alternatives in the 'we' form.

1 *Llevamos un árbol de Navidad.*
2 *Comemos champán.*
3 *Celebramos regalos para los niños.*
4 *Vivimos una cena deliciosa.*

(*Answers:* Decoramos, Bebemos, Traemos/Compramos, Preparamos)

Check answers. Ask students to summarise the 'we' form endings for **-ar**, **-er** and **-ir** verbs.

4 Lee los textos. Copia y completa la tabla.

Reading. Students copy out the table. They read the three texts on different festivals and complete the table with the details in English.

Answers

	festival	time of year	decorations	food eaten	other details
Marcelo	Diwali	October/November	coloured lights, garlands	delicious dishes and very good sweets	give presents to the family, people wear new clothes, let off firecrackers and fireworks
María	Christmas	24 December	Christmas tree, crib	turkey	go to Mass, other friends come, have turkey for dinner
Lía	Feria de Abril	April	–	fried fish, sherry	wear traditional flamenco dress, dance, sing, eat and drink, there are bullfights every evening

➕ Students list all the verbs in the texts in exercise 5, categorising them by person (I, he/she, we, etc.). They then translate them into English.

5 Con tu compañero/a, habla de la fiesta que prefieres.

Speaking. In pairs: students talk about their favourite festival, taking it in turn to ask and answer questions. A framework is supplied.

⭐ ResultsPlus
Tip box on including adjectives in speaking and writing.

6 Escribe un texto sobre tu festividad preferida.

Writing. Students write a text on their own favourite festival or celebration, using the questions in exercise 5 to structure it.

Tip box on improving writing: using present-tense verbs in the 'we' form, connectives and adjectives.

📀 Students research another Spanish festival or celebration on the internet (e.g. Semana Santa, las Fallas, la Tomatina) and write out in English three interesting facts about it.

Plenary

Put the class into teams. Ask the class to choose a festival or other celebration. Each team takes it in turn to say something about the festival, using the language of the unit. A correct sentence using the 'we' form of the present tense wins 2 points.

Cuaderno Verde, page 21

1

Answers

(*b*) En la 'Tomatina de Buñol', lanzamos tomates a los (*f*) espectadores. Empezamos la fiesta a las once y terminamos (*d*) a las doce exactamente. Este año lanzamos más de cien (*e*) mil kilos de tomates. Después preparamos una (*a*) cena especial y comemos jamón con (*c*) tomate. ¡Hay un ambiente increíble!

2

Answers

1 *celebramos* **2** decoramos **3** lanzamos
4 tenemos **5** bailamos **6** lo pasamos fenomenal

Cuaderno Verde, page 22

1

Answers

Normalmente mi hermana Ana y yo **(1)** *tenemos* clase de flamenco los sábados por la mañana y **(2)** **bailamos** durante dos horas. ¡Lo **(3)** **pasamos** muy bien! Después siempre **(4)** **vamos** al centro comercial. Me **(5)** **gusta** comprar ropa en una tienda moderna. Ana **(6)** **compra** maquillaje a menudo. A mediodía **(7)** **comemos** en una cafetería. Generalmente **(8)** **tomo** un bocadillo de jamón y Ana siempre **(9)** **come** un bocadillo de tortilla de patata. A veces **(10)** **bebemos** limonada. **(11)** **Volvemos** a casa y mi madre **(12)** **prepara** la cena. Luego, por la noche Ana **(13)** **sale** con sus amigos y yo **(14)** **voy** al cine con mi amiga Olivia. Me encantan las películas románticas…

2

Answers

1	escuchar	I listen	*escucho*
2	bailar	I dance	**bailo**
3	comprar	you buy	**compras**
4	comer	he/she eats	**come**
5	beber	I drink	**bebo**
6	salir	you go out	**sales**
7	ir	I go	**voy**
8	hacer	I do/make	**hago**

I listened	*escuché*
I danced	**bailé**
you bought	**compraste**
he/she ate	**comió**
I drank	**bebí**
you went out	**saliste**
I went	**fui**
I did/made	**hice**

2 Prueba oral: Tourist information (Student Book pp. 36–37)

Topics revised	Resources
● Talking about tourism	CD 5, tracks 5–7

Overview

Read through the task box at the top of the page and outline for students how this section works. They will hear a Speaking controlled assessment model interaction in three parts and do exercises focused on the language used. These exercises, along with the advice/activities on how to improve speaking performance in Results Plus, will help them prepare to take part in a role-play style interaction of their own on the topic.

Before listening

As exercise 1 requires students to ask as well as answer a number of questions, you could do the following pre-listening task on questions. Write up the following:

a *¿Habla usted español?*
b *¿En qué puedo ayudarle?*
c *¿Qué hay de interés en Oxford?*
d *¿Cuánto tiempo va a pasar en Oxford?*
e *¿Le gustan los deportes?*
f *¿Le gusta la historia?*
g *¿A qué hora abre el castillo?*
h *¿Por dónde se va al castillo?*
i *¿Me puede usted recomendar un restaurante?*
j *¿Qué pasa durante la Navidad aquí?*

Working in pairs, students decide (1) what each question means and (2) predict which ones will be used in the recording by Jade (playing the tourist office assistant) and which will be used by the examiner (playing the tourist.)

Point out the use of the **usted** form in formal situations.

(*Answers:*
a *Do you speak Spanish?*
b *How can I help you?*
c *What is there of interest in Oxford?*
d *How much time are you going to spend in Oxford?*
e *Do you like sports?*
f *Do you like history?*
g *At what time does the castle open?*
h *How do you get to the castle?*
i *Can you recommend a restaurant?*
j *What happens here at Christmas?*

Jade's/tourist office assistant's questions:
b, d, e, f
Examiner's/tourist's questions:
a, c, g, h, i, j)

1 You are going to listen to Jade, an exam candidate, taking part in the above interaction. Jade is playing the role of the tourist information officer. In which order do you hear these phrases or questions?

Listening. Explain to the students that they will hear a sample of the kind of role-play style interaction they are expected to have in the Speaking controlled assessment.

Students listen and note the sentences/questions in the order they hear them.

Audioscript *Track 5*

Part 1

– *Buenos días. ¿Habla usted español?*
– *Sí, claro. ¿En qué puedo ayudarle?*
– *A ver... ¿qué hay de interés en Oxford?*
– *Pues, hay muchos lugares de interés y monumentos antiguos muy bonitos. También hay museos muy interesantes, el Ashmolean, por ejemplo. Además, hay muchos parques, cines, bares y restaurantes. Es una ciudad animada con buen ambiente por lo general. Me gusta mucho. ¿Cuánto tiempo va a pasar en Oxford?*
– *Voy a pasar una semana en Oxford.*
– *¿Le gustan los deportes?*
– *Me gusta hacer natación y en invierno me gusta patinar.*
– *Muy bien. Hay una piscina en el centro y también hay una pista de hielo.*

Answers

g, e, c, d, b, h, a, f

✚ Play the recording again, pausing after each noun/adjective or adjective/noun phrase. Students explain why the adjective has the ending it does.

2 Listen to part 2 of Jade's interaction and note down the words that fill the gaps.

Listening. Students now listen to the second part of Jade's interaction and complete the gap-fill version of the transcript. The answers are supplied in random order for support.

With a confident class you could ask students to read the text and try to work out plausible answers first, then use the recording to check.

Audioscript *Track 6*

Part 2

– *¿Le gusta la historia?*
– *Sí, me **encanta** la historia.*
– *Pues, en Oxford **hay** un castillo impresionante. El **año pasado** subí a la torre y **saqué** muchas fotos. Fue*

estupendo. **También** *cogí un autobús turístico. Primero* **visité** *unos colegios y luego fui al parque. Lo que más me gustó fue 'Christ Church College'.* **Fue** *muy interesante.*

- *¿A qué hora abre el castillo?*
- *El castillo* **abre** *todos los días a las diez. Cierra a las cinco y media.*
- *¿Por dónde se va al castillo?*
- *A ver. No está* **lejos**. *Primero siga todo recto. Tome la primera calle a la izquierda y está a la* **derecha**.

Answers

Also in bold in the audioscript.

1 me encanta **2** hay **3** El año pasado **4** saqué
5 También **6** visité **7** Fue **8** abre **9** lejos
10 derecha

---

3 Now listen to part 3 of Jade's interaction and rewrite the jumbled words in bold.

Listening. Students listen to the third and final part of Jade's interaction and write out the words that are given as anagrams. A confident class could attempt to work out the words first, and then use the recording to check their answers.

Audioscript *Track 7*

Part 3

- *¿Me puede usted recomendar un restaurante?*
- *Mi restaurante preferido es un restaurante italiano en el centro. Se llama 'Molto bene'. La especialidad de la casa es la pizza. ¡Qué rica!*
- *¿Qué pasa durante la Navidad aquí?*
- *Me gusta mucho la Navidad. Es una fiesta importante en Oxford. Ponemos luces y un árbol en el centro comercial. Es típico comer pavo. Este año creo que voy a cocinar pasteles o dar fotos a mi familia y a mis amigos. Hay un ambiente especial. ¡Lo vamos a pasar bomba!*

Answers

1 restaurante, centro **2** rica **3** Navidad **4** fiesta
5 comer **6** pasteles, amigos **7** especial **8** bomba

⭐ ResultsPlus

The Results Plus support for speaking activities is differentiated, allowing students to identify and work towards their target level: covering the basics, Grade C, increasing their marks. Encourage students to adopt the techniques in these sections in all extended speaking activities.

Read through and discuss the Results Plus section together.

4 Now it's your turn! Prepare your answers to the task and then do the interaction with your partner or your teacher.

Speaking. Students participate in a role-play interaction on a travel and tourism theme in the style of a controlled assessment task. They should use all the support supplied, here and elsewhere on the spread:

- the Results Plus advice on the language to include
- Jade's responses, adapted to talk about themselves
- the English notes in the task box, p. 36
- their answers to exercises 1–3.

Each student takes part in an interaction as the person answering the questions. If they are working with a partner, they will take turns asking and answering.

If possible, record the interactions or have the students record themselves. They can then swap recordings with a partner, listen to each other's version and offer comments on how it might be improved. A simple marking system is suggested (one/two/three stars for listed categories). Students should then identify two or three areas which they would like to improve next time they do an extended speaking task.

2 Prueba escrita (Student Book pp. 38–39)

Topics revised

● Writing about a Spanish festival

1 Read the text and put these topics into the order of the text.

Reading. Students read the text and reorder the topics (**a–e**) as they are mentioned.

Answers

b, e, a, c, d

2 Find these expressions in Spanish in the text.

Reading. Students reread the text and identify the Spanish versions of the English expressions listed.

Answers

1 …una fiesta muy importante.
2 …hay un ambiente especial.
3 Tiene lugar en diciembre…
4 Es típico comer pavo.
5 …si hace buen tiempo…
6 ¡Lo pasamos fenomenal!
7 …pasé dos semanas en Madrid…
8 …cené ternera asada…
9 Fue increíble.
10 ¡Va a ser genial!

3 Find six adjectives in the text that Naomi uses to describe festivals or atmosphere.

Reading. Students reread the text and find six adjectives used by Naomi to describe festivals or atmosphere.

Answers

Any six: importante, especial, típico, fenomenal, increíble, guay, genial

4 Choose the four sentences which are correct.

Reading. Students reread the text and identify which four of the statements supplied about it are correct.

Answers

1, 4, 5, 8

5 You might be asked to write about a celebration as a controlled assessment task. Use the Results Plus to help you prepare your account.

Students read through the language support material supplied in preparation for doing their own extended writing task in exercise 6.

⊛ ResultsPlus

The Results Plus section gives students the support they need to structure and improve their writing. The support is differentiated, allowing students to identify and work towards their target level: covering the basics, Grade C, increasing their marks. Encourage students to adopt the kind of approach taken in this section in all extended writing activities.

6 Now write a full account of your favourite celebration.

Writing. Students write their own text about their favourite celebration in the style of a controlled assessment task (at least 100 words). As well as the Results Plus guidelines on the language to include, they should use all the support supplied here:

● Naomi's text, adapted to refer to themselves
● the sample structure for the text.

7 Check carefully what you have written.

Writing. Students check their own work using the list of features supplied.

• This section helps students develop their listening and reading skills in preparation for the exam.

Resources

CD 5, tracks 8–10

LEER

1 Read this welcome message on the TV in your hotel bedroom. Answer the questions. *(2 marks)*

Reading. Students read the text and answer the comprehension questions in English.

These questions approximate to Grade E. Warn students that in each case there may initially appear to be more than one possible answer, but the inappropriate ones can be eliminated because of a clear negative.

> **Answers**
> **1** swimming pool
> **2** *Any one of:* you can't smoke in the room; you can't smoke in the bar; you can smoke in the (hotel) garden

⭐ ResultsPlus

Tip box on reading the question carefully and using this as a guide to read carefully for negatives.

2 Look at the list below of activities in Seville. Which would most interest each tourist? Write a letter for each person. *(1 mark for each person)*

Reading. Students read the list of activities. They then read what each person likes and match the person to the appropriate activity.

The text required to answer the first three questions approximates to Grade D, as it contains reasonably familiar vocabulary or cognates. For the last three questions, the text approximates to Grade C, as it contains some unfamiliar vocabulary and requires some association of vocabulary.

> **Answers**
> **1** d **2** h **3** c **4** e **5** a **6** g

⭐ ResultsPlus

Tip box on reading strategies: looking for paraphrases, related vocabulary and cognates.

ESCUCHAR

3 Listen to Miguel talking about his holiday in Seville. Answer the questions. *(6 marks)*

Listening. Students listen to Miguel talking about his holiday in Seville and answer the comprehension questions in English.

Questions 1, 3, and 4 approximate to Grade G as they require simple word recognition. The other questions approximate to Grade F because of the vocabulary (questions 2 and 6) and the location of the key information (question 5).

Audioscript *Track 8*

1 *Fui a Sevilla en agosto.*
[Repeated as above]
2 *Pasé una semana allí.*
[Repeated as above]
3 *Fui con mis amigos.*
[Repeated as above]
4 *El primer día visité la catedral.*
[Repeated as above]
5 *Pasé dos horas en el museo.*
[Repeated as above]
6 *Mi restaurante favorito estaba cerca del parque.*
[Repeated as above]

> **Answers**
> **1** August **2** a week **3** his friends **4** the cathedral
> **5** two hours **6** near the park

⭐ ResultsPlus

Tip box on approaching listening tasks in the exam.

4 Listen to Miguel giving more information about his holiday. Choose the correct letter. *(3 marks)*

Listening. Students listen to Miguel giving more information about Seville and answer the multiple-choice picture questions.

These questions approximate to Grade E. The stimulus material is now a little longer and contains ideas other than those specifically tested.

Audioscript *Track 9*

1 *Fui en avión porque es rápido y hay vuelos baratos.*
[Repeated as above]
2 *El viaje fue, pues, normal. Lo pasé bien.*
[Repeated as above]

3 *Cuando llegué, hizo mucho sol. Pues, Sevilla es famosa por su buen tiempo, ¿no?*
[Repeated as above]

Answers

1 a **2** b **3** b

 Results Plus

Tip box on listening for distractors and negatives.

5 Some young people are talking about their hotel. What do they mention? Put a cross in the correct box. *(4 marks)*

Listening. Students copy out the table. They listen to four young people talking about their hotel and put a cross in the correct box for each speaker, to indicate what he/she is talking about.

The first two questions approximate to Grade D as they are reasonably straightforward, with fairly accessible phrases and adjectives. The last two questions approximate to Grade C as they require a clear understanding of the language in the context.

Audioscript *Track 10*

1 Andrés
– *¿Qué opinas del hotel, Andrés?*
– *Pienso que las habitaciones son muy cómodas. Me gusta mucho la vista bonita desde mi balcón.*
[Repeated as above]

2 Beatriz
– *¿Qué piensas tú, Beatriz?*
– *El aire acondicionado es fenomenal. Desgraciadamente el ascensor no funciona.*
[Repeated as above]

3 Carlos
– *¿Estás de acuerdo, Carlos?*
– *Pues, en mi opinión el bar está sucio. Por la noche el ruido de la discoteca es horrible.*
[Repeated as above]

4 Diana
– *¿Y cuál es tu opinión, Diana?*
– *Los camareros son buenos. El precio de la comida es caro.*
[Repeated as above]

Answers

	the view	the lifts	the restaurant	the noise	the pool
Andrés	X				
Beatriz		X			
Carlos				X	
Diana			X		

 Results Plus

Tip box on listening for distractors.

● Self-access reading and writing

A Reinforcement

1 Match up the questions and answers.

Reading. Students match the questions and answers.

Answers

1 d 2 b 3 a 4 c 5 e

2 Read the advert and answer the questions below in English.

Reading. Students read the text and answer the comprehension questions in English.

Answers

1 an impressive collection of Spanish art
2 Mondays   3 10:00   4 14:00   5 20:00

3 Write out the words in the word snakes with the correct punctuation. Then match the sentences to the pictures.

Writing. Students write out the word snakes as sentences, then match each sentence to the correct picture.

Answers

1 De primer plato voy a tomar calamares. – **h**
2 Por favor, me falta un cuchillo. – **c**
3 De segundo plato voy a tomar jamón serrano. – **d**
4 Por favor, me falta un tenedor. – **a**
5 El vaso está sucio. – **g**
6 Por favor, no hay aceite. – **e**
7 De postre voy a tomar helado. – **b**
8 No hay vinagre. – **f**

4 Read the text. What opinion does Juan have of the restaurant? Write P (positive), N (negative), or P+N (positive and negative).

Reading. Students read the text, then note the opinion of the person who wrote it: P (positive), N (negative) or P + N (a mixture of both).

Answers

P+N

B Extension

1 Match the sentences to the symbols.

Reading. Students match up the sentences to the correct pictures.

Answers

1 e 2 f 3 c 4 a 5 d 6 b

2 Translate the phrases in red above into English.

Reading. Students reread the sentences in exercise 1 and translate the words in red into English.

Answers

1 I'm scared.
2 I prefer to go by car
3 because it's cheap
4 because it's not expensive
5 I prefer to go on foot
6 for this reason I take a taxi

3 Read the text and then answer the questions below in English.

Reading. Students read Antonia's text and answer the comprehension questions in English.

Answers

1 Paris
2 one day
3 went on a bus tour, bought souvenirs in shops, went up the Eiffel Tower
4 on foot
5 veal/beef steak and apple tart
6 lots of photos she took

4 Write a passage about a day you spent in London. Use the phrases in blue in the text from exercise 3 to help you structure your text.

Students write their own passage about a day trip to London, supported by the phrases in blue from exercise 3 and the prompts supplied.

Module 3 A clase (Student Book pages 44–61)

Unit	Main topics and objectives	Grammar	Skills
Repaso 1 Las asignaturas (pp. 44–45)	• Giving opinions on school subjects • Using a range of verbs to express opinions	Adjectives Verbs of opinion (**gustar, encantar, interesar**)	Using the definite article with **me gusta**; not using it with **tengo** or **estudio** Making adjectives agree Improving written texts
Repaso 2 En clase (pp. 46–47)	• Describing your school routine • Using the present tense with time expressions	The present tense	Understanding times when reading and listening
1 ¿Cómo es tu insti? (pp. 48–49	• Describing your school • Using the present tense	The present tense	Listening for negative opinions and statements
2 ¿Qué llevas en el cole? (pp. 50–51)	• Describing your school uniform • Using colour adjectives correctly	Colour adjectives	Improving speaking by using a variety of structures Using exclamations to sound more authentic
3 Las normas del insti (pp. 52–53)	• Describing school rules and problems at school • Using phrases with the infinitive	The near future tense	Using a variety of structures
4 ¡Los profesores! (pp. 54–55)	• Describing teachers • Using comparatives (more/less than)	Comparatives	Recognising cognates Using qualifiers to add more detail
Prueba oral: School life (pp. 56–57)	Exam speaking practice	Revision	
Prueba escrita (pp. 58–59)	Exam writing practice	Revision	
Te toca a ti (pp. 176–177)	Self-access reading and writing		

Repaso 1 *Las asignaturas* (Student Book pages 44–45)

Main topics and objectives

- Giving opinions on school subjects
- Using a range of verbs to express opinions

Grammar

- Adjectives
- Verbs of opinion (**gustar, encantar, interesar**)

Key language

el comercio
el dibujo
el español
el francés
el inglés
el teatro

la educación física
la geografía
la historia
la religión
la tecnología
los idiomas
las ciencias
las matemáticas

me gusta(n)
me encanta(n)
me gusta(n) mucho
no me gusta(n) nada
odio
me interesa(n)
Mi asignatura preferida es...

porque es.../son...
aburrido/a(s)
difícil(es)

divertido/a(s)
entretenido/a(s)
fácil(es)
guay(s)
interesante(s)
práctico/a(s)
útil(es)

lunes, martes, miércoles, jueves,
 viernes, sábado, domingo
¿Cuándo tienes...?
¿Qué día tienes (inglés)?
Tengo (inglés) los martes.

Resources

CD 2, track 2
Cuaderno Verde, page 25
Gramática 206, 210

Starter 1

To review the vocabulary for school subjects; to review *me gusta(n)*

Write up the following. Give students 3 minutes to translate the sentences into English.

1 *Me gusta el dibujo.*
2 *No me gustan nada las matemáticas.*
3 *Odio la religión.*
4 *Me gusta mucho la educación física.*

Check answers. Then ask students how they would say 'I don't like (art)' and 'I like (science)'.

1 Escribe la palabra para cada dibujo.

Writing. Students label each of the pictures of school subjects, using the words supplied. There are three distractors. Ask students to translate these into English after you check answers to the activity.

> **Answers**
>
> **a** la educación física **b** el teatro **c** el comercio
> **d** el dibujo **e** la tecnología **f** las matemáticas
> **g** las ciencias **h** el español **i** la geografía
> **j** el francés

2 Lee las frases. Identifica si la opinión es positiva (P) o negativa (N).

Reading. Students read the six sentences and identify whether the opinion expressed in each is positive (P) or negative (N). A language box is supplied for support.

> **Answers**
>
> **1** *P* **2** N **3** N **4** P **5** P **6** P

➕ Students translate the sentences into English and then write three more along the same lines in Spanish, using the language box for support.

3 Escucha. Copia y completa la tabla. (1–5)

Listening. Students copy out the table. They listen to five people talking about their school timetables and complete the table with the details in English.

Audioscript *Track 2*

1 – ¿Qué estudias?
   – *Estudio matemáticas, pero no me gustan porque son aburridas y son también muy difíciles.*
2 – ¿Te gusta el español?
   – *Me encanta el español porque es divertido y es bastante interesante.*
3 – ¿Qué estudias?
   – *Los lunes tengo ciencias. Me encantan porque son prácticas y son también bastante fáciles.*
4 – ¿Te gusta la religión?
   – *Pues… odio la religión porque es difícil y no es útil.*
5 – ¿Prefieres el inglés o la historia?
   – *Prefiero el inglés. Es mi asignatura preferida porque es fácil y es guay.*

Answers

	subject	opinion ☺ ☹	why (adjectives used)
1	*maths*	☹	*boring, very difficult*
2	Spanish	☺	fun, quite interesting
3	science	☺	practical, quite easy
4	RE	☹	difficult, not useful
5	English	☺	easy, cool (favourite subject)

✚ Students write sentences giving their opinion of two school subjects.

G Grammar

Use the Grammar box to review adjective agreement.

R Prompt with a subject, e.g. *la música*. Students respond with an opinion, e.g. *La música es guay.* You could make it more challenging by omitting the definite article in your prompts.

Starter 2

To review days of the week

Write up the days of the week in jumbled order. Give students 2 minutes to write them out in the correct chronological order.

4 Con tu compañero/a, pregunta y contesta.

Speaking. In pairs: using the pictures prompts from exercise 1, students take it in turn to ask and answer questions about their school timetables. A sample exchange is given, with the text they need to change underlined.

⭐ ResultsPlus

Tip box on using the definite article with **me gusta** and not using it with **tengo** or **estudio**, plus agreement of adjectives.

5 Lee el correo de Luis y contesta a las preguntas.

Reading. Students read Luis's email and answer the comprehension questions in English.

Answers

1 biology   **2** it's interesting and he loves the animal world   **3** he likes languages because he's interested in other cultures   **4** Rafa is not interested in either   **5** they are practical subjects

G Grammar

Use the Grammar box to review the different forms of **me gusta(n)**, and the similar verbs **encantar** and **interesar**. Contrast these with other verbs of opinion like **odiar** and **preferir**, which don't contain a pronoun.

R Students tell you which subjects they are interested in, using **me interesa(n)**.

6 Write a paragraph in Spanish giving your opinions of school subjects.

Writing. Students write a paragraph giving their own opinions of the subjects they study.

⭐ ResultsPlus

Tip boxes on improving written texts: giving details (e.g. times), including a variety of opinions using different verbs, using **porque es/son** to extend sentences, using a range of adjectives with correct agreements and including other people's opinions.

🐚 If you have links with a school in Spain, use the activities in this module as a cue for students to discuss their experiences of school. See p. 38 for suggestions on linking up with a partner school to exchange information.

Plenary

Ask students to summarise how the verb **gustar** works, and to give you two other verbs that behave like this (**encantar** and **interesar**). Put the class into teams and have the teams take it in turn to respond in Spanish when you prompt in English, e.g. 'He is interested in art.' An answer with the correct pronoun wins 1 point; one which also includes the correct verb ending (e.g. **interesa** or **interesan**) wins 2 points.

Cuaderno Verde, page 25

1

Answers

1 Me gustan las matemáticas porque son fáciles.
2 A mí me encantan los idiomas porque son útiles.
3 Odio las ciencias porque son difíciles.
4 No le gusta el dibujo porque es complicado.
5 Me gusta mucho la educación física porque es práctica.
6 Pedro prefiere la historia porque es muy interesante.

2

Answers

1 I **like** maths because it is **easy**.
2 I **love languages** because they are **useful**.
3 I **hate** science because it is **difficult**.
4 **He/she does not like** art because it is **complicated**.
5 I **like** PE a lot because it is **practical**.
6 Pedro **prefers** history because it is **very interesting**.

3

Answers (sample)

Pepe: ¿Te gusta la geografía?
Sara: ☺ ✓ No, *prefiero* la religión porque es *muy interesante*.
Pepe: ¿Te gusta la historia?
Sara: ☺☺☺ Sí, me **encanta** porque es…
Pepe: ¿Qué opina Miguel de la tecnología?
Sara: ☹☹ **Odia** la tecnología porque **es**…
Pepe: Y a Julia, ¿le gusta el comercio?
Sara: Sí, ☺ **le gusta** porque es… y también ☺☺ **le gustan** mucho las matemáticas porque **son**…

3 Repaso 2 *En clase* (Student Book pages 46–47)

Main topics and objectives
- Describing your school routine
- Using the present tense with time expressions

Grammar
- The present tense

Key language
la primavera
el verano
el otoño
el invierno
En (verano)...
Por la tarde/la mañana...
Normalmente...
Nunca...
Siempre...
A menudo...

¿Cómo vas al colegio?
Voy al colegio/instituto...

Vuelvo del colegio/instituto...
a pie/andando
en coche/autobús/metro/tren/
  bicicleta/moto/autocar
Me gusta ir (en autobús)...
Prefiero ir (en coche)...
cuando hace buen/mal tiempo
cuando llueve
porque es cómodo/rápido/barato

¿A qué hora empiezan/terminan
  tus clases?
Empiezan/Terminan...
a la una/las dos, etc.
y/menos cuarto
y/menos cinco, diez, veinte, etc.
y media
de la mañana
de la tarde

¿Qué haces...?
en clase
en el recreo

a la hora de comer
después del colegio

En clase...
escucho al profe/a la profe
hablo/leo/uso el diccionario/
  escribo mucho

A la hora de comer/En el recreo/
  En verano/En invierno...
juego al tenis/al fútbol
hago natación
voy al club de ajedrez/idiomas
canto en el coro
toco en la orquesta

Resources
CD 2, tracks 3–6
Cuaderno Verde, page 26

Starter 1

To review expressions of frequency

Write up the following, jumbling the order of the second column. Give students 3 minutes to match the Spanish and English versions.

normalmente	normally
por la mañana	in the morning
a menudo	often
nunca	never
en verano	in summer
por la tarde	in the afternoon
en invierno	in winter
siempre	always

Check answers.

1 Escucha y lee el texto. Completa las frases.

Reading. Students read Catarina's text about transport to and from school, then complete the sentences in English summarising it.

Audioscript *Track 3*

Por la mañana en invierno voy al instituto en autobús, pero en verano voy andando cuando hace buen tiempo. Nunca voy en metro porque no me gusta. Por la tarde vuelvo a casa en tren con mi amigo Felipe. Él siempre coge el tren y es divertido. Mi hermana va al instituto en bicicleta a menudo, pero en invierno va conmigo en autobús.

Answers
1 In winter Catarina usually goes to school by **bus**.
2 She walks to school in **summer**.
3 She does not like going by **tube/underground**.
4 She goes by train with her friend Felipe in **the afternoon**.
5 Her sister often goes to school by **bicycle**.
6 Her sister goes by bus in **winter**.

2 Write a paragraph about how you get to and from school. Use the questions and answers below to help you structure your writing.

Writing. Students write a paragraph about how they get to and from school, using the framework and the language box supplied.

R In pairs, students practise a dialogue using the framework and their own written responses from exercise 2.

⭐ ResultsPlus

Tip box on understanding times, in preparation for exercise 3.

3 Listen and write down the correct letter. (1–6) Listen again. What happens at each time?

Listening. Students listen to six conversations and note the correct time for each one, using the clocks supplied (**a–f**). They listen again and write down in English what happens at the specified time.

63

Audioscript *Track 4*

1 – ¿A qué hora empiezan las clases?
  – Empiezan a las ocho de la mañana.
2 – ¿A qué hora terminan las clases?
  – Terminan a las cinco y veinte de la tarde.
3 – ¿A qué hora es el recreo?
  – El recreo es a las diez y media de la mañana.
4 – ¿A qué hora vuelves a casa?
  – Vuelvo a casa a las cuatro y media de la tarde.
5 – ¿A qué hora tienes ciencias?
  – Tengo ciencias a las ocho y media de la mañana.
6 – ¿A qué hora coges el autobús?
  – Cojo el autobús a las cuatro menos cuarto.

Answers

1 *a – classes start* 2 d – classes finish 3 b – break
starts 4 f – go home 5 e – have science
6 c – catch the bus

R In pairs, students practise reading aloud the
times (**a–f**).

Starter 2

**To review times; to review vocabulary for
talking about the school day**

Write up the following. Give students 3 minutes
to complete each sentence with an appropriate
time, e.g. *a las ocho y media*. You could do the
first one as a model for support.

1 *Las clases empiezan…*
2 *El recreo empieza…*
3 *Tengo español…*
4 *La hora de comer termina…*
5 *Vuelvo del instituto…*

Ask students to read their sentences aloud, with
the rest of the class giving feedback as necessary
on their accuracy.

4 Lee y completa el diálogo con palabras
del cuadro. Luego escucha y comprueba tus
respuestas.

Listening. Students read and complete the gap-
fill dialogues, using the words supplied. They
then listen to check their answers. There are two
distractors.

Audioscript *Track 5*

– ¿A qué hora empiezan tus clases?
– Muy temprano… Empiezan a las **ocho** de la mañana.
– ¿Qué **haces** en clase normalmente?
– **Siempre** escucho al profe, pero también hablo con mis
  amigos.
– ¿Qué tienes que llevar a clase?
– Siempre llevo mi **estuche**, unos bolígrafos y una regla.
  También necesito mis cuadernos y mis **libros**.
– ¡Claro! ¿Qué haces a la hora de comer?

– Todos los **miércoles** voy al club de ajedrez, y a veces
  juego al fútbol en el patio.
– ¿Qué haces después del **instituto**?
– De vez en cuando voy al club de **informática**, y hago mis
  deberes.

Answers

Also in bold in the audioscript.
1 ocho 2 haces 3 Siempre 4 estuche 5 libros
6 miércoles 7 instituto 8 informática

⭐ ResultsPlus

R Students write down and translate into
English the underlined verbs in the dialogue.

Encourage students to note and use these verbs
when writing on this subject. Can they identify
any other verbs that would be useful in this
context?

5 Escucha. Copia y completa la tabla en inglés.
(1–5)

Listening. Students copy out the table. They listen
to five conversations about school and complete the
table with the details in English.

Audioscript *Track 6*

1 – ¿Qué haces después del instituto?
  – Pues… normalmente los jueves hago natación con mis
    amigos.
2 – ¿Qué haces en clase normalmente?
  – No me gustan las clases, entonces hablo con mis
    amigos y a veces leo.
3 – ¿Qué haces a la hora de comer?
  – Generalmente juego al fútbol y escucho música. Los
    lunes juego al tenis.
4 – ¿Qué necesitas llevar a clase?
  – Llevo cuadernos, libros, mi estuche, mi calculadora y
    mi móvil.
5 – ¿A qué hora empiezan tus clases?
  – Muy temprano… Llego a las ocho, pero las clases
    empiezan a las ocho y cuarto de la mañana.

Answers

	topic	details
1	A	goes swimming with friends on Thursdays
2	C	talks to friends, reads
3	E	plays football and listens to music; plays tennis on Mondays
4	D	exercise books, books, pencil case, calculator, mobile phone
5	B	classes start at quarter past 8, arrives at 8 am

6 Con tu compañero/a, pregunta y contesta.

Speaking. In pairs: students put together a dialogue,
taking it in turn to ask and answer questions using
the picture prompts. A framework and a language
box are supplied.

Students can go on to put together further dialogues, making up their own details.

Plenary

Ask students to remember the key verbs covered in exercise 4 and to give you sentences about school featuring them.

Review times by prompting in Spanish for students to respond in English. You could then increase the level of challenge by giving English prompts.

Cuaderno Verde, page 26

1

Answers

(f) En verano voy andando al instituto a menudo **(a)** porque hace sol. En invierno no hace buen **(c)** tiempo y siempre cojo el **(b)** autobús. En primavera vuelvo en metro por la **(h)** tarde porque es rápido. Mi amiga Celia nunca **(g)** va en tren al instituto. Por **(e)** la mañana mi hermano va al trabajo a **(d)** pie, pero por la tarde vuelve en autobús.

2

Answers

1 *en verano*   **2** a menudo   **3** siempre   **4** por la tarde
5 en primavera   **6** nunca   **7** por la mañana

1 ¿Cómo es tu insti? (Student Book pages 48–49)

Main topics and objectives
- Describing your school
- Using the present tense

Grammar
- The present tense

Key language

En mi cole/colegio/instituto...
(no) hay...
(no) tenemos...
un campo de fútbol

un comedor
un gimnasio
un patio
un salón de actos
una biblioteca
una piscina
una pista de atletismo/tenis
una sala de profesores
unos laboratorios
unos vestuarios
unas aulas

bueno/a(s)
grande(s)

malo/a(s)
pequeño/a(s)
antiguo/a(s)
moderno/a(s)

Lo bueno es que...
Lo malo es que...

Resources

CD 2, tracks 7–10
Cuaderno Verde, page 27
Gramática 192

Starter 1

To review the vocabulary for school facilities

Give students 3 minutes to do exercise 1 on p. 48.

1 Look at the plan of the school and find the correct phrase for each number. (There are two phrases too many.)

Reading. Students look at the plan of the school, then identify each of the numbered sections (**1–10**) using the labels **a–l**. There are two distractors.

> **Answers**
>
> **1** h **2** a **3** j **4** f **5** c
> **6** d **7** k **8** b **9** e **10** i

2 ¿Qué se menciona? Escucha e identifica las dos letras correctas del ejercicio 1. (1–5)

Listening. Students listen to five people talking about their schools and note the two facilities mentioned each time, using the captions in exercise 1 (**a–l**).

Audioscript *Track 7*

1 – ¿Cómo es tu colegio?
  – Es bueno porque hay muchas instalaciones. Hay una pista de atletismo y podemos nadar en la piscina.
2 – ¿Cómo es tu colegio?
  – Tenemos unos laboratorios excelentes. Lo malo es que no hay campo de fútbol.
3 – ¿Te gusta tu instituto?
  – Sí, me gusta porque hay muchas aulas grandes. También hay un salón de actos fantástico.
4 – ¿Cómo es tu cole?
  – Lo bueno es que tenemos un gimnasio grande, pero no hay vestuarios modernos.
5 – ¿Hay buenas instalaciones en tu instituto?
  – Hay malas instalaciones. Por ejemplo, no hay un buen patio y no me gusta la biblioteca porque es pequeña.

> **Answers**
>
> **1** j, i **2** a, h **3** c, k **4** e, l **5** b, f

⭐ ResultsPlus

Tip box on listening for negative opinions and statements, in preparation for exercise 3.

3 Escucha otra vez. ¿Positivo (P), negativo (N) o positivo y negativo (P+N)? (1–5)

Listening. Students listen to the recording for exercise 2 again. This time they note whether each speaker's opinion is positive (**P**), negative (**N**) or a mixture of both (**P + N**). A language box is supplied.

Audioscript *Track 8*

As exercise 7.

> **Answers**
>
> **1** P **2** P+N **3** P **4** P+N **5** N

R Students use the language box on **lo bueno es**... (etc.) to come up with three statements about their own school.

4 Lee la pagina web de Mónica. Busca estas frases en español.

Reading. Students read Mónica's webpage, then identify the Spanish versions of the English sentences listed.

Cultural note
- ESO = la Educación Secundaria Obligatoria (Key Stages 3 and 4)
- segundo de la ESO (Year 9), tercero de la ESO (Year 10), cuarto de la ESO (Year 11)

> **Answers**
>
> **1** Hay cuatrocientos alumnos aproximadamente.
> **2** Fue construido en los años sesenta.
> **3** Antes mi colegio era muy malo.
> **4** Lo malo es que…
> **5** ¡Es una lástima!
> **6** Mi colegio es una 'ecoescuela'.
> **7** Reciclamos mucho papel.

Starter 2

To review useful expressions for giving opinions

Write up the following. Give students 3 minutes to rewrite each sentence twice so that it makes sense: the first time changing the structure at the start of the sentence (**Lo bueno es que**, etc.); the second time changing the detail at the end of the sentence.

1 *Lo bueno es que llueve todos los días.*
2 *Lo malo es que no hacemos los deberes.*

Hear answers, asking students to translate their sentences into English.

5 Decide whether these statements are true (T), false (F) or not mentioned (NM) in Mónica's text.

Reading. Students reread the text in exercise 4 and decide whether the statements about it are true (T) or false (F) or contain information not mentioned in the text.

> **Answers**
>
> **1** F **2** T **3** NM **4** NM **5** T

6 Listen and note down the information Juan gives about the following topics. (1–3)

Listening. Students listen to Juan talking about his school and note in English what he says about (1) the school generally (2) the facilities there and (3) his opinion of the school.

🔊 Audioscript *Track 9*

1 *Voy a un cole público masculino en el norte de España. Está especializado en música. Es un cole pequeño con trescientos alumnos.*
2 *Tenemos aulas, un salón de actos y un patio, pero no tenemos instalaciones para practicar deporte. Por ejemplo, no tenemos piscina y el gimnasio es viejo.*
3 *Me gusta mi instituto porque tengo muchos amigos aquí. También me encanta la música y en el cole hay una orquesta y un coro que son muy buenos.*

> **Answers**
>
> **1** boys' state school, specialises in music, small – 300 pupils
> **2** classrooms, drama studio/hall, playground; doesn't have good sports facilities, e.g. no pool, old gym
> **3** likes the school as he has lots of friends there; loves music – good orchestra and choir at the school

🔊 Pronunciation

Play the recording. Practise saying the Spanish/English cognates together.

Audioscript *Track 10*

En el gimnasio hacemos atletismo.
Los laboratorios son muy modernos.

7 Con tu compañero/a, haz un diálogo.

Speaking. In pairs: students put together a dialogue about their school. A framework is supplied.

8 Lee las frases. Escoge la palabra correcta.

Reading. Students read and complete the sentences by choosing the correct word from the two options given each time.

> **Answers**
>
> **1** va **2** Es **3** es **4** Tenemos **5** tiene

🄶 Grammar

Use the Grammar box to review the present tense (singular + 'we' forms) of **ir**, **ser** and **tener**.

9 Escribe un blog de tu colegio.

Writing. Students write a blog entry describing their school.

🔊 You could consider setting up a class or school blog, working in conjunction with your ICT department.

Plenary

Ask students to tell you what the good/bad things about their school are, using **Lo bueno es que...** and **Lo malo es que...**

Cuaderno Verde, page 27

1

> **Answers**
>
> **1** I **2** F **3** I **4** M **5** M **6** F

2

> **Answers**
>
> **1** Mi colegio **es** moderno.
> **2** Vicente **va** al gimnasio.
> **3** **Tiene** buenas instalaciones.
> **4** **Voy** al colegio en coche.
> **5** **Tenemos** un comedor antiguo.
> **6** Cada aula **tiene** una pizarra interactiva.

2 ¿Qué llevas en el cole? (Student Book pages 50–51)

Main topics and objectives

- Describing your school uniform
- Using colour adjectives correctly

Grammar

- Colour adjectives

Key language

En el cole...
llevo/tengo que llevar...
me gustaría llevar...
un jersey
un vestido
una blusa
una camisa
una camiseta
una chaqueta

una chaqueta de punto
una corbata
una falda
una gorra
una sudadera
unos pantalones
unos vaqueros
unos calcetines
unos zapatos
unas botas
unas zapatillas de deporte
unas medias

blanco
amarillo
negro
morado
rojo
verde
gris
azul

marrón
naranja
rosa
claro/oscuro

anticuado, bonito, cómodo, elegante, fácil, feo, incómodo, práctico
¡Qué feo!
¡Qué guay!
¡Qué suerte!
¡Qué horror!
¡Qué vergüenza!

Resources

CD 2, tracks 11–13
Cuaderno Verde, pages 28–29
Gramática 210

Starter 1

To review vocabulary for clothes; to review adjective agreement

Write up the following for support. Give students 3 minutes to write a sentence describing what they wear to school on a typical day. (If your school has a uniform, they can either describe this or pretend that they are free to choose what they wear and invent the details.) Remind them as necessary to include the relevant articles and to check adjective agreement. Alternatively, you could supply the articles for support.

Llevo...

falda medias pantalones camisa corbata
vaqueros chaqueta zapatos zapatillas jersey
vestido

negro azul verde naranja

Hear some answers, asking students to translate them into English. Ask students to summarise the rules of adjective agreement and position, using the four different colours shown above.

1 Escucha. ¿Quién habla? (1–6)

Listening. Students listen to four people talking about what they wear to school. Using the pictures in exercise 1, they identify the speaker each time.

Audioscript *Track 11*

1 *Me gusta mi uniforme. Llevo unos pantalones grises y una camisa blanca.*
2 *Mi uniforme es muy feo. Llevo una falda gris y una blusa amarilla.*

3 *No llevo uniforme. Normalmente llevo vaqueros y un jersey verde.*
4 *Odio mi uniforme. Llevo un vestido y una chaqueta de punto azul oscuro.*
5 *Llevo unas medias blancas y zapatos negros. ¡Buagh!*
6 *Llevo una chaqueta azul, pero lo bueno es que no llevo corbata.*

Answers

1 *Gustavo* **2** Maya **3** Carlos **4** Silvia
5 Maya **6** Gustavo

2 Escucha otra vez y escribe los colores en inglés. (1–6)

Listening. Students listen to the recording in exercise 1 again and write the colours they hear in English.

Answers

1 grey, white **2** grey, yellow **3** green
4 dark blue **5** white, black **6** blue

Audioscript *Track 12*

As exercise 1.

G Grammar

Use the Grammar box to review adjective agreement. Remind students that most adjectives in Spanish (including all colours) follow the noun.

R Students work in pairs, taking it in turn to prompt with an item in English (e.g. 'a black skirt') and to respond in Spanish (e.g. *una falda negra*).

⭐ ResultsPlus

💾 Suggest students use the computer to summarise and learn grammar. Putting information like this together will help them remember key language points and will also be a useful reference when it comes to revising for the exam.

They could draw and fill in a grid in a word-processing, spreadsheet or DTP package, along the following lines:

masculine singular	feminine singular	masculine plural	feminine plural	position
rojo				
verde				
azul				

Encourage them to use different colours for the different genders (e.g. blue for masculine, pink for feminine, etc.); they may be able to picture the colour when they are trying to remember the gender of a word. They could also highlight endings of words by using the highlight function or underlining them.

They can also use this approach to test themselves, by making a blank copy of the grid and filling it in from scratch, then checking it against the reference version they created.

Starter 2

To review verb expressions followed by an infinitive

Write up the following, omitting the text in brackets. Give students 3 minutes to identify which of these sentences are grammatically correct and to correct those which are not.

1 *Tengo que llevo una corbata fea. (llevar)*
2 *Tengo que hacer mis deberes.*
3 *Me gustaría llevar vaqueros.*
4 *Me gusta juego al tenis. (jugar)*

3 Using the pictures, have conversations with your partner about what you wear and what you would like to wear.

Speaking. In pairs: students discuss what they wear to school and what they would like to wear, given a free choice. They take it in turn to ask and answer. A framework is supplied.

⭐ ResultsPlus

Tip box on using **tengo que/me gustaría** + the infinitive.

4 Lee los blogs y escribe las frases en español.

Reading. Students read the three blogs and identify the Spanish versions of the English sentences.

Answers

a Es superfeo
b Es tan anticuado.
c ¡Qué vergüenza!
d pero a mí no me importa
e También es barato.
f ¡Qué guay!
g ¡Lo odio!
h No es cómodo.

5 Lee los blogs del ejercicio 4 otra vez. Copia y completa la tabla en inglés.

Reading. Students copy out the table. They reread the texts in exercise 4 and complete the table with the details in English.

Answers

	uniform items	adjectives used
1	blue skirt orange blouse grey tights black or brown shoes	really ugly, old-fashioned
2	black trousers white shirt red jacket	practical cheap easy
3	(stripy) dress dark green cardigan grey trousers yellow sweatshirt	not comfortable

6 Copy the grid from exercise 5. Listen and fill it in again. (1–5)

Listening. Students copy out the table in exercise 5 again. They listen to five conversations about school uniform and complete the table with the details in English.

Audioscript *Track 13*

1 – *¿Llevas uniforme?*
– *Sí, llevo uniforme y no me gusta nada porque es muy feo. Tenemos que llevar unos pantalones negros y una camisa blanca.*
2 – *¿Llevas uniforme?*
– *Sí, llevamos uniforme, pero a mí no me importa. Llevamos una falda azul oscuro y una camiseta roja. Es muy elegante y práctico.*
3 – *¿Qué opinas de tu uniforme?*
– *Pues es barato y práctico, pero no me gusta. Llevo unos pantalones grises, una camiseta amarilla y una chaqueta azul. ¡Qué vergüenza!*
4 – *A mí me encanta porque es fácil y cómodo. Llevamos un vestido negro, una camisa gris y unos zapatos negros. ¡Qué suerte!*

5 – ¿Qué opinas de tu uniforme?
– Es incómodo y muy anticuado. Llevamos unos pantalones verdes y una camisa azul claro. ¡Qué horror!

Answers

	uniform items	adjectives used
1	black trousers, white shirt	ugly
2	dark blue skirt, red T-shirt	elegant, practical
3	grey trousers, yellow T-shirt, blue jacket	cheap, practical
4	black dress, grey shirt, black shoes	easy, comfortable
5	green trousers, light blue shirt	uncomfortable, old-fashioned

7 Write a paragraph about your uniform or what you wear to school.

Writing. Students write a paragraph about their own uniform, or what they wear to school if there is no uniform. A language box is supplied.

⭐ ResultsPlus

Tip box on using exclamations to sound more authentic.

Plenary

Ask students to summarise the rules of adjective agreement, giving the endings of the various different kinds of adjective types in this unit.

Then ask them to tell you the verbs/verb expressions followed by the infinitive used in this unit. Can they give examples of these verbs with infinitives <u>not</u> used in the unit?

Cuaderno Verde, pages 28–29

1

Answers

```
              15
       1 v  e  s  t  i  d  o
    2 c  a  l  c  e  t  i  n  e  s
       3 s  u  d  a  d  e  r  a
              n
    4 c  a  m  i  s  e  t  a
              5 f  a  l  d  a
              o
    6 g  o  r  r  a
              m
       7 m  e  d  i  a  s
       8 j  e  r  s  e  y
    9 b  o  t  a  s
          10 c  h  a  q  u  e  t  a
 11 p  a  n  t  a  l  o  n  e  s
 12 z  a  p  a  t  i  l  l  a  s  d  e  d  e  p  o  r  t  e
          13 z  a  p  a  t  o  s
       14 c  o  r  b  a  t  a
```

2

Answers

blanco/marrón/azul/claro/negro/oscuro/rosa/amarillo/ naranja/rojo/morado/verde/feo/cómodo/práctico/fácil/ anticuado/barato/elegante/incómodo/gris

3

Answers

1 Llevo una falda mo**rada**. Es bastante bonita y có**moda**.
2 Odio mi chaqueta ro**ja**/ro**sa** porque es muy anti**cuada**.
3 No me gustan las medias marr**ones** porque son muy fe**as**.
4 Me encantan los pantalones gri**ses** porque son muy ele**gantes**.
5 Me gustaría llevar una sudadera ne**gra** porque es muy prá**ctica**.
6 No me gustaría llevar una corbata porque es muy in**cómoda**.

4

Answers

1 ¡Qué guay!
2 ¡Qué horror!
3 ¡Qué suerte!
4 ¡Qué mal!
5 ¡Qué vergüenza!
6 ¡Qué bien!

3 Las normas del insti (Student Book pages 52–53)

Main topics and objectives
- Describing school rules and problems at school
- Using phrases with the infinitive

Grammar
- The near future tense

Key language
(No) Se debe/(No) Se permite/(No) Está prohibido...
escuchar en clase
hacer los deberes
llegar a tiempo
llevar uniforme

comer chicle
correr en los pasillos
escuchar música/tu MP3 en clase
llevar maquillaje/joyas/piercings/ zapatillas de deporte
leer correos electrónicos en la sala de informática
mandar mensajes en clase
salir del instituto durante la jornada escolar
ser desobediente
usar el móvil en clase

Los alumnos tienen que ser puntuales y amables.

En el futuro/El año que viene, voy a...

tener problemas
ver ataques físicos en el patio
tener muchos exámenes

el acoso escolar
un problema serio
hacer novillos
El estrés va a continuar.
Además...

Resources
CD 2, tracks 14–16
Cuaderno Verde, pages 30–31
Gramática 200

Starter 1

To introduce vocabulary for talking about problems at school; to practise using reading strategies

Write up the following, jumbling the order of the second column. Give students 3 minutes to match the halves and translate the completed sentences into English.

No se debe...

1	*correr*	*en los pasillos*
2	*escuchar*	*música en clase*
3	*llevar*	*zapatillas de deporte*
4	*comer*	*chicle*
5	*usar*	*el móvil en clase*

Check answers.

1 Escribe una norma para cada dibujo.

Writing. Students write a caption for each picture, saying what you must (pictures **a–d**, on green background) and mustn't (pictures **e–l**, on red background) do at school.

> **Answers**
>
> **a** *Se debe escuchar en clase.*
> **b** Se debe hacer los deberes.
> **c** Se debe llevar uniforme.
> **d** Se debe llegar a tiempo.
> **e** No se debe llevar maquillaje.
> **f** No se debe escuchar música en clase.
> **g** No se debe llevar zapatillas de deporte.
> **h** No se debe llevar joyas.
> **i** No se debe llevar piercings.
> **j** No se debe comer chicle.
> **k** No se debe correr en los pasillos.
> **l** No se debe usar el móvil en clase.

2 Escucha y escribe las letras correctas del ejercicio 1. (1–5)

Listening. Students listen to five people talking about rules at school and for each speaker match the rules mentioned to the appropriate pictures in exercise 1.

Audioscript *Track 14*

1 *En mi colegio se debe hacer los deberes, pero no se debe llevar joyas.*
2 *En mi insti se debe llegar a tiempo, pero no se debe correr en los pasillos.*
3 *En mi escuela se debe escuchar al profesor en clase, pero no se debe escuchar música.*
4 *En mi instituto se debe llevar uniforme, pero no se debe llevar zapatillas de deporte.*
5 *En mi colegio no se debe llevar piercings y no se debe llevar maquillaje.*

> **Answers**
>
> **1** b, h **2** d, k **3** a, f **4** c, g **5** i, e

3 Con tu compañero/a, pregunta y contesta.

Speaking. In pairs: students take it in turn to ask and answer questions about rules at school. The questions and openings for the answers are supplied for support.

➕ Students include an opinion on the school rules they are discussing.

Starter 2

To review the present and near future tenses ('I' form)

Write up the following, omitting the words in brackets. Give students 3 minutes to copy and complete the table. They can work in pairs for support.

Hoy…	Mañana…
voy	(voy a ir)
(llevo)	voy a llevar
veo	(voy a ver)
(vivo)	voy a vivir
tengo	(voy a tener)
(soy)	voy a ser
bebo	(voy a beber)
(corro)	voy a correr
hago	(voy a hacer)

Check answers, asking students to translate the verbs into English. Can they explain how the near future is formed?

4 Read the Spanish school rules. Does your school have these rules? Write ✓ or ✗ for each one.

Reading. Students read the school rules and note with a tick or a cross whether or not each is a rule in their own school.

⊛ ResultsPlus

Tip box on using a variety of structures for interest.

5 Escucha y escribe la letra correcta. (1–3)

Listening. Students listen to three people talking about problems at school and identify what each is talking about, using the pictures **a–c**.

Audioscript *Track 15*

1 En mi colegio hay bastante violencia entre los alumnos. El acoso escolar es un problema serio. En el futuro vamos a ver ataques físicos en el patio.

2 Tengo mucho estrés en el colegio. El año que viene vamos a tener exámenes y el estrés va a continuar.

3 Mi amigo Alonso no va al colegio. Prefiere ir al parque o al centro comercial. Siempre hace novillos. El año que viene Alonso va a tener problemas.

> **Answers**
> **1** b **2** a **3** c

G Grammar

Use the grammar box to review the near future tense.

6 Listen again and note down in English what will happen in the future. (1–3)

Listening. Students listen to the recording in exercise 5 again and note the three predictions of what will happen in the future. A language box is supplied.

Audioscript *Track 16*

As exercise 5.

> **Answers**
> **1** We are going to see physical attacks in the playground.
> **2** We are going to have exams and the stress is going to continue.
> **3** Alonso is going to have problems.

7 Write a paragraph about the rules and problems in your school.

Writing. Students write a paragraph about their own school, giving details of the rules and problems, both current and future. Encourage them to include their opinions. A language box is supplied.

Plenary

Encourage the class to talk about school problems (both current and future), prompting in English as necessary.

Cuaderno Verde, pages 30–31

1

> **Answers**
> ✓
> Se permite llevar maquillaje/piercings y piercings/maquillaje.
> Se permite usar el móvil en el insti.
> Se debe escuchar en clase.
> Se debe ser amable/obediente y obediente/amable.
>
> ✗
> No se debe llevar uniforme.
> No se debe llevar joyas.
> Está prohibido salir del insti durante la jornada.
> Está prohibido comer chicle en clase.
> No se debe usar el móvil en clase.
> No se permite mandar mensajes en clase.

2

Answers

1 *In the future Juan is not going to be stressed.*
En el futuro Juan no **va a tener** estrés.
2 *Tomorrow Ana is going to arrive on time.*
Mañana Ana **va a llegar** a tiempo.
3 *In the future we are going to see physical attacks.*
En el futuro **vamos a ver** ataques físicos.
4 *Tomorrow we are not going to wear uniform.*
Mañana no **vamos a llevar** uniforme.
5 *Next year you are going to leave school earlier.*
El año que viene **vas a salir** del colegio antes.
6 *In the future I am going to do my homework.*
En el futuro **voy a hacer** los deberes.
7 *Next year you are not going to have exams.*
El año que viene no **vas a tener** exámenes.
8 *Tomorrow we are going to listen to music in class.*
Mañana **vamos a escuchar** música en clase.

3

Answers

a Bullying is a problem. **4**
b The pupils cheat in exams. **3**
c There are sometimes fights in the playground. **5**
d Pupils are never on time. **7**
e Pupils are very disobedient. **8**
f Juan hates his school. *1*
g Juan is not going to school tomorrow. **9**
h Homework is never done. **6**
i Juan is stressed by exams. **2**

4 ¡Los profesores! (Student Book pages 54–55)

Main topics and objectives
- Describing teachers
- Using comparatives (more/less than)

Grammar
- Comparatives

Key language
paciente
impaciente
trabajador(a)
perezoso/a
antipático/a
simpático/a

listo/a
tonto/a
pesimista
optimista
raro/a
normal
tolerante
severo/a
aburrido/a
divertido/a

Mi profesor(a) de (español) es…
más/menos (paciente) que…
mejor que…
peor que…
tan (listo/a) como…

¿Qué opinas del profesor de (ciencias)?
Creo que…

demasiado
muy
bastante
un poco
poco

Estoy de acuerdo. ¡Claro!
No estoy de acuerdo. ¡Qué va!

Resources
CD 2, tracks 17–19
Cuaderno Verde, pages 32–33
Gramática 212

Starter 1

To review adjectives

Give students, in pairs, 3 minutes to do the following quiz on adjectives without looking at their books. Tell them they cannot use the same adjective twice. They need to come up with:

- 3 adjectives where you change **-o** in the masculine form to **-a** to make the feminine form
- 3 adjectives where the masculine and feminine forms are the same.

Check answers. Ask students to summarise when adjectives change ending and how, and to tell you where adjectives appear in a sentence: before or after the noun?

1 Look at the list of words below. What do they mean? Look up any that you don't understand in the *Vocabulario* section. How would you describe each of these teachers in Spanish?

Reading. Students read through the list of adjectives and translate them into English, using reading strategies (e.g. looking for cognates, using context, using logic) and the *Vocabulario* section for any they are unable to work out. They then choose adjectives to describe the teachers pictured.

> **Answers**
> *See exercise 2.*

⭐ ResultsPlus

Tip box on reading strategies: looking for cognates.

2 Look at the words in exercise 1 again and find 6 pairs of opposites.

Reading. Students group the adjectives from exercise 1 in pairs of opposites.

> **Answers**
>
> paciente – impaciente: patient – impatient
> trabajador(a) – perezoso/a: hardworking – lazy
> antipático/a – simpático/a: unpleasant – nice
> listo/a – tonto/a: clever – stupid
> pesimista – optimista: pessimistic – optimistic
> raro/a – normal : strange – normal
> tolerante – severo/a: tolerant – strict
> aburrido/a – divertido/a: boring – fun

⭐ ResultsPlus

Point out to the class that noting and learning pairs of words in this way makes it easier to remember them.

R Students take it in turn to prompt with an adjective in English and to give the Spanish (both masculine and feminine forms).

3 Escucha y escribe las asignaturas y la descripción del profesor/de la profesora. (1–6)

Listening. Students listen to six people talking about their teachers and note for each the subject and the adjective used to describe the teacher.

Audioscript *Track 17*

1 Me gusta mucho mi profesor de matemáticas porque es bastante paciente.
2 Odio a mi profesora de inglés porque es demasiado severa.
3 Creo que mi profesor de alemán es un poco antipático.
4 En mi opinión, mi profesor de ciencias es muy tolerante.
5 Creo que mi profesora de español es poco lista.
6 No me gusta nada mi profesor de historia porque es demasiado pesimista.

Answers

1 *matemáticas – paciente*
2 *inglés – severa*
3 *alemán – antipático*
4 *ciencias – tolerante*
5 *español – (poco) lista*
6 *historia – pesimista*

⭐ ResultsPlus

Tip box on using qualifiers (**demasiado, muy,** etc.) to add more detail to descriptions.

4 Escribe frases sobre tus profes.

Writing. Students write five or six sentences describing their own teachers. An example is given.

Starter 2

To review comparatives

Write up the following. Give students 2 minutes to complete each sentence and translate it into English.

1 *Franz Ferdinand es más entretenido que...*
2 *Kaká es menos famoso que...*
3 *Rafael Nadal es mejor que...*
4 *Hacer de canguro es peor que...*
5 *Jugar con el ordenador es tan interesante como...*

Check answers. Ask students to summarise the comparative structures and how they are used. Remind them as necessary that adjectives used in the comparative must agree.

5 Escucha y completa las frases. (1–4)

Listening. Students listen to four people comparing teachers at their school and write down the missing word to complete each sentence.

Audioscript *Track 18*

1 *Mi profesor de inglés es más **simpático** que mi profesor de matemáticas.*
2 *Mi tutor es más **paciente** que mi profesor de ciencias.*
3 *Mi profe de matemáticas es menos **severo** que mi profe de inglés.*
4 *Mi profe de español es tan **aburrido** como mi profe de francés.*

Answers

Also in bold in the audioscript.
1 simpático 2 paciente 3 severo 4 aburrido

G Grammar

Use the Grammar Box to review comparatives.

R Using the comparative structures shown in the Grammar box, students in pairs compare friends and/or famous people.

6 Copia y completa las frases del ejercicio 5 con *tus* opiniones.

Writing. Students rewrite the sentences in exercise 5, adapting them to give their own opinions.

7 Read the text and answer the questions in English. Look at the text again. What do you think the phrases in bold type mean?

Reading. Students read Lalo and Jade's chat, then answer the questions in English. Some vocabulary is glossed for support.

Answers

1 Señora Torres is Lalo's new ICT teacher.
2 She is a bit strict and quite unpleasant.
3 She got cross because Lalo spoke with his partner.
4 He missed break.
5 She's lazier.

Phrases in bold: creo que – *I believe*, no estoy de acuerdo – *I don't agree*, Estoy harto de – *I'm fed up with*

➕ Students identify all the adjectives in the text in exercise 7, writing out the masculine and feminine form of each one.

8 Escucha. Copia y completa la tabla. (1–5)

Listening. Students copy out the table. They then listen to a conversation (in five parts) between two teachers who are discussing their colleagues, and complete the table with the details. A language box is supplied for support.

Audioscript *Track 19*

1 – *Hola, Marisol, ¿cómo estás?*
   – *Muy bien, pero un poco cansada. Hoy tengo seis horas de clase.*
   – *¡Qué horror! Oye, ¿qué opinas del profesor de geografía?*
   – *Creo que es bastante trabajador – me gusta. ¿Y tú?*
   – *Estoy de acuerdo, enseña bien.*
2 – *Y ahora... ¿qué te parece la profesora de inglés?*
   – *Pienso que es una persona muy paciente.*
   – *¿Ah sí? Pues yo no estoy de acuerdo. Creo que es bastante antipática y a los alumnos no les gusta.*
3 – *Bueno... ¿Qué opinas del profesor Martínez?*
   – *¿Qué asignatura enseña?*
   – *Es el profesor de teatro.*
   – *¡Ah sí, claro! Pues... a mí me parece que es trabajador.*
   – *No estoy de acuerdo. El señor Martínez es el profesor más perezoso del instituto.*
4 – *Pues... vamos a hablar de los profesores de idiomas. ¿Qué te parece el profesor de francés?*
   – *Para mí es el mejor del instituto. Enseña bien y los alumnos aprenden mucho.*

– *Estoy de acuerdo. Sin duda, es un buen profesor. También creo que es muy inteligente.*
– *Sí, es verdad. Enseña muy bien.*

5 – *Finalmente, ¿qué opinas de la profesora de educación física?*
– *La odio. Pienso que es la peor profesora del instituto. ¡Es tan aburrida!*
– *¡Qué va! No estoy de acuerdo contigo. Me encanta porque es muy divertida.*

Answers

	Who are the teachers talking about?	Do they agree or disagree? (A/D)
1	*geography teacher*	A
2	English teacher	D
3	drama teacher	D
4	French teacher	A
5	PE teacher	D

9 ¡A debate! Habla con tu compañero/a de tus profesores.

Speaking. In pairs: students discuss their teachers using the debate phrases from exercise 8 and the language box supplied.

Plenary

Ask students to summarise how the comparative is formed. Then ask for suggestions in English of bands, films, CDs, books, magazines, websites, computer games, mobiles, etc., and write these up. Students take it in turn to compare one of the English items in Spanish, using either the comparative or the superlative.

Cuaderno Verde, page 32

1

Answers

b	i	d	o	n	n	l	i	s	t	o	m
a	q	i	m	p	a	c	i	e	n	t	e
s	u	v	c	e	j	x	z	v	s	m	n
t	m	e	j	o	r	m	d	e	t	i	o
a	á	r	a	r	o	u	y	r	r	n	s
n	s	t	a	n	p	y	p	o	c	o	a
t	x	i	t	á	t	u	c	e	o	s	r
e	b	d	e	m	a	s	i	a	d	o	z
x	t	o	g	e	u	a	n	t	s	j	l
t	r	a	b	a	j	a	d	o	r	f	x

1 Mi profesora de música es **más divertida** que mi profe de inglés.
2 Mi tutor es **menos severo** que mi director.
3 Mi profe de historia es **demasiado impaciente**.
4 Mi profesor de geografía es un **poco raro**.
5 Normalmente mis profesores son **muy trabajadores**.
6 Mi profesor de educación física es **mejor** que mi profesor de música.
7 Mi profesor de matemáticas es **peor** que mi profesor de teatro.
8 Mi profe de español es **bastante listo**.

Cuaderno Verde, page 33

1

Answers

1 *Me gusta**n** las ciencias porque son interesante**s**.*
2 Me encant**a** el teatro porque es muy divertid**o**.
3 Mi hermano **va** al instituto en metro porque es rápid**o**.
4 Odio el uniforme porque es incómod**o** y es muy fe**o**.
5 Mi profesor de inglés **es** muy estrict**o**, pero es bastante simpátic**o**.
6 Creo que la música es muy entretenid**a** y no es aburrid**a**.
7 Mi profe de religión **es** más impacient**e** que mi profe de historia.

2

Answers

(1) *Creo* que mi colegio no (2) **es** aburrido! No (3) **llevo** uniforme escolar y se (4) **permite** llevar vaqueros. Me (5) **gusta** llevar vaqueros, una sudadera y zapatillas de deporte porque (6) **son** muy cómodos. No (7) **se debe** llevar piercings o joyas, pero mañana (8) **voy** a llevar maquillaje. ¡Qué guay! En mi colegio no (9) **está** prohibido llevar el móvil y me (10) **encanta** escuchar música en clase. Me gusta el teatro porque (11) **es** divertido y mis profes (12) **son** muy simpáticos. Nunca (13) **tengo** deberes el fin de semana.

Prueba oral: School life (Student Book pp. 56–57)

Topics revised
● Talking about school

Resources
CD 5, tracks 11–13

Overview

Read through the task box at the top of the page and outline for students how this section works. They will hear a Speaking controlled assessment model presentation in three parts and do exercises focused on the language used. These exercises, along with the advice/activities on how to improve speaking performance in Results Plus, will help them prepare to give a presentation of their own on the topic.

1 You are going to listen to Daniel, an exam candidate, giving a presentation. Listen to part 1 and choose the correct option to complete each sentence.

Listening. Explain to the students that they will hear a sample of the kind of presentation they are expected to have in the Speaking controlled assessment.

They listen to the first part of the presentation and complete the sentences by choosing from the three options given each time.

Audioscript *Track 11*

Part 1
Buenos días. Voy a un colegio mixto. Hay setecientos alumnos y cien profesores. El colegio tiene buenas instalaciones. Por ejemplo, hay un gimnasio moderno y una piscina grande. Lo bueno es que hay un campo de fútbol. Lo malo es que no tenemos un patio grande.

Las clases empiezan a las nueve menos cuarto y terminan a las tres y media. Mi asignatura preferida es el teatro porque es bastante divertido y el profesor es simpático. Odio el alemán porque es demasiado difícil. Tengo que llevar uniforme. Llevo una camisa gris, una corbata azul y unos pantalones negros. Me gusta mi uniforme porque es práctico, pero la camisa es un poco fea.

Answers
1 mixto **2** 700 **3** un campo de fútbol
4 nueve menos cuarto **5** el teatro **6** negros
7 práctico

✚ Students listen to the recording again and note the words/expressions Daniel uses to give opinions.

(*Answers:* Lo bueno es que…, Lo malo es que…, preferida, odio, me gusta)

2 Listen to part 2 of Daniel's presentation and note down the words that fill the gaps.

Listening. Students now listen to the second part of Daniel's presentation and complete the gap-fill version of the transcript.

With a confident class you could ask students to read the text and try to work out plausible answers first, then use the recording to check. Discuss whether alternative answers the students came up with could also be correct in the context.

Audioscript *Track 12*

Part 2
– *¿Qué actividades haces después del instituto?*
– *Bueno… **voy** al club de informática los jueves y **canto** en el coro los lunes. **También** tenemos actividades a la hora de comer. Voy al club de ajedrez los **viernes** y voy al club de idiomas los miércoles. El año **pasado** fui al club de fotografía **pero** prefiero el club de informática porque es más fácil.*
– *¿Te gustan tus profesores?*
– *Pues sí, me **gustan** mis profesores. Hay unos profesores que son **muy** simpáticos pero mi profesor de matemáticas es un poco **impaciente**. Mi profesora preferida es mi profesora de francés porque es bastante optimista y **nunca** es severa. Sus clases son muy entretenidas porque me interesan otras culturas.*

Answers
Also shown in bold in audioscript.
1 voy **2** canto **3** También **4** viernes **5** pasado
6 pero **7** gustan **8** muy **9** impaciente **10** nunca

✚ Students find examples of the following in Daniel's replies in the audioscript for exercise 2: preterite, opinions, reasons, negatives, adjectives, time and frequency expressions, connectives and qualifiers. Point out that including details like these will earn them extra marks in the exam.

(*Answers:*
Preterite: fui
Opinions: me gustan, preferida, me interesan
Reasons: porque es…
Negatives: nunca
Adjectives: fácil, simpáticos, impaciente, preferida, optimista, severa, entretenidas
Time and frequency expressions: los jueves, los lunes, los miércoles, el año pasado, nunca
Connectives: y, también, pero, porque
Qualifiers: más, muy, un poco, bastante)

3 Now listen to part 3 of Daniel's assessment and correct the underlined mistake in each of the following sentences.

Listening. Students listen to the third and final part of Daniel's assessment and correct the mistake in each sentence, highlighted by an underline.

Audioscript *Track 13*

Part 3

– *¿Tienes muchas normas en tu colegio?*

– *Tenemos muchas normas, pero en mi opinión son bastante importantes. Por ejemplo, no se permite usar el móvil en clase y está prohibido llevar joyas.*

– *¿Cómo vas al colegio?*

– *Pues, a menudo voy al colegio a pie o en bicicleta. Prefiero ir en bici porque es más rápido que ir a pie. Pero me gusta ir en autobús o en coche cuando hace mal tiempo. Mi hermano siempre va en autobús porque es muy perezoso.*

– *¿Qué vas a hacer el año que viene?*

– *El año que viene voy a estudiar inglés, español y teatro, pero no voy a tener exámenes. ¡Qué guay!*

Answers

1 móvil **2** joyas **3** bicicleta **4** mal
5 autobús **6** español

⭐ ResultsPlus

The Results Plus support for speaking activities is differentiated, allowing students to identify and work towards their target level: covering the basics, Grade C, increasing their marks. Encourage students to adopt the techniques in these sections in all extended speaking activities.

Read through and discuss the Results Plus section together.

4 Now it's your turn! Prepare and give a presentation on your school to your teacher or partner.

Speaking. Students give a presentation on school in the style of a controlled assessment task. They should use all the support supplied, here and elsewhere on the spread:

- the Results Plus advice on the language to include
- Daniel's responses, adapted to talk about themselves
- the English points in the task box, p. 56
- their answers to exercises 1–3.

Each student gives the presentation. If they are working with a partner, they will take turns presenting and commenting.

If possible, record the presentations or have the students record themselves. They can then swap recordings with a partner, listen to each other's version and offer comments on how it might be improved. A simple marking system is suggested (one/two/three stars for listed categories). Students should then identify two or three areas which they would like to improve next time they do an extended speaking task.

Topics revised

● Writing about school

1 Read the text and choose the correct title for each paragraph.

Reading. Students read Julio's text and identify the correct title (from **a–e**) for each paragraph.

> **Answers**
>
> **First paragraph** – e
> **Second paragraph** – c
> **Third paragraph** – a
> **Fourth paragraph** – b
> **Fifth paragraph** – d

2 Find the equivalent of these expressions in Spanish in the text.

Reading. Students reread the text in exercise 1 and find the Spanish versions of the ten English phrases listed.

> **Answers**
>
> 1 … cuando hace mal tiempo…
> 2 … siempre va en autobús.
> 3 Mi cole es público.
> 4 Creo que los profesores son muy simpáticos…
> 5 El colegio tiene unas instalaciones impresionantes.
> 6 Lo bueno es que…
> 7 Además hay dos piscinas…
> 8 Me interesan los deportes…
> 9 Mi asignatura preferida es…
> 10 …el año que viene voy a ir a Francia.

3 Read the text again. Find three more examples of each of the following…

Reading. Students reread the text and find three examples of each of the following, not mentioned in the answers to exercise 2: present-tense verb or verbs expressing an opinion, adjectives, preterite verbs.

> **Answers**
>
> *Any three of each.*
> **Present tense/opinions:** hace, es, son, tenemos, me llamo, vivo, voy, prefiero, tiene, me interesan, juego, hago, canto, no me gustan, hablo
> **Adjectives:** perezoso, severa, gracioso, grande, fantástico, guay, entretenido, francesa, mal, público, simpáticos, impresionantes
> **Preterite:** hice, gané, canté

4 Read the text again and answer the questions in English.

Reading. Students reread the text and answer the comprehension questions in English.

> **Answers**
>
> 1 60
> 2 *Any one of:* swimming, football
> 3 sings in the choir
> 4 he sang songs from it
> 5 drama – it's very entertaining
> 6 with a French family
> 7 he doesn't speak French well

5 You might be asked to write about your school as a controlled assessment task. Use the Results Plus to help you prepare your account.

Students read through the language support material supplied in preparation for doing their own extended writing task in exercise 6.

✪ ResultsPlus

The Results Plus section gives students the support they need to structure and improve their writing. The support is differentiated, allowing students to identify and work towards their target level: covering the basics, Grade C, increasing their marks. Encourage students to adopt the kind of approach taken in this section in all extended writing activities.

6 Now write a full account of your school.

Writing. Students write their own text about their school in the style of a controlled assessment task (at least 100 words). As well as the Results Plus guidelines on the language to include, they should use all the support supplied here:

● Julio's text, adapted to refer to themselves
● relevant language from throughout the module
● the sample structure for the text.

7 Check carefully what you have written.

Writing. Students check their own work using the list of features supplied.

● Self-access reading and writing

A Reinforcement

1 Copy out the sentences and complete them with the correct letters. Then write each sentence in English.

Reading. Students copy and complete the sentences with the gap-fill words, then translate them into English.

Answers

1 *Voy en bicicleta. – I go by bike.*
2 *¿Vas en autocar? – Do you go by coach?*
3 *Juan va en coche. – Juan goes by car.*
4 *Vamos en tren. – We go by train.*
5 *Lucas y Ana María van a pie. – Lucas and Ana María walk/go on foot.*

2 Copy out the sentences and complete them with the correct times. Then write each sentence in English.

Reading. Students copy and complete the gap-fill sentences using the picture prompts. They then translate the sentences into English.

Answers

1 Tengo matemáticas a las **siete y media**. *I have maths at 7.30.*
2 Tienen inglés a las **diez y cuarto**. *They have English at 10.15.*
3 Tenemos alemán a las **dos menos cuarto**. *We have German at 1.45.*
4 María tiene dibujo a las **nueve y veinte y cinco**. *María has art at 9.25.*

3 Read the texts and complete the timetable with the missing subjects.

Writing. Students read the texts and use them to identify the missing subjects in the timetable.

Answers

A dibujo **B** informática **C** historia **D** ciencias
E geografía **F** geografía **H** educación física

4 Write out your own timetable for Thursday and Friday in Spanish.

Writing. Students write out in Spanish the subjects they have on a Thursday and Friday.

B Extension

1 Read each opinion and complete the sentence with an appropriate adjective. Be careful with the adjective endings! Then change the sentence to give your own opinion.

Reading. Students read and complete the sentences with an appropriate adjective from those supplied, making the adjectives agree. They then rewrite the sentences to give their own opinion of the subjects.

2 Copy and complete the sentences with the correct words from the box. Then write the sentences in English.

Reading. Students copy and complete the gap-fill sentences, using the words supplied. They then translate the sentences into English.

Answers

1 Me **encantan** las matemáticas porque no son difíciles.
 I love maths because it isn't difficult.
2 Mi profesor de ciencias es bastante **severo**.
 My science teacher is quite strict.
3 Siempre llevo una **falda** gris y una camiseta azul.
 I always wear a grey skirt and a blue T-shirt.
4 Las clases **empiezan** a las ocho y media todos los días.
 Classes start at 8.30 every day.
5 No voy al club de **ajedrez** porque no me interesa.
 I don't go to chess club because I'm not interested.

3 Read José's text and find the Spanish for the phrases that follow.

Reading. Students read the text and identify in it the Spanish versions of the English expressions listed.

Answers

1 muchos alumnos
2 Hay muchas reglas.
3 No se permite mandar mensajes (con el móvil).
4 Hay acoso escolar.
5 Mi colegio era (muy) bueno.

4 Answer the questions about José's text in English.

Students answer in English the comprehension questions about the text in exercise 4.

Answers

1 ten
2 it's big/has lots of students; has lots of rules
3 *any two:* wearing jewellery is forbidden; listening to your MP3 player is forbidden in class; sending texts isn't permitted
4 jeans and a T-shirt
5 bullying

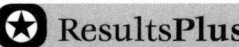 **ResultsPlus**

Tip box on using a dictionary or the *Vocabulario* section when reading, and noting down useful vocabulary for learning.

Module 4 ¡Perdidos! (Student Book pages 62–81)

Unit	Main topics and objectives	Grammar	Skills
Repaso Mi familia (pp. 62–63)	• Talking about yourself and your family • Using possessive adjectives	Using possessive adjectives	Developing vocabulary learning skills: words with gender change Listening for higher numbers
1 Los supervivientes (pp. 64–65)	• Giving basic information about yourself • Using **ser** and **estar**	Using **ser** and **estar**	Developing listening skills: predicting what you might hear
2 La vida cotidiana (pp. 66–67)	• Talking about daily routine • Using reflexive verbs	Using reflexive verbs	Using **desde hace** with the present tense to express how long
3 Las tareas (pp. 68–69)	• Talking about chores • Understanding negatives	Negatives	Listening for negatives Using negatives in writing to extend what you say
4 Otro accidente (pp. 70–71)	• Describing people's personalities • Talking about relationships	Adjectives	Listening for paraphrases and negatives Adjective agreement
5 Un año después (pp. 72–73)	• Talking about plans • Using the near future tense and other phrases with the infinitive	The near future tense Verbs followed by the infinitive	Listening for negatives Extending answers
Prueba oral: Family photograph (pp. 74–75)	Exam speaking practice	Revision	
Prueba escrita (pp. 76–77)	Exam writing practice	Revision	
Leer y escuchar (Modules 3–4) (pp. 78–79)	Listening and reading skills	Revision	
Te toca a ti (pp. 178–179)	Self-access reading and writing		

Main topics and objectives

- Talking about yourself and your family
- Using possessive adjectives

Grammar

- Using possessive adjectives

Key language

Mi cumpleaños es (el 13 de febrero).
enero/febrero/marzo/abril/mayo/ junio/julio/agosto/septiembre/ octubre/noviembre/diciembre

(No) Soy...
alto/a
bajo/a
delgado/a
gordo/a

guapo/a
feo/a

Tengo los ojos...
azules/marrones/grises/verdes
Tengo el pelo...
blanco/castaño/gris/negro/ pelirrojo/rubio/moreno
largo/corto
liso/rizado/ondulado
Es calvo.
Tengo pecas.
Llevo gafas.
Tiene barba/bigote.

el abuelo
el hermanastro
el hermano
el hijo
el marido
el padrastro

el padre
el primo
el tío

la abuela
la hermana
la hermanastra
la hija
la madre
la mujer
la madrastra
la prima
la tía

Nací/Nació el (12) de (mayo) de (2000).

mi(s), tu(s), su(s)

Resources

CD 2, tracks 20–21
Cuaderno Verde, page 36

Starter 1

To revise key verb forms in the present tense

Write up the following, leaving gaps for the underlined verbs. Give students 3 minutes to supply the correct words. If necessary, supply the verbs in random order for support.

Mi cumpleaños <u>es</u> el 8 de agosto.
¿Cuántos años <u>tienes</u>?
<u>Soy</u> bajo, pero mi hermana es alta.
<u>Tengo</u> el pelo negro y corto.
Mis hermanos <u>tienen</u> los ojos marrones.
¿Cómo <u>es</u> tu pelo?

Check answers.

1 Lee y empareja las preguntas y las respuestas.

Reading. Students read and match the questions and answers.

```
Answers
1 c  2 d  3 e  4 a  5 b
```

2 Escucha. Copia y completa la tabla en inglés. (1–3)

Listening. Students copy out the table. They listen to three people talking about themselves and complete the table with the details in English.

Audioscript *Track 20*

1 – *¿Cuándo es tu cumpleaños?*
  – *Mi cumpleaños es el 13 de febrero.*
   ¿Cuántos años tienes?
  – *Tengo quince años.*

– *¿Cómo eres?*
– *Soy alto y delgado.*
  ¿Cómo es tu pelo?
– *Tengo el pelo rubio y rizado.*
  ¿De qué color son tus ojos?
– *Tengo los ojos azules.*

2 – *¿Cuándo es tu cumpleaños?*
  – *Mi cumpleaños es el 22 de noviembre.*
   ¿Cuántos años tienes?
  – *Tengo diecisiete años.*
   ¿Cómo eres?
  – *Soy bajo y delgado.*
   ¿Cómo es tu pelo?
  – *Tengo el pelo negro y liso.*
   ¿De qué color son tus ojos?
  – *Tengo los ojos marrones.*

3 – *¿Cuándo es tu cumpleaños?*
  – *Mi cumpleaños es el 3 de junio.*
   ¿Cuántos años tienes?
  – *Tengo dieciséis años.*
   ¿Cómo eres?
  – *Soy guapa. Tengo pecas.*
   ¿Cómo es tu pelo?
  – *Tengo el pelo pelirrojo y largo.*
   ¿De qué color son tus ojos?
  – *Tengo los ojos verdes. Llevo gafas.*

	birthday	age	description	hair	eyes
1	13 February	15	tall, thin	blond, curly	blue
2	22 November	17	short, thin	black, straight	brown
3	3 June	16	pretty, freckles	red, long	green, glasses

3 Con tu compañero/a, pregunta y contesta utilizando las preguntas del ejercicio 1.

Speaking. Using the questions in exercise 1, students describe themselves. They take it in turn to ask and answer questions. A language box is supplied for support.

4 Match up the pairs of words that go together. What do they mean?

Reading. Students group the family words in pairs and translate them into English.

> **Answers**
>
> padre – madre (father – mother)
> hermano – hermana (brother – sister)
> abuelo – abuela (grandfather – grandmother)
> tío – tía (uncle – aunt)
> primo – prima (cousin)
> hijo – hija (son – daughter)
> marido – mujer (husband – wife)
> padrastro – madrastra (stepfather – stepmother)

⭐ **ResultsPlus**

Tip box on tackling patterns in words for family members.

Starter 2

To review vocabulary for describing people; to review adjective agreement

Write up the following, leaving a gap for all the words in brackets. Give students 3 minutes to fill in the gaps, selecting from the words supplied underneath.

Mi (hermana) se llama Ana. (Nació) el 12 de mayo de 2000. (Es) muy guapa. Tiene los (ojos) marrones y el pelo (negro) y ondulado. Lleva (gafas).

hermano hermana Nació Tiene Es Cuándo ojos ojo negro negra gafas barba

5 You are Pedro. Listen and write down in Spanish which member of your family is being described.

Listening. Students imagine they are Pedro. They listen to him talk about his family and use the family tree to identify which family member he is describing each time. To challenge the students, you could pause the recording during the description in each case to see if they can work out the answer from fewer clues.

Audioscript *Track 21*

1 *Nació el 28 de julio de 1968. Tiene el pelo rizado, negro y gris, y los ojos azules.*
2 *Nació el 6 de agosto de 1935. Tiene el pelo corto y castaño. Tiene los ojos marrones y lleva gafas.*
3 *Nació el 31 de julio de 1978. Tiene el pelo moreno y liso. Tiene los ojos marrones y tiene barba.*
4 *Nació el 11 de diciembre de 1933. Es un poco calvo. Tiene el pelo blanco y liso, y los ojos negros. Tiene un gran bigote blanco. Es divertido.*
5 *Nació el 15 de junio de 1953. Tiene poco pelo y es de color gris. También tiene bigote. Tiene los ojos marrones.*

6 *Nació el 17 de diciembre de 1994. Tiene los ojos azules y el pelo rubio, largo y liso.*
7 *Nació el 18 de abril de 1971. Tiene el pelo largo y castaño.*
8 *Nació el 21 de febrero de 1955. Tiene el pelo largo, moreno y liso. Es muy guapa.*

> **Answers**
>
> 1 *mi tío, Federico*
> 2 mi abuela, Luisa
> 3 mi hermano, Leandro
> 4 mi abuelo, Martín
> 5 mi padre, Alejandro
> 6 mi hermana, Viviana
> 7 mi tía, Rosana
> 8 mi madre, Juliana

⭐ **ResultsPlus**

Tip box on tackling higher numbers/dates.

➕ Ask students to close their books. Read out the year (or the whole date) of birth for each person in the family tree in exercise 4 for students to write down.

6 Copy out the texts about Pedro's family and correct the factual mistakes.

Reading. Students copy and correct the texts about three members of Pedro's family.

> **Answers**
>
> 1 Mi abuelo se llama Martín. Tiene el pelo **blanco y liso**, y los ojos **negros**. Tiene **un gran bigote blanco**. Nació el once **de diciembre de 1933**.
> 2 Mi hermana se llama **Viviana**. Tiene el pelo **rubio, largo y liso**, y los ojos **azules**. Nació el **diecisiete** de diciembre de **1994**.
> 3 Mi tío se llama Federico. Tiene el pelo **rizado, negro y gris**, y los ojos azules. Nació el **veintiocho** de julio de **1968**.

G Grammar

Use the Grammar box to review possessive adjectives (singular and plural).

R Prompt with different family members and a possessive adjective in English (e.g. 'her brother'). Students give the correct Spanish version.

7 Write descriptions of yourself and two other members of your family.

Writing. Students write a description of themselves and two other members of their family. Sentence openings and a language box are supplied.

Plenary

Challenge the class to remember all of the vocabulary for family members introduced in this unit.

Then ask them to give you all the different forms of the possessive adjective. Ask them to come up with expressions using these with different Spanish nouns, translating each one into English (e.g. *tu libro* – your book).

Cuaderno Verde, page 36

1

Answers

1 el padre – **father**
2 **la madre** – mother
3 los padres – parents
4 el hermano – **brother**
5 **la hermana** – sister
6 **el abuelo** – grandfather
7 la abuela – **grandmother**
8 los abuelos – grandparents
9 el tío – **uncle**
10 **la tía** – aunt
11 **el primo** – cousin (male)
12 la prima – **cousin (female)**
13 el padrastro – **stepfather**
14 **la madrastra** – stepmother
15 el hermanastro – **stepbrother**
16 **la hermanastra** – stepsister
17 **el hijo** – son
18 la hija – **daughter**

2

Answers

1 *Mi tío es el hijo de mi abuelo.*
2 Mi **padre es** el **hermano** de **mi tío**.
3 Tu **hermanastra es** la **hija** de **tu** madre.
4 Su **primo es** el hijo de **su tía**.
5 **Mi hermano** es **el hijo** de **mis padres**.
6 **Su abuelo** es **el padre** de **su madre**.

3

Answers

Me llamo Amparo. Soy baja. Tengo el pelo rubio y los ojos azules. Nací el veintiséis de febrero de 1995. Vivo con mi madre. Mi madre se llama Rosa. Es delgada. Tiene el pelo pelirrojo y los ojos marrones. Nació el diez de diciembre de 1959. Mi tío Marco es el hermano de mi madre. Es alto. Tiene el pelo rubio y los ojos azules. Lleva gafas.

Main topics and objectives

● Giving basic information about yourself
● Using **ser** and **estar**

Grammar

● Using **ser** and **estar**

Key language

Soy...
alemán/ana, colombiano/a, escocés/esa, español/a, francés/esa, galés/esa, inglés/esa, irlandés/esa, mexicano/a, peruano/a

Tengo... años.

Soy...
abogado/a, diseñador(a), mecánico/a, estudiante
alegre
ambicioso/a
creativo/a
duro/a
energético/a
honesto/a
inteligente
optimista
paciente
perezoso/a
tolerante (con...)
tranquilo/a
trabajador(a)
También soy... pero no soy...
Tengo mucho sentido de humor.

Me parezco a...
Me llevo bien con...
Tengo una relación problemática con...

Estoy...
casado/a
divorciado/a
separado/a
soltero/a

Resources

CD 2, tracks 22–23
Cuaderno Verde, page 37
Gramática 192

Starter 1

To introduce vocabulary for talking about relationships; to use reading strategies

Write up the following, jumbling the order of the second column. Give students 3 minutes to match the columns.

1 *Estoy soltera*   *pero espero encontrar pronto a mi chico ideal.*

2 *Estoy casado*   *con una mujer maravillosa.*

3 *Estoy separada*   *porque no me llevo bien con mi marido.*

Check answers, asking students to translate the completed sentences into English. Ask students to explain how they matched the columns and worked out the meanings.

1 Listen and read the texts on the survivors of the plane crash. Note down each person's nationality and job.

Listening. Students read the newspaper article about the plane crash and listen to the recording about the people who survived it, following the text at the same time. They note in English each person's nationality and job.

Cultural note

The **bachillerato** is the equivalent of studying for A Levels in the UK.

Audioscript *Track 22*

Catástrofe aérea
Un avión de pasajeros de la aerolínea Mundial se estrelló el jueves 15 de octubre en el océano Pacífico. No se conocen las causas del accidente y no se sabe si hay supervivientes.

Leonora
Soy española. Soy una persona creativa y paciente. Me parezco a mi padre. Soy diseñadora gráfica. Aquí en la isla tengo una vida tranquila. Hay problemas, pero estoy feliz.

Inmaculada
Soy colombiana. Soy abogada. Soy una persona energética y honesta. Tengo una relación problemática con mi madre. Estoy separada.

Benedicto
Soy peruano. Soy estudiante de medicina. Tengo mucho sentido del humor. Por lo general soy tolerante y optimista. Vivo con mi mamá y mi hermana. De momento estoy soltero, pero espero encontrar pronto a mi chica ideal.

Eugenio
Soy estadounidense, de Los Ángeles. Soy mecánico y me encanta mi trabajo. Soy trabajador. No soy nada perezoso. Estoy casado con una mujer maravillosa. La quiero mucho.

Alicia
Soy peruana y soy la hermana menor de Benedicto. Estudio bachillerato y quiero ir a la universidad. Soy ambiciosa y alegre. Afortunadamente me llevo bien con mi hermano.

Answers

Leonora – Spanish, graphic designer
Inmaculada – Colombian, lawyer
Benedicto – Peruvian, medical student
Eugenio – American, mechanic
Alicia – Peruvian, student

2 Read the texts again. Make notes about each person's character.

Reading. Students reread the texts in exercise 1 and write in English the adjectives used by each person to describe his/her character.

Answers

Leonora – *creative*, patient
Inmaculada – energetic, honest
Benedicto – good sense of humour, tolerant, optimistic
Eugenio – hardworking, never lazy
Alicia – ambitious, cheerful

G Grammar

Use the Grammar box to review when **ser** and **estar** are used.

3 Now look for these expressions about relationships in the texts (they are all in green).

Reading. Students identify the Spanish for key phrases in the texts in exercise 1, as shown in green.

Answers

1 Estoy separada.
2 Estoy soltero.
3 Estoy casado.
4 Tengo una relación problemática con mi madre.
5 Me parezco a mi padre.
6 Me llevo bien con mi hermano.

Starter 2

To review the 'I' form of key verbs for talking about yourself

Write up the following. Give students 3 minutes to write a short profile of themselves, using full sentences to answer the questions supplied.

¿Cómo te llamas?
¿De dónde eres?
¿Cuántos años tienes?
¿Cómo es tu carácter?

Hear some answers. Invite constructive feedback from the rest of the class on the accuracy of the language, in particular the verb forms.

4 Con tu compañero/a, mira estos perfiles. Pregunta y contesta.

Speaking. In pairs: students read the profiles of Rigoberta and Diego and take it in turn to ask and answer questions as though they were these people. The questions and answer openings are supplied for support.

⭐ ResultsPlus

Tip box on listening skills: predicting the kind of language which comes up; listening for negatives.

5 Listen and complete each sentence with the correct option. (1–3)

Listening. Students listen to three people talking about themselves and complete the sentences by selecting the correct option (from three) each time.

Audioscript *Track 23*

1 *Me llamo Juan y soy el hermano mayor de Inma. Inma es una persona muy inteligente. Es una chica guay que es muy trabajadora. Nunca es perezosa. También tiene mucho sentido del humor.*
2 *Me llamo Mónica. Leonora es mi hermana y le echo de menos. Pero creo que va a sobrevivir porque es tranquila y también tiene una personalidad muy fuerte.*
3 *Soy Silvia, la mujer de Eugenio. Mi marido es una persona muy sincera y optimista. Es verdad que no es siempre paciente. Nos conocimos en la fiesta de una amiga en 2003 y nos casamos dos años más tarde.*

Answers

1a older brother   **1b** intelligent and hardworking
1c a good sense of humour
2a sister   **2b** calm and strong
3a optimistic   **3b** 2003   **3c** two

6 Write a description of another person who has been stranded on the island.

Writing. Students write a description of another person stranded on the island, inventing details of his/her character and relationships. A language box is supplied.

 This could be done on computer using a word-processing or DTP package, with students incorporating pictures or photos into their texts.

Plenary

Ask the class to summarise when the verbs **ser** and **estar** are used.

Give Spanish expressions with **ser** and **estar** as prompts, mixing correct and incorrect versions (e.g. **soy creativo**/**soy divorciado**, etc.). Ask students to tell you whether or not each is correct.

Cuaderno Verde, page 37

1

Answers

1 María y Diego **son** peruanos.
2 Yo no **soy** creativa.
3 Nosotros **estamos** divorciados.
4 Hoy yo **estoy** muy contento.
5 Pedro **está** casado y **es** colombiano.
6 Ana **es** abogada y **es** muy ambiciosa.

2

> **Answers**
>
> **1** What are you like as a person? *d*
> **2** Are they married? **f**
> **3** What is your name? **a**
> **4** Where is she from? **g**
> **5** How old are you? **c**
> **6** Inma, how are you today? **h**
> **7** Are they students? **e**
> **8** Does he have children? **b**

3

> **Answers**
>
> **1** *Es muy alegre y ambiciosa.*
> **2** Es creativo, no es serio y es muy inteligente.
> **3** Es la hermana menor de José.
> **4** Es diseñador.
> **5** No, Bea no está casada. Está soltera.
> **6** No, José no está casado. Está soltero.

2 La vida cotidiana (Student Book pages 66–67)

Main topics and objectives
- Talking about daily routine
- Using reflexive verbs

Grammar
- Using reflexive verbs

Key language
Me despierto temprano.
Me levanto.
Me ducho.
Me lavo los dientes.

Me baño en el mar.
No me peino.
No me afeito nunca.
Me visto.
Desayuno fruta.
Meriendo a las cuatro.
Ceno pescado.
Me acuesto a las...

más tarde
por la tarde
desde hace un año
Lo peor es...

Resources
CD 2, tracks 24–25
Cuaderno Verde, pages 38–39
Gramática 194

Starter 1

To review reflexive verbs used for daily routine

Use ActiveTeach to display the language boxes accompanying exercise 1 on p. 66 (*Me despierto*, etc.). Alternatively, write up the sentences.

Give students 3 minutes working in pairs to identify all the reflexive verbs in the text and translate them into English. You could do the first one as a model.

1 Escucha a Eugenio y lee.

Listening. Students listen to Eugenio describing his daily routine, following the text at the same time.

Audioscript *Track 24*

– *¿A qué hora te levantas, Eugenio?*
– *Me despierto temprano, a las cinco y media, y luego me levanto a las seis de la mañana.*
– *¿Qué haces por la mañana?*
– *Primero me ducho, luego me lavo los dientes y me baño en el mar, pero no me peino y no me afeito nunca. Después me visto.*
– *¿Qué comes durante el día?*
– *Desayuno fruta. A las cuatro de la tarde meriendo y más tarde ceno pescado.*
– *¿A qué hora te acuestas?*
– *Me acuesto a las nueve de la tarde.*

G Grammar

Use the Grammar box to review reflexive verbs, in the context of actions you do to yourself. Draw attention to the fact that some of these verbs are also stem-changing verbs; you could use this as an opportunity to review stem-changing verbs in more detail.

+ Students translate into Spanish: we get up, you get dressed, she goes to bed, they wake up (*nos levantamos, te vistes, se acuesta, se despiertan*).

2 Contesta a las preguntas en inglés.

Reading. Students reread the text in exercise 1 and answer the comprehension questions in English.

Answers
1 5:30 am **2** 6 am **3** fruit **4** 4 pm **5** fish **6** 9 pm

3 Listen to Alicia. Are the statements below true (T) or false (F)?

Listening. Students listen to Alicia talking about her daily routine on the island and identify whether the statements about what she says are true (T) or false (F).

Audioscript *Track 25*

1 *Me levanto a las siete y media de la mañana. Primero me baño en el mar y después desayuno fruta. La fruta de la isla es estupenda.*
2 *Por las tardes ceno pescado y fruta. Después me ducho y me acuesto muy tarde a medianoche.*
3 *Meriendo a las cinco normalmente. A menudo como fruta con leche de coco. También me peino porque no quiero tener el pelo como Eugenio. ¡Qué horror!*

Answers
1a F **1b** F **1c** T **2a** F **2b** T **3a** F **3b** T

Starter 2

To review reflexive verbs for daily routine

Give students 2 minutes to write down as many reflexive verbs to describe daily routine as they can. Tell them that they encountered nine in the first part of the unit (introduced in exercise 1) so this should be their target.

4 Estás en la isla. Con tu compañero/a, pregunta y contesta.

Speaking. In pairs: students pretend they are stranded on the island. They take it in turn to ask and answer questions about their daily routine. A framework with picture prompts is supplied.

ResultsPlus
Tip box on **desde hace** + present tense to say how long.

5 Lee el diario de Benedicto y termina las frases en inglés.

Reading. Students read the text and complete the sentences summarising it in English.

Answers

1 brushes his teeth 2 tea 3 Inma 4 8 pm
5 fish 6 goes to bed 7 he bathes in the sea
8 have a shower

6 Copy out the words in red in the text and write their meaning in English.

Reading. Students write out and translate into English the words in red in the text.

Answers

desde hace un año – for a year
Primero por la mañana – first in the morning
desde hace unos meses – for some months
Más tarde – later
luego – then
Después – then, later, next
Normalmente – normally
de vez en cuando – from time to time
a las diez y media – at 10:30
en verano – in summer
en invierno – in winter

✚ Students choose three activities they do and write a sentence for each saying how long they have been doing it using **desde hace**.

7 Describe la rutina diaria de una persona perdida en una isla. Utiliza estas frases.

Writing. Students imagine they are a person stranded on an island and write a description of their daily routine and life on the island. A structure is supplied for support.

Plenary

Ask the class to summarise how reflexive verbs work and to give you examples of the different verbs from the unit used in different persons. Then play a chain game round the class: the first person says what he/she does every day using a reflexive verb; the next person repeats that and adds another reflexive verb; and so on round the class.

Cuaderno Verde, pages 38–39

1

Answers

1 se levanta
2 desayuna piña
3 se viste
4 cena pescado
5 merienda
6 se ducha
7 se despierta temprano
8 se lava los dientes
9 se baña
10 se acuesta
11 no se peina y no se afeita

2

Answers

1 *I get up* – me levanto
2 *they do their hair* – se peinan
3 *he washes* – se lava
4 *you (tú) go to bed* – te acuestas
5 *he gets dressed* – se viste
6 *you (tú) have a bath* – te bañas
7 *you (plural) wake up* – os despertáis
8 *we have a shower* – nos duchamos

3

Answers

1 *Se levanta **temprano**.*
2 **Se baña** cuando hace calor.
3 **Se lava** los dientes.
4 Bebe **té**.
5 **Benedicto es su mejor amigo.**
6 Trabaja en **el jardín**.
7 **No** le gusta el pescado.
8 Cena **pescado**.

3 Las tareas (Student Book pages 68–69)

Main topics and objectives
- Talking about chores
- Understanding negatives

Grammar
- Negatives

Key language
Lavo los platos.
Hago la cama.
Limpio mi dormitorio.
Arreglo mis cosas.
Cocino.

Pongo la mesa.
Quito la mesa.
Pesco.
Trabajo en el jardín.
Paso la aspiradora.
Plancho la ropa.

No (limpio).
No hago nada.
Nunca (lavo los platos).
Nadie (pasa la aspiradora).
Tampoco (pongo la mesa)/No (pongo la mesa) tampoco.
No (paso la aspiradora) ni (plancho).

Resources
CD 2, tracks 26–27
Cuaderno Verde, pages 40–41
Gramática 214

Starter 1

To review vocabulary for household tasks

Write up the following, omitting the underline (here to show the answers only). Give students 3 minutes to identify the correct verb in each sentence and to translate the sentences into English.

1 Hago/<u>Pongo</u> la mesa.
2 <u>Trabajo</u>/Cocino en el jardín.
3 <u>Paso</u>/Quito la aspiradora.
4 Lavo/<u>Hago</u> la cama.
5 <u>Plancho</u>/Pesco la ropa.

1 Escucha. ¿Qué tareas hacen Leonora y Eugenio? Escribe las letras correctas. (1–2)

Listening. Students listen to Leonora and Eugenio talking about their daily chores and note the letters of the correct pictures (from **a–k**).

Audioscript *Track 26*

1 – ¿Qué tareas haces en la isla, Leonora?
– Hago mi cama, arreglo mis cosas y limpio mi dormitorio todos los días.
– ¿Algo más?
– Normalmente pongo y quito la mesa para los otros. Lavo los platos también. Pero no cocino. No me gusta nada cocinar.
2 – Y tú, Eugenio, ¿qué tareas haces en la isla?
– Todos los días, pesco. Me encanta pescar. De vez en cuando trabajo en el jardín.
– ¿Y qué no haces?
– Pues… no paso la aspiradora. ¿Qué más? No plancho la ropa. No tenemos ni aspiradora, ni plancha, je, je.

Answers
1 Leonora: b, d, c, f, g, a   **2 Eugenio:** h, i

R Working in pairs, students take it in turn to prompt and complete a sentence from exercise 1, e.g. student 1: *Limpio…* student 2: *… mi dormitorio*.

✪ ResultsPlus
Tip box on listening out for negatives.

G Grammar
Use the Grammar box to review negatives before students do exercise 2.

2 Escucha a Benedicto e Inma. ¿Qué tareas *no* hacen? Escribe las letras del ejercicio 1. (1–2)

Listening. Students listen to Benedicto and Inma and identify the tasks they don't do, from the pictures in exercise 1 (**a–k**).

Audioscript *Track 27*

1 – Y tú, Benedicto, ¿qué tareas haces en la isla?
– A ver … de vez en cuando pongo la mesa, pero eso es todo. No hago la cama, ni arreglo mi dormitorio. Nunca cocino y tampoco lavo los platos.
– ¿Eres un poco perezoso, entonces? ¿No haces nada?
– No soy perezoso, pero tengo problemas en este momento.
2 – E Inma. ¿Qué no te gusta hacer en la isla?
– Pues… hago mi cama y limpio mi dormitorio, pero hay cosas que no me gusta hacer. Por ejemplo, nunca pesco. No cocino tampoco. Nadie pasa la aspiradora y nadie plancha la ropa – es imposible en la isla.

Answers
1 Benedicto: b, c *or* d, e, a   **2 Inma:** h, e, j, k

R Students working in pairs take it in turn to prompt using the pictures in exercise 1 and a negative (e.g. *e* – never) and to respond with a sentence (e.g. *Nunca cocino*).

Starter 2

To review vocabulary for household tasks

Give students 3 minutes working in pairs to write down in Spanish as many of the household tasks as they can remember, without looking at their books.

Pairs swap answers to check, awarding 1 point for each correct task. The pair with the most points are the winners.

3 Escribe las frases en español.

Writing. Students write captions for the pictures.

> **Answers**
>
> 1 *No pesco.*
> 2 No pongo la mesa ni lavo los platos.
> 3 Nadie hace la cama.
> 4 Nunca cocino.
> 5 No plancho la ropa.
> 6 No arreglo mis cosas ni trabajo en el jardín.

4 Lee los textos y escoge el verbo correcto.

Reading. Students read and complete the gap-fill texts using the verbs supplied.

> **Answers**
>
> 1 limpio   2 arreglo   3 trabajo   4 pongo   5 quito
> 6 lavo   7 paso   8 hace   9 Hago   10 voy
> 11 habla   12 ayuda

5 Con tu compañero/a, imagina que eres otra persona de la isla. Pregunta y contesta.

Speaking. In pairs: students imagine that they are stranded on the island and take it in turn to ask and answer questions about what they normally do/don't do. The questions and answer openings are supplied for support.

⭐ ResultsPlus

Tip box on using negatives in writing to extend what you say or write.

6 Imagine you are on the island. Write a paragraph about the jobs you do on the island and the jobs you do back at home.

Writing. Students imagine they are stranded on the island. They write a paragraph about the jobs they do there and the jobs they usually do at home. They should include details of jobs they <u>don't</u> do as well.

Plenary

Ask students to summarise the negative structures used in the unit.

Go round the class asking students to tell you what jobs they don't do. Each student has to use a different negative from the student before him/her.

Cuaderno Verde, pages 40–41

1

> **Answers**
>
> **Leonora:**
> Hago la cama.
> Limpio mi dormitorio.
> Arreglo mis cosas.
> Quito la mesa.
> No plancho la ropa.
>
> **Eugenio:**
> Pesco en el mar.
> Preparo la cena.
> Pongo la mesa.
> Lavo los platos.
> No paso la aspiradora.

2

Answers

N	O	N	L	N	A	D	A
F	T	A	M	P	O	C	O
N	G	U	O	K	F	A	T
A	V	I	N	U	N	C	A
D	H	L	A	D	A	N	M
A	J	W	D	Q	D	P	P
T	O	N	F	N	A	N	O
A	D	I	E	M	F	J	C
S	R	E	I	D	A	N	O

no 5, nothing 4, no one 1, neither 2, never 1

3

> **Answers**
>
> 1 No plancho la ropa.
> 2 No limpio nunca.
> 3 Nadie prepara la cena.
> 4 Nunca quito la mesa.
> 5 No pongo la mesa tampoco.
> 6 No trabajo ni pesco.
> 7 No hago nada.
> 8 Nunca lavo los platos.

4 Otro accidente (Student Book pages 70–71)

Main topics and objectives
- Describing people's personalities
- Talking about relationships

Grammar
- Adjectives

Key language
(No) Era muy/poco...
agresivo/a
alegre

amable
egoísta
generoso/a
introvertido/a
maleducado/a
optimista
pesimista
simpático/a
sincero/a
valiente

Para mí...
En mi opinión...
Pienso que...

Estoy de acuerdo.
No estoy de acuerdo.

Resources
CD 2, tracks 28–30
Cuaderno Verde, page 42

Starter 1

To review adjectives for describing character

Give students 3 minutes working in pairs to write down as many adjectives as possible that can be used to describe a person's character. They should give both the masculine and feminine singular forms.

1 Empareja el español con el inglés.

Reading. Students match the Spanish adjectives with the correct English translation.

Answers
1 a **2** c **3** f **4** j **5** b **6** e **7** g
8 k **9** l **10** h **11** i **12** d

⭐ ResultsPlus
Tip box on listening for paraphrases in exercise 2.

2 Listen and read the sentences. Write an adjective from the box above that applies to each person. (1–6)

Listening. Students listen to six people being described and note for each person an appropriate adjective in English (from **a–l** in exercise 1).

Audioscript *Track 28*

1 Mi hermana nunca piensa en otras personas.

2 Mi mejor amigo me compra cosas todo el tiempo. Hace regalos a todo el mundo.

3 Mi amiga es una persona muy tímida y un poco nerviosa. No le gustan las fiestas o las situaciones con mucha gente.

4 Mi mujer nunca es positiva y espera lo peor en todas las situaciones.

5 Mis hijos nunca tienen miedo.

6 Mi abuela es una persona muy positiva y por lo general espera lo mejor.

Answers
1 selfish **2** generous **3** introverted
4 pessimistic **5** brave **6** optimistic

3 Write a paragraph about someone you know. Change the words in brackets to apply to them.

Writing. Students write a description of a friend or family member, adapting the text supplied.

⭐ ResultsPlus
Tip box on checking adjective agreement.

Starter 2

To review adjectives for describing character

Use ActiveTeach to display the words numbered 1–12 accompanying exercise 1 on p. 70. Alternatively, ask students to look at this text in their books.

Give students 3 minutes to group the adjectives under the headings **Positive quality** and **Negative quality**.

Check answers, asking students to translate all the adjectives into English.

4 Escucha y lee.

Listening. Students listen to the story of an accident that happened on the island, following the text at the same time.

Audioscript *Track 29*

a El día del accidente, nos levantamos temprano porque hacía sol.

b Fuimos a la playa. Eugenio fue a pescar y nosotras fuimos a buscar conchas. Benedicto estaba nervioso y se quedó en la cabaña.

c Una hora después, Inma fue a buscar a Benedicto.

d Normalmente Alicia no nada en el mar, pero esa mañana decidió bañarse conmigo.

e *En la casita, Benedicto habló con Inma. Por fin, Benedicto le declaró a Inma su amor, y le dio un gran beso.*

f *De repente, Eugenio vio algo en el agua y empezó a gritar: '¡Tiburón, tiburón! ¡Alicia, Leonora! ¡Hay un tiburón!'*

g *Yo salí enseguida pero Alicia se quedó en el agua. Luego el agua se llenó de sangre. Era la sangre de Alicia.*

h *Benedicto e Inma vinieron corriendo. Alicia estaba inconsciente.*

i *Benedicto limpió y curó la herida de su hermana. Benedicto era estudiante de medicina antes del accidente. Alicia tenía fiebre. Eugenio dijo: '¡Va a morir, va a morir!'*

✚ Translate the text into English, as an oral exercise round the class.

5 Listen to these speakers talking about the people on the island.

Listening. Students listen to the conversation about the people on the island and answer the comprehension questions in English.

Audioscript *Track 30*

– *¿Cómo era Benedicto en tu opinión?*
– *Para mí Benedicto era introvertido, pero era sincero también porque declaró su amor a Inma. Además, al final fue muy valiente porque ayudó a su hermana.*
– *¿E Inma?*
– *Pues… primero era alegre y amable. No era nada egoísta porque fue a buscar a Benedicto.*
– *¿Y cómo era Eugenio?*
– *En mi opinión Eugenio no era nada optimista al final, no, al contrario, era muy pesimista.*

> **Answers**
> - Benedicto, Inma and Eugenio
> - Benedicto – introverted, sincere, brave
>   Inma – cheerful, kind
>   Eugenio – pessimistic

6 Read the story again and decide which personal qualities each character showed. Discuss them with your partner.

Speaking. In pairs: students discuss how the characters in the story behaved and what this showed about their personalities. A sample exchange and a language box are supplied.

✚ Ask students to predict what they think is going to happen next in the story and why.

Plenary

Put the class into teams and challenge them to remember all of the adjectives used to describe people's personalities in the unit. The team with the most correct answers (and – in the event of a draw – which finishes first) is the winner.

Cuaderno Verde, page 42

1

> **Answers**
>
> Sábado
> Todos nos despertamos muy temprano. Hacía sol y fuimos a la playa. Eugenio y Benedicto fueron a pescar y Leonora, Alicia y yo fuimos a buscar conchas. Me gusta Leonora porque siempre es muy *amable*. A veces Alicia no es muy <u>simpática</u> porque es un poco <u>egoísta</u>.
>
> Benedicto decidió bañarse, pero de repente gritó: '¡Aaaay!' Un momento después salió del agua con una medusa enorme en la pierna derecha.
>
> Normalmente Eugenio es <u>introvertido</u> y no es una persona <u>agresiva</u>. Cogió un palo y, con mucho cuidado, le quitó la medusa de la pierna a Benedicto. Al principio a Benedicto le dolía mucho y yo era muy <u>pesimista</u>. Leonora, que es muy <u>generosa</u>, lavó la pierna de Benedicto con agua del mar. Después de unos minutos vi que Benedicto estaba bien, así que yo me sentí más <u>optimista</u>. También Alicia estaba más <u>positiva</u> y <u>alegre</u>.
>
> Benedicto es muy <u>valiente</u> y nunca tiene miedo, pero en el futuro ¡no va a bañarse más en el mar!

2

> **Answers**
> **1** *Leonora*   **2** Alicia   **3** Alicia   **4** Eugenio   **5** Eugenio
> **6** Inma   **7** Leonora   **8** Inma   **9** Alicia   **10** Benedicto

5 Un año después (Student Book pages 72–73)

Main topics and objectives

- Talking about plans
- Using the near future tense and other phrases with the infinitive

Grammar

- The near future tense
- Verbs followed by the infinitive

Key language

Adjectives to describe personality

¿Qué vas a hacer?
¿Cuál es la primera cosa que vas a hacer?

Primero…, luego…, después…
Voy a beber champán…
Voy a comer chicle y patatas fritas…
Voy a dormir veinte horas…
Voy a llamar a mi madre…
Voy a ducharme…
Voy a afeitarme…
Me gustaría viajar…
Me gustaría estudiar…
Quiero comprar un coche nuevo…
Quiero buscar un trabajo…
Voy a casarme…

¿Qué tipo de persona eres ahora?
En mi opinión/Pienso que soy una persona…

Ahora soy mucho más/menos…
También/Además soy…
tolerante
generoso/a
paciente
optimista

¿Qué quieres hacer en el futuro?
En el futuro voy a…
Me gustaría…
Quiero…
porque…

Resources

CD 2, tracks 31–32
Cuaderno Verde, pages 43–44
Gramática 200

Starter 1

To review infinitives of key verbs

Write up the following. Give students 3 minutes to write the infinitive forms of all the verbs shown. They can work in pairs for support.

voy	llamo	como	busco
bebo	viajo	vivo	soy
duermo	compro	hago	tengo

Check answers, asking students to translate the verbs.

1 Read the text below, then write a few sentences in English about the rescue.

Reading. Students read the newspaper report and write a short summary of it in English.

Answers (sample)

Five people found on a desert island in the Pacific Ocean. A ship's captain spotted them on the beach. He contacted the emergency services and a helicopter came to rescue them.

ResultsPlus

Tip box on listening for negatives.

2 Escucha. Copia y completa la tabla. (1–4)

Listening. Students copy out the table. They listen to four of the survivors being interviewed about what they are going to do and complete the table with the details (from pictures **a–k**).

Ask students to explain why some of the infinitives here end in **-me**.

Audioscript *Track 31*

1 – *¿Qué vas a hacer, Benedicto?*
  – *A ver, primero voy a ducharme… luego voy a llamar a mi madre y después voy a comer chicle y patatas fritas…*
2 – *¿Y tú, Inma? ¿Qué vas a hacer? ¿Cuál es la primera cosa que vas a hacer?*
  – *Creo que primero voy a beber champán… luego… me gustaría estudiar, no quiero ser abogada ahora… y después tal vez voy a casarme.*
3 – *¿Cuál es la primera cosa que vas a hacer, Eugenio?*
  – *No voy a beber champán. No señor. Primero voy a afeitarme por supuesto y voy a ver a mi mujer. Luego voy a dormir veinte horas… y después quiero comprar un coche nuevo…*
4 – *¿Y tú, Leonora? ¿Cuál es la primera cosa que vas a hacer?*
  – *Primero yo también voy a beber champán… luego quiero buscar un trabajo. Esto es muy importante. Y después, no tengo ningún plan… me gustaría viajar. No quiero estudiar o casarme.*

Answers

	primero	luego	después
Benedicto	e	d	b
Inma	a	h	k
Eugenio	f	c	i
Leonora	a	j	g

G Grammar

Use the grammar box to review the formation of the near future tense, along with other verb + infinitive structures that can be used to talk about the future.

Starter 2

To review the near future tense

Write up the following. Give students 3 minutes to write a sentence about future plans using each of the three expressions.

Voy a... Quiero... Me gustaría...

Hear answers. Invite constructive feedback from the rest of the class.

3 Con tu compañero/a, pregunta y contesta.

Speaking. Students imagine they are survivors from the desert island and take it in turn to ask and say what they are going to do. A framework with picture prompts is supplied.

4 Lee el texto. Contesta a las preguntas en inglés.

Reading. Students read Benedicto's account of his life after the island, then answer the comprehension questions in English.

Answers

1 more tolerant, less introverted
2 their problems, what makes them happy
3 he thinks he's a stronger person
4 have a family, travel with Inma
5 be a doctor

5 Lee el texto otra vez. ¿Qué significan las palabras en rojo?

Reading. Students reread the text in exercise 4 and translate the words in red into English.

Answers

en mi opinión – *in my opinion*
ahora – *now*
También – *also*
pienso que – *I think that*
además – *moreover, besides*
En el futuro – *in the future*
porque – *because*

⭐ ResultsPlus

Tip box on extending sentences and adding variety in speaking and writing.

6 Escucha. Apunta los siguientes datos en inglés.

Listening. Students listen to Alicia being interviewed on life after the island, then note in English (1) what she is like now and (2) what she is planning for the future.

Audioscript *Track 32*

– *Alicia, ¿qué tipo de persona eres ahora después de tu experiencia en la isla?*
– *Creo que soy un poco más paciente y más realista también.*
– *¿Qué vas a hacer en el futuro?*
– *No pienso en el futuro, solo vivo el momento. Creo que no voy a trabajar. Quizás voy a estudiar. Y me gustaría viajar el año que viene con mi novio.*

Answers

1 She is more patient and realistic.
2 She's not going to get a job. She might study. She would like to travel (next year) with her boyfriend.

7 Escribe una entrevista con una persona perdida en una isla desierta.

Writing. Students write an interview with a person stranded on a desert island. A language box is supplied.

💭 Students could produce their interview on computer. Once they have prepared a first draft, they should look at a partner's text on screen and highlight (using underline or a different colour) any errors they spot, without saying what the error is or correcting it. Students then correct their own texts and prepare a second draft.

Plenary

Go round the class asking students at random one of the questions in the language box in exercise 7. Ask the rest of the class to confirm whether the right tense is used in each response.

Cuaderno Verde, page 43

1

Answers

a I would like to help more. **4**
b I want to work. **6**
c I want to have a shave. **3**
d What are you are going to do? **1**
e I'm never going to eat fish again! **5**
f I am going to talk a lot with my wife. **2**

2

Answers

1 *Soy paciente y tolerante.*
2 Voy a beber champán y voy a hablar mucho con mi mujer, Ana.
3 Voy a ducharme y voy a afeitarme./Me voy a duchar y me voy a afeitar.
4 Quiero comer filetes.
5 Voy a trabajar como mecánico.
6 No. Me gustaría/Quiero ser ingeniero.
7 Quiero ir a Egipto.
8 Voy a viajar en barco.

Cuaderno Verde, page 44

1

Answers

1 Carlota y Marco no *son* españoles, tampoco **son** ingleses.
2 ¿Cómo **eres** (tú) ?
3 Miguel y María no **están** casados.
4 ¿Cuándo **es** tu cumpleaños?
5 Nosotros no **somos** ni creativos, ni trabajadores.
6 Yo **soy** una persona más fuerte ahora.
7 Mi amiga no **está** casada; **está** separada.
8 Hoy yo no **estoy** contenta.

2

Answers

sebañan/<u>no</u>/televantas/<u>nunca</u>/meducho/<u>ni</u>/seviste/<u>tampoco</u>/sedespiertan/<u>ni</u>/seacuestan/<u>nada</u>/mepeino/<u>nadie</u>

3

Answers

Alicia:
Ahora soy mucho más fuerte. (**1**) **Voy a ser** más independiente y no (**2**) **voy a vivir** más en casa de mi madre. Primero (**3**) **me gustaría terminar** mis estudios, y después (**4**) **quiero buscar** un buen trabajo. Luego (**5**) **voy a viajar** mucho porque (**6**) **me gustaría ver** el mundo.

Inma:
Soy una persona optimista y pienso que soy generosa. Benedicto (**1**) **va a terminar** sus estudios de medicina. (**2**) **Me gustaría trabajar** con Benedicto porque también (**3**) **quiero ayudar** a los demás. En el futuro (**4**) **voy a casarme** con Benedicto y (**5**) **vamos a formar** una familia.

Topics revised	Resources
• Talking about family • Talking about holidays	CD 5, tracks 14–16

Overview

Read through the task box at the top of the page and outline for students how this section works. They will hear a Speaking controlled assessment model discussion in three parts and do exercises focused on the language used. These exercises, along with the advice/activities on how to improve speaking performance in Results Plus, will help them prepare to take part in a discussion of their own on the topic.

Before listening

Students could predict what questions the examiner might ask about the photo. Once they have completed exercises 1, 2 and 3, they could compare their list of predicted questions with the ones the examiner actually asked.

1 You are going to listen to Ellie, an exam candidate, having a conversation about the photo. Listen to part 1 and choose the correct word to complete each sentence.

Listening. Explain to the students that they will hear a sample of the kind of discussion they are expected to have in the Speaking controlled assessment.

They listen to the first part of the discussion and complete the sentences by choosing from the three options given each time.

Audioscript *Track 14*

Part 1

– ¿Dónde fue sacada esta foto?
– Fue sacada cerca de la casa de mi familia en Alicante.
– ¿Cuándo fue sacada?
– Fue sacada el verano pasado. Fuimos de paseo por el campo. Hizo mucho calor.
– ¿Quién está en la foto?
– Mi padre, mi madrastra… y la chica enfrente es mi hermanastra. Mi hermanastra es alta y guapa. Tiene diecisiete años. Es enérgica y optimista. También es muy inteligente. No es perezosa. El chico de la foto es mi hermano. Se llama Bobby y tiene doce años. Por lo general mi hermano es sincero. Tiene mucho sentido del humor. Pero a veces es un poco introvertido.

Answers

1 Alicante 2 verano 3 diecisiete
4 perezosa 5 sincero 6 introvertido

➕ Students listen again and identify the adjectives, explaining the gender and number for each one, noting MS (masculine singular), FS (feminine singular), MP (masculine plural) or FP (feminine plural).

(*Answers:* pasado (MS – verano); alta, guapa, enérgica, optimista, inteligente, perezosa (FS – mi hermanastra); sincero, introvertido (MS – mi hermano))

2 Listen to part 2 of Ellie's conversation and note down the words that fill the gaps.

Listening. Students now listen to the second part of Ellie's discussion and complete the gap-fill version of the transcript. The answers are supplied in random order for support.

With a confident class you could ask students to read the text and try to work out the answers first, then use the recording to check.

Audioscript *Track 15*

Part 2

– ¿Te llevas bien con tu familia por lo general?
– Sí, **me llevo** bien con mi familia pero de vez en cuando no me llevo bien con mi madrastra. **Es** generosa pero a veces es un poco impaciente. **Nunca** está feliz. Es una persona difícil. Mi padre es muy **ambicioso** y trabaja mucho **pero** me llevo bien con él. En mi opinión es bastante guapo. **Tiene** el pelo castaño y los ojos marrones.
– ¿Te gustaría casarte o tener niños?
– Pues… sí. Un **día** me gustaría casarme y también me gustaría tener niños. **Voy** a tener una familia grande porque la familia es **importante** en mi vida. Creo que voy a tener cinco niños. No me **gustaría** ser soltera.

Answers

Also in bold in the audioscript.
1 me llevo 2 Es 3 Nunca 4 ambicioso 5 pero
6 Tiene 7 día 8 Voy 9 importante 10 gustaría

3 Now listen to part 3 of Ellie's conversation. In which order does she use these phrases?

Listening. Students listen to the third and final part of Ellie's discussion and note the order in which she uses sentences **a–f**.

Audioscript *Track 16*

Part 3

– ¿Tienes que hacer tareas en tu casa?

– Claro. Normalmente hago la cama y arreglo mis cosas todos los días. Nunca preparo la cena. A mi madrastra le gusta cocinar, pero yo lavo los platos con mi hermano y con mi hermanastra.

– ¿Qué tareas hiciste el fin de semana pasado?

– A ver, el sábado me desperté bastante tarde y me levanté a las nueve de la mañana. Primero limpié mi dormitorio un poco y luego hice la cama. Más tarde fui de compras. Por la tarde puse la mesa y después de la cena lavé los platos. No me gusta nada lavar los platos. ¡Qué aburrido!

Answers

b, e, a, c, f, d

 ResultsPlus

The Results Plus support for speaking activities is differentiated, allowing students to identify and work towards their target level: covering the basics, Grade C, increasing their marks. Encourage students to adopt the techniques in these sections in all extended speaking activities.

Read through and discuss the Results Plus section together.

---

4 Now it's your turn! Choose your own photo and then prepare to talk about it with your partner or your teacher.

Speaking. Students participate in a discussion about a holiday photo in the style of a controlled assessment task. They should use all the support supplied, here and elsewhere on the spread:

- the Results Plus advice on the language to include
- Ellie's responses, adapted to talk about themselves
- the English notes in the task box, p. 74
- their answers to exercises 1–3.

Each student takes part in a discussion as the person answering the questions. If they are working with a partner, they will take turns asking and answering.

If possible, record the discussions or have the students record themselves. They can then swap recordings with a partner, listen to each other's version and offer comments on how it might be improved. A simple marking system is suggested (one/two/three stars for listed categories). Students should then identify two or three areas which they would like to improve next time they do an extended speaking task.

Prueba escrita (Student Book pages 76–77)

Topics revised
- Writing about relationships

1 Read the text and choose the correct title for each paragraph.

Reading. Students read the text and choose the correct title (from **a–d**) for each paragraph (**1–4**). Some vocabulary is glossed for support.

Answers

1 c **2** d **3** b **4** a

2 Find the equivalent of these expressions in Spanish in the text.

Reading. Students reread the text and identify the Spanish versions of the English expressions listed.

Answers

 1 Soy alta y delgada.
 2 Tengo un hermano gemelo que se llama…
 3 No me llevo bien con mi padre.
 4 …me vuelve loca.
 5 …a veces puede ser agresivo…
 6 Tengo una relación problemática con mi familia…
 7 El verano pasado trabajé…
 8 No me gustó nada. ¡Nunca jamás!
 9 En el futuro me gustaría trabajar como dependienta…
10 Luego voy a viajar.

3 Find five sentences in the text that have a negative in them.

Reading. Students identify five sentences in the text which feature a negative. They should start with their answers to exercise 2 (two negatives appear here).

Answers

No me llevo bien con mi padre.
No me gustó nada.
¡Nunca jamás!
No soy muy paciente.
Voy a hacer muchas cosas en mi vida pero ¡nunca me voy a casar, nunca voy a tener hijos!

4 Answer the following questions in English.

Reading. Students answer in English the comprehension questions about Lucy's text in exercise 1.

Answers

1 16; 9 December
2 green
3 10 years ago
4 He always says no.
5 her uncle, Christian, and her half-brother/stepbrother Bobby
6 (quite) energetic, independent, brave, not very patient
7 in a clothes shop
8 get married, have children

5 You might be asked to write about your family as a controlled assessment task. Use the Results Plus to help you prepare your account.

Students read through the language support material supplied in preparation for doing their own extended writing task in exercise 6.

✪ ResultsPlus

The Results Plus section gives students the support they need to structure and improve their writing. The support is differentiated, allowing students to identify and work towards their target level: covering the basics, Grade C, increasing their marks. Encourage students to adopt the kind of approach taken in this section in all extended writing activities.

6 Now imagine you are a character in a soap opera and write a full account of your family.

Writing. Students write their own text about family relationships in the style of a controlled assessment task (at least 100 words). As well as the Results Plus guidelines on the language to include, they should use all the support supplied here:

- Lucy's text, adapted to refer to themselves
- the sample structure for the text.

7 Check carefully what you have written.

Writing. Students check their own work using the list of features supplied.

● This section helps students develop their listening and reading skills in preparation for the exam.

Resources

CD 5, tracks 17–20

LEER

1 Read this letter from Isabel, who is writing about her family. Answer the questions. *(4 marks)*

Reading. Students read Isabel's letter, in which she writes about her family, and answer the comprehension questions in English.

Questions 1 and 2 are very straightforward and target Grade G. Questions 3 and 4 are a little more demanding and target Grade F.

> **Answers**
> **1** How are you? **2** teacher
> **3** (wears) glasses **4** short

★ ResultsPlus

Tip box on tackling reading tasks in the exam: using the fact that the answers appear in the text in the same order as the questions are asked.

2 Read Vicente's advert for penfriends in England and answer the questions. Write the correct letter. *(2 marks)*

Reading. Students read Vicente's advert and answer the multiple-choice questions.

This task approximates to Grade E: the questions are fairly straightforward but vocabulary needs to be picked carefully out of the text in order to match the answer options.

> **Answers**
> **1** b **2** a

★ ResultsPlus

Tip box on tackling reading tasks in the exam: taking time to match options to the text.

3 Read these teacher's comments and answer the questions. Write down the person's name each time. *(4 marks)*

Reading. Students read the texts and identify in the questions which follow who is being described each time. There are two distractors.

This task approximates to Grade D. Some vocabulary items are mentioned twice in this text but the meaning changes because of negatives.

> **Answers**
> **1** Alicia **2** Emilio **3** Blanca **4** Pedro

★ ResultsPlus

Tip box on reading carefully in order to choose the appropriate piece of information.

4 Daniel's daily routine. Read the text and write the correct letter. *(4 marks)*

Reading. Students read Daniel's text and answer the multiple-choice questions.

This task approximates to Grade C. There is a lot of information to understand, including some redundant language. Most sentences are fairly long and contain some complex structures.

> **Answers**
> **1** b **2** a **3** c **4** a

★ ResultsPlus

Tip box on distinguishing important and unimportant language: recognising times and working out a sequence of events.

ESCUCHAR

5 Listen to Rosa talking about her school routine and answer the questions. *(3 marks)*

Listening. Students listen to Rosa and answer the comprehension questions.

Audioscript *Track 17*

1 *Mis clases empiezan a las ocho y media.*
  [Repeated as above]
2 *Durante el recreo hablo con mis amigos.*
  [Repeated as above]
3 *Después de las clases voy al club de música.*
  [Repeated as above]

These three questions require the understanding of more than one word and approximate to Grade F.

> **Answers**
> **1** 8:30 **2** talks to her friends **3** music club

6 Listen to Francisco and Yolanda talking about their favourite school subjects. Which day do you think they each prefer? Write the correct letter. *(1 mark for each person)*

Listening. Students listen to two people talking about their school subjects and look at the schedule. They identify which day each person prefers.

This task requires matching simple vocabulary and approximates to Grade E.

Audioscript *Track 18*

– *¿Qué asignaturas prefieres, Francisco?*
– *Me gustan mucho las ciencias. Son divertidas.*
– *Y a ti Yolanda, ¿qué asignaturas te gustan más?*
– *Prefiero los idiomas. Son muy interesantes.*
  [Repeated as above]

Answers

1 Francisco – d   **2** Yolanda – b

⭐ ResultsPlus

Tip box on listening for related vocabulary.

7 Listen to Ernesto talking about his school. What does he say are the best and worst aspects? Write the correct letter. *(2 marks)*

Listening. Students listen to Ernesto and identify the best and worst aspects of his school from the topics listed.

These questions approximate to Grade D. Two of the three options are mentioned in each question. The information given about one of them may be tempting, but the language makes it clear which one is 'best' or 'worst'.

Audioscript *Track 19*

1 *El salón de actos es grande y moderno, pero la biblioteca es genial porque tiene unos libros estupendos.*
  [Repeated as above]
2 *Los laboratorios son malos porque no tenemos muchos recursos, pero el comedor es fatal. ¡No hay suficiente sitio para todos!*
  [Repeated as above]

Answers

1 a   **2** c

⭐ ResultsPlus

Tip box on listening carefully in order to distinguish between two pieces of information.

8 Carmen, Javier and Lucía talk about household chores. Write down the chore each finds difficult. *(1 mark for each person)*

Listening. Students listen to three people talking about household chores and identify the chore each one finds difficult.

These questions use a number of negative expressions which significantly affect the answer. They approximate to Grade C.

Audioscript *Track 20*

1 – *¿Ayudas mucho en casa, Carmen?*
– *Sí, todos los días hago mi cama sin problema. Limpiar mi dormitorio no es nada fácil porque siempre está desordenado.*
  [Repeated as above]
2 – *¿Y qué haces tú, Javier?*
– *No mucho. A veces paso la aspiradora porque no es difícil. No plancho nunca mis camisas. Creo que es muy complicado.*
  [Repeated as above]
3 – *¿Qué dices tú, Lucía?*
– *Pues trabajar en el jardín es imposible para mí. Sin embargo soy una persona práctica y sé cocinar muy bien.*
  [Repeated as above]

Answers

1 Carmen – cleaning bedroom
2 Javier – ironing (shirts)
3 Lucía – gardening/working in the garden

⭐ ResultsPlus

Tip box on listening carefully for negative expressions.

● Self-access reading and writing

A Reinforcement

1 Answer these questions for the people below in full sentences.

Writing. Students look at the profiles for Luis and Angélica and answer the questions as though they were each of them, using full sentences. Some vocabulary is glossed for support.

> **Answers**
>
> **Luis**
> Tengo dieciséis años.
> Soy de México/mexicano.
> Tengo los ojos azules.
> Tengo el pelo rubio.
> Normalmente soy sincero y tolerante.
> Pero puedo ser tranquilo y pesimista.
>
> **Angélica**
> Tengo catorce años.
> Soy de Estados Unidos/estadounidense.
> Tengo los ojos marrones.
> Tengo el pelo castaño.
> Normalmente soy egoísta y un poco agresiva.
> Pero puedo ser valiente y optimista.

2 Read the text and write a clock time for each picture.

Writing. Students read the text and write the correct time for each picture.

> **Answers**
>
> **a** *6:30 am* **b** 6:50 am **c** 7:05 am
> **d** 4:30 pm **e** 8:15 pm **f** 9:30 pm

B Extension

1 Follow the lines to find the words and write them out. Then match the English to the Spanish.

Reading. Students complete the words by following the coloured lines. They then match each word to the correct English translation.

> **Answers**
>
> **1** agresivo – aggressive
> **2** alegre – cheerful
> **3** amable – kind
> **4** egoísta – selfish
> **5** generoso – generous
> **6** introvertido – introverted
> **7** maleducado – rude
> **8** optimista – optimistic
> **9** pesimista – pessimistic
> **10** simpático – friendly/nice
> **11** sincero – sincere
> **12** valiente – brave

2 Read these texts and then answer the questions.

Reading. Students read the texts about three different people and identify who is being described each time.

> **Answers**
>
> **1** Laura **2** Aitor **3** Laura **4** Magec
> **5** Aitor **6** Magec

3 Read Alicia's diary and answer the questions below in English.

Reading. Students read the text and answer the comprehension questions in English.

> **Answers**
>
> **1** winter **2** spring **3** winter **4** summer **5** winter

Module 5 Los trabajos (Student Book pages 82–99)

Unit	Main topics and objectives	Grammar	Skills
Repaso A trabajar (pp. 82–83)	• Revising jobs and places where people work • Revising masculine and feminine nouns	Revising masculine and feminine nouns	Omitting definite article when saying what job you do Dictionary skills Improving your pronunciation of cognates
1 ¿Trabajas los sábados? (pp. 84–85)	• Describing part-time jobs • Using **tener que** followed by the infinitive	Using **tener que** + the infinitive	Distinguishing between confusable spoken forms
2 Prácticas laborales (pp. 86–87)	• Describing work experience • Using the preterite and the imperfect tense	Using the preterite and the imperfect tense	Using a range of tenses
3 El futuro (pp. 88–89)	• Describing future plans • Using a variety of verbs to refer to the future	Talking about the future Using **si** clauses	Using a range of tenses
4 Mi currículum vitae (pp. 90–91)	• Understanding job adverts and writing a CV • Using the preterite	The preterite	Using reading strategies Using the preterite to talk about past experience
5 La entrevista (pp. 92–93)	• Conducting a job interview • Forming the perfect tense	The perfect tense	Conducting a job interview
Prueba oral: Work/ study placement (pp. 94–95)	Exam speaking practice	Revision	
Prueba escrita (pp. 96–97)	Exam writing practice	Revision	
Te toca a ti (pp. 180–181)	Self-access reading and writing		

5

Repaso *A trabajar* (Student Book pages 82–83)

Main topics and objectives

- Revising jobs and places where people work
- Revising masculine and feminine nouns

Grammar

- Revising masculine and feminine nouns

Key language

¿En qué trabaja usted?
Soy…/Trabajo como/de…
abogado/a
camarero/a
carpintero/a
cocinero/a
enfermero/a
ingeniero/a

jardinero/a
mecánico/a
médico/a
peluquero/a

conductor(a)
diseñador(a)
profesor(a)

cantante
comerciante
dentista
futbolista
periodista
recepcionista
soldado
actor/actriz
dependiente/a

en…
un estadio

un garaje
un hospital
un hotel
un instituto
un jardín
un restaurante
un taller
un teatro
una carnicería
una comisaría
una clínica
una oficina
una peluquería
una tienda de ropa

Resources

CD 3, tracks 2–3
Cuaderno Verde, page 47
Gramática 208

Starter 1

To review/introduce vocabulary for jobs

Write up the following. Give students working in pairs 3 minutes to order the jobs, starting with the one they'd most like to do and finishing with the one they'd least like to do.

camarero/a
cocinero/a
conductor(a)
enfermero/a
ingeniero/a
peluquero/a
profesor(a)
cantante
futbolista
dependiente/a

When they have finished, check students know what all the jobs are in English. Ask students to explain how they worked out any new words, reminding them as necessary of the various reading strategies. Take a class vote (by show of hands for favourite/least favourite) to identify the most and least popular jobs.

1 Lee y completa las frases con los lugares correctos. (1–6)

Reading. Students read and complete the sentences about where people work. A language box listing the places is supplied for support. There are two distractors.

Answers

1 jardín **2** peluquería **3** clínica **4** estadio
5 restaurante **6** hotel

⭐ ResultsPlus

Tip box on omitting the article when you say what job you do.

2 Escucha e identifica el trabajo y el lugar. (1–8)

Listening. Students listen to eight people talking about their jobs and identify the job and place of work for each. A language box is supplied.

After playing the recording, review when the **usted** form is used.

Audioscript *Track 2*

1 – *¿En qué trabaja usted?*
  – *Soy periodista y trabajo en una oficina.*
2 – *¿En qué trabaja usted?*
  – *Trabajo como abogado. Normalmente trabajo en una oficina.*
3 – *¿Qué hace usted?*
  – *Soy enfermera. Trabajo en un hospital.*
4 – *¿Qué hace usted?*
  – *Soy dentista. Trabajo en una clínica en Barcelona.*
5 – *¿Dónde trabaja usted?*
  – *Trabajo en el jardín de un hotel de cinco estrellas. Soy jardinera.*
6 – *¿En qué trabaja usted?*
  – *Soy cantante, pero trabajo en un teatro.*
7 – *¿En qué trabaja usted?*
  – *Trabajo como mecánico en un garaje, en Madrid.*
8 – *¿Dónde trabajas?*
  – *Trabajo en una tienda de ropa. Soy dependienta.*

Answers

1 *periodista – una oficina*
2 abogado – una oficina
3 enfermera – un hospital
4 dentista – una clínica
5 jardinera – (el jardín de) un hotel
6 cantante – un teatro
7 mecánico – un garaje
8 dependienta – una tienda (de ropa)

G Grammar

Use the Grammar box to review the masculine and feminine forms of nouns such as job titles.

Starter 2

To review masculine and feminine nouns

Write up the following. Give students 2 minutes to give the feminine forms of the nouns.

mecánico
diseñador
cantante
dentista
médico
dependiente
profesor

(*Answers:* mecánica, diseñadora, cantante, dentista, médica, dependienta, profesora)

Check answers, asking students to give the English for each job. You could also ask them to give you other examples of job nouns which behave in the same way (e.g. end in **-o** with feminine in **-a**, etc.).

★ ResultsPlus

Tip box on dictionary skills in preparation for exercise 3.

3 Traduce al español. Usa el diccionario si lo necesitas.

Writing. Students copy the sentences and translate them into Spanish, using a dictionary as necessary.

Answers

1 *Mi padre es bombero.*
2 Mi hermana es soldado.
3 Soy veterinario/a.
4 Mi amigo/a es granjero/a.
5 Mi vecino/a es obrero/a.
6 Mi hijo es cartero.
7 Miguel es electricista.

4 Lee los textos. Copia y completa la tabla en inglés.

Reading. Students copy out the table. They read the texts and complete the table with the details in English.

Answer

name	job	opinion & reason	place of work	extra information
Dario	actor	loves job, very exciting, never boring	TV studio (in Mexico)	money and creativity important
Mariana	cashier	doesn't like job at all, quite heavy going	hypermarket (near Malaga)	always very busy
Brisa	air hostess	likes it a lot, varied and fun	the (Spanish) airline Iberia	travels to Europe, Africa, Latin America

5 Talk about a job that someone in your family does. Answer the questions. Then write down the information using full sentences.

Speaking. Students choose a member of their family and talk about the job he/she does, using the questions and answer openings supplied.

Pronunciation

Play the recording. Practise saying the Spanish/English cognates together.

Audioscript *Track 3*

– *secretario*
– *actriz*
– *clínica*
– *médico*
– *dentista*
– *policía*
– *actor*

➕ Students choose a member of their family and write a paragraph about the job he/she does, using the questions in exercise 5 to help structure their writing.

Plenary

Challenge students to name as many jobs as they can, giving you both the masculine and feminine forms. Tell them that more than 20 different jobs are mentioned in the unit, to give them a target.

Cuaderno Verde, page 47

1

Answers

x	c	d	p	q	i	p	d	r	j	g
b	i	v	e	ñ	a	d	o	r	a	s
b	m	x	l	z	b	n	s	k	r	e
m	é	q	u	w	o	t	i	o	d	c
e	d	u	q	e	g	w	z	l	i	r
c	i	s	u	i	a	a	í	s	n	e
á	c	d	e	q	d	c	a	h	e	t
n	a	v	r	y	o	m	l	f	r	a
i	p	r	o	f	e	s	o	r	a	r
c	s	r	a	c	t	r	i	z	o	i
o	j	t	c	a	m	a	r	e	r	o

1 oficina – *el abogado*
2 teatro – la actriz
3 garaje – el mecánico
4 hospital – la médica
5 instituto – la profesora
6 oficina – el secretario
7 restaurante – el camarero
8 peluquería – el peluquero
9 jardín – la jardinera

2

Answers

(**d**) *Soy azafata de la aerolínea Iberia. Me gusta tener responsabilidades.* Mi madre trabaja en una (**h**) clínica, es dentista. Le encanta su trabajo porque es muy (**b**) interesante. Mi padre es actor y trabaja en un (**c**) teatro. Lo bueno es que a veces actúa en programas (**a**) de televisión. Le gusta su trabajo porque es variado. Mi (**f**) hermana mayor es recepcionista en un (**e**) hotel de lujo. Siempre está muy (**i**) ocupada. Mi hermano es ingeniero. Para él, tener un (**g**) trabajo creativo es muy importante.

5 1 ¿Trabajas los sábados? (Student Book pages 84–85)

Main topics and objectives

- Describing part-time jobs
- Using **tener que** followed by the infinitive

Grammar

- Using **tener que** + infinitive

Key language

Reparto periódicos.
Hago de canguro.
Trabajo como…
dependiente/a
camarero/a
jardinero/a

socorrista
Lavo coches.

Los sábados…
Por las mañanas/tardes…
Todos los días…
Los fines de semana…
tengo que…
cuidar a niños
vender zapatos/ropa
servir comida a los clientes
vigilar a la gente que nada en la
    piscina
levantarme temprano
coger el autobús
ser puntual

Trabajo de (nueve) a (seis).
Gano (diez) euros a la hora.
Los clientes son…
(No) gano mucho/Gano poco.

Resources

CD 3, tracks 4–5
Cuaderno Verde, page 48

Starter 1

To review time expressions

Write up the following. Give students 2 minutes to translate the sentence openings into English.

1 Los fines de semana…
2 Por las mañanas…
3 Todos los días…   tengo que trabajar mucho.
4 Los sábados…
5 Por las tardes…

Check answers, asking students to translate the end of the sentence too.

1 Escucha. Copia y completa la tabla. (1–5)

Listening. Students copy out the table. They listen to five people talking about their jobs and fill in the details in Spanish.

Audioscript *Track 4*

1 – ¿Tienes un trabajo a tiempo parcial?
  – Trabajo como peluquero.
  – ¿Cuándo trabajas?
  – Trabajo los fines de semana.
  – ¿Cuánto ganas?
  – Gano seis euros a la hora.
2 – ¿Tienes un trabajo a tiempo parcial?
  – Trabajo como cajero los sábados.
  – ¿Cuánto ganas?
  – Gano ocho euros a la hora.
3 – ¿Trabajas los fines de semana?
  – No. Trabajo los jueves.
  – ¿Qué haces?
  – Trabajo como dependiente.
  – ¿Cuánto ganas?
  – Trabajo de cinco de la tarde a nueve y media de la noche, pero sólo gano treinta euros en total.
4 – ¿Trabaja usted los fines de semana?
  – Sí. Trabajo todos los domingos.
  – ¿En qué trabaja usted?

  – Trabajo de camarera en un restaurante.
  – ¿Cuánto gana usted?
  – Gano siete euros a la hora.
5 – ¿Qué hace usted para ganar dinero?
  – Trabajo de jardinero.
  – ¿Cuándo trabaja usted?
  – Trabajo los fines de semana.
  – ¿Cuánto gana usted?
  – Gano cuarenta y cinco euros al día.

Answers

	¿Trabajo?	¿Cuándo?	¿Cuánto ganas?
1	*peluquero*	*los fines de semana*	*6€ a la hora*
2	cajero	los sábados	8€ a la hora
3	dependiente	los jueves	30€ en total
4	camarera	los domingos	7€ a la hora
5	jardinero	los fines de semana	45€ al día

★ ResultsPlus

Tip box on distinguishing between spoken forms that are easily confused (¿**Cuándo**…? and ¿**Cuánto**…?).

2 Lee las descripciones y escribe la letra correcta.

Reading. Students read the descriptions and identify the correct picture for each one (from a–g).

Answers

1 b **2** a **3** d **4** e **5** c **6** g **7** f

3 Read the dialogue with your partner. Then make up another dialogue, using the pictures or your own ideas.

Speaking. In pairs: students read the dialogues shown, taking it in turn to ask and answer the questions. They then make up their own dialogue together, replacing the details using the picture prompts or with their own ideas. A language box is supplied for support.

Starter 2

To review *tener que* + the infinitive

Write up the following. Give students 3 minutes to translate each of the five sentences into Spanish. (Supply **tener que** as necessary for support.)

I have to…
get up early.
catch the bus.
be on time.
sell shoes.

Check answers. Ask students to identify the verb form used after **tener que**.

G Grammar

Use the Grammar box to review **tener que** + the infinitive.

R Students write five sentences on what they have to do every day, using **tener que** + the infinitive.

4 Read Mónica's email and choose the four statements that apply.

Reading. Students read Mónica's email and the seven statements in English about it, then identify the four statements that are correct. Some vocabulary is glossed for support.

Answers
2, 4, 5, 7

5 Lee el texto otra vez. Copia y completa la tabla en inglés. (P = opinión positiva, N = opinión negativa, P+N = opinión positiva y negativa.)

Reading. Students copy out the table. They reread the text and fill in the details of Mónica's opinions (positive – P, negative – N or a mixture of positive and negative – P + N).

Answers

	pay	working hours	clothes	duties	people
P/N/ P+N	P	N	N	P+N	N
details	8€/hour	every Saturday from 8 am to 6:30 pm	has to be well dressed; prefers wearing jeans and trainers	interesting but difficult; has to answer the phone and sometimes makes coffee for the clients	very serious and sometimes a little unpleasant

6 Escucha. ¿Qué hacen? Escribe P, N o P+N. (1–4)

Listening. Students listen to four people talking about their jobs. They note what each person does in English and his/her opinion of the job (positive – P, negative – N or a mixture of positive and negative – P + N).

Audioscript *Track 5*

1 – *¿En qué trabajas, Jimena?*
  – *Pues soy dependienta y tengo que vender libros en una librería.*
  – *¿Qué opinas de tu trabajo?*
  – *La gente es muy simpática y mi jefe es muy paciente.*
2 – *Y tú, Javier. ¿Qué tal tu trabajo?*
  – *Trabajo como socorrista. La piscina donde yo trabajo está muy sucia, pero el horario es bueno.*
3 – *¿En qué consiste tu trabajo, Zaida?*
  – *Cuido a animales en un centro veterinario.*
  – *¿Te gusta?*
  – *Es duro y no gano mucho.*
4 – *¿Trabajas los fines de semana?*
  – *Sí, claro. Trabajo como recepcionista.*
  – *¿Te gusta tu trabajo, Rafael?*
  – *Me encanta porque los clientes son interesantes.*

Answers

1 shop assistant – sells books, P
2 lifeguard at a swimming pool, P + N
3 looks after animals in a veterinary centre, N
4 receptionist, P

7 You are working part-time in a shoe shop. Include positive and negative opinions as you write about…

Writing. Students write about their part-time job in a shoe shop. Details of what to include are supplied. They should include both positive and negative opinions. Encourage them to look at how Mónica has used connectives in the text in exercise 4 and to follow this as a model.

Plenary

Ask students to tell you how **tener que** is used. Ask for examples using this structure, either with language from the unit or vocabulary from elsewhere in the course.

Cuaderno Verde, page 48

1

Answers

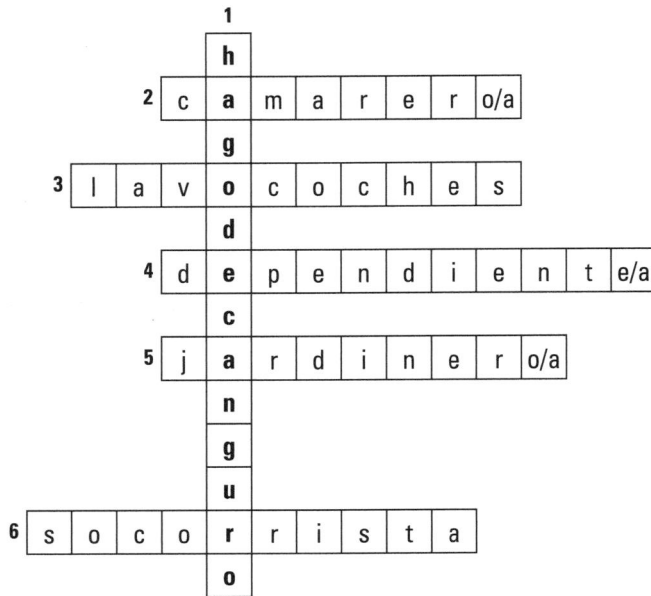

1 *Hago de canguro.*
2 Soy camarera/o.
3 Lavo coches.
4 Soy dependiente/a
5 Soy jardinero/a.
6 Soy socorrista.

2

Answers

1 a veces tengo que
2 normalmente tengo que servir
3 lo mejor es que
4 es mejor que trabajar
5 lo peor es trabajar

3

Answers

1 She is a waitress.
2 It's easy and she doesn't have to get up early.
3 She works at weekends.
4 Working in winter, when clients are more unpleasant.

2 Prácticas laborales (Student Book pages 86–87)

Main topics and objectives
- Describing work experience
- Using the preterite and the imperfect tense

Grammar
- Using the preterite and the imperfect tense

Key language
Hice mis prácticas laborales...
Trabajé...
en una escuela
en una oficina
en un polideportivo
en una empresa inglesa
en un hotel
Fui a trabajar a una tienda de ropa.

Months of the year
Era...
moderno/a, antiguo/a, grande, pequeño/a
Mi jefe era... y...
Los clientes eran...
callado/a(s)
respetuoso/a(s)
serio/a(s)
Escribí..., Ayudé..., Hablé..., Contesté..., Vendí..., Serví..., Di..., Mandé...
Aprendí mucho/poco.

No aprendí nada.
Por ejemplo, aprendí a trabajar en equipo, ayudar a/hablar con la gente, servir..., contestar...

Resources
CD 3, tracks 6–7
Cuaderno Verde, page 49
Gramática 196, 198

Starter 1

To review the preterite; to introduce vocabulary for talking about work experience

Write up the following, omitting the underline. Give students 3 minutes to identify the correct verb form for each sentence.

El año pasado...
1 ...*hice/hacer mis prácticas laborales en una oficina.*
2 ...*trabajo/trabajé en una tienda.*
3 ...*fui/voy a una empresa inglesa.*
4 ...*mandar/mandé correos electrónicos.*
5 ...*escribo/escribí cartas.*

Check answers, asking students to translate the sentences in the preterite into English.

1 Escucha y escribe el nombre correcto. (1–6)

Listening. Students listen to six people talking about their work experience and, using the pictures and speech bubbles, identify who is speaking each time.

Audioscript *Track 6*

1 *Trabajé como secretaria. Contesté llamadas telefónicas, escribí cartas y mandé correos. Fue un poco aburrido.*
2 *En mis prácticas laborales trabajé como camarero. Serví comida y bebida a los clientes, por supuesto. Me encantó.*
3 *Trabajé como profesora. Ayudé a los niños en las clases de dibujo y matemáticas. Me gusta mucho trabajar con niños.*
4 *Hice mis prácticas laborales aquí en Mallorca. Hablé en inglés con los clientes de Inglaterra. Lo pasé bien.*
5 *Hice mis prácticas en un centro comercial. Vendí vaqueros y camisas y lo pasé fatal. Los clientes eran antipáticos.*
6 *En mis prácticas laborales jugué al tenis y di clases de natación. Fue muy divertido.*

Answers
1 *Lilia* **2** Emilio **3** Eva **4** Inmaculada
5 Jorge **6** José

✛ Students listen again and note whether the opinions expressed are positive or negative in each case.

2 Read the phrases and write down who may have done this activity as part of their work experience (Eva, Jorge, Lilia, José, Inmaculada or Emilio). Justify your answer.

Reading. Students read the sentences and identify who is speaking each time, using the people in exercise 1.

Answers *(sample)*

Students may come up with more than one answer for some items: the important thing is that they should be able to justify their responses.

1 *Lilia – you write letters and send emails in an office*
2 *Eva, Jorge, José, Emilio – you would find children in a school, a shop, a leisure centre or a restaurant*
3 *Jorge, Inmaculada, Emilio – you might deal with English people in a shop, an English company or a restaurant*
4 *Lilia, Inmaculada – you answer telephone calls in an office*
5 *José – you sell jeans in a clothes shop*
6 *Emilio – you serve food and drinks in a restaurant*
7 *José – you give swimming lessons in a leisure centre*

3 Con tu compañero/a, pregunta y contesta. Utiliza los dibujos.

Speaking. In pairs: students ask and answer questions about work experience using the picture prompts supplied.

Starter 2

To review the preterite

Write up the following and give students 3 minutes to rewrite the sentences, replacing the present tense verbs with verbs in the preterite.

1 *Ayudo a los niños.*
2 *Hago mis prácticas laborales en una oficina.*
3 *Trabajo en una tienda.*
4 *Vendo vaqueros.*
5 *Hablo con los clientes.*

(*Answers:* ayudé, hice, trabajé, vendí, hablé)

4 Lee e identifica los verbos en el pretérito.

Reading. Students read the text and list all the verbs in the preterite.

Answers

hice, pasé, fue, trabajé, tuve, ayudé, limpié, serví, organicé, aprendí

➕ Students identify the verbs in the imperfect tense in the text, and translate them into English.

5 Lee otra vez y contesta a las preguntas.

Reading. Students reread the text in exercise 4 and answer the comprehension questions in English. Some vocabulary is glossed for support.

Answers

1 in a hospital
2 she had a great time; it was a little hard
3 very nice
4 very good; a little strict at times
5 *Any two of:* helped patients, cleaned the ward, served tea
7 a birthday party for Theo, a sick child
8 to work in a team; to talk with patients

G Grammar

Use the Grammar box to review the preterite and the imperfect before students do exercise 6.

6 Listen to Miguel talking about his work experience and make notes under the following headings.

Listening. Students listen to Miguel talking about his work experience and note the following details in English: what the building, boss and clients were like, what his responsibilities were and what he learnt.

Audioscript *Track 7*

1 *Hice mis prácticas laborales en una tienda de deportes. La tienda es bastante pequeña y está en el centro de la ciudad, al lado de un supermercado.*
2 *Mi jefe era muy serio, pero bastante tolerante.*
3 *El problema más grande del trabajo fueron los clientes. Eran tan maleducados y a veces agresivos. ¡Fue terrible!*
4 *Tuve muchas responsabilidades. Serví a los clientes, vendí ropa deportiva y contesté llamadas telefónicas. Aprendí a hablar con los clientes difíciles.*

Answers

1 Building – quite small shop
2 Boss – very serious but quite tolerant
3 Clients – so rude and sometimes aggressive
4 Responsibilities and what he learnt – served clients, sold sports clothes and answered the phone; learnt to speak with difficult clients

7 Escribe sobre tus prácticas.

Writing. Students write a short text on their own work experience (real or imagined). A language box is supplied.

⭐ ResultsPlus

🖱 Suggest students use the computer to summarise and learn grammar. The computer is also useful for self-testing: students could set up a table with verbs in different tenses, copying from the verb tables at the back of the Student Book then deleting all or some of the Spanish forms. They key in the missing verb forms, then compare their version with the original, complete table.

Plenary

Ask students to summarise when the preterite and the imperfect are used.

Go round the class. Students take it in turn to say something that they did during their work experience, using the preterite.

Cuaderno Verde, page 49

1

Answers

1	I did	*hice*
2	it was	fue
3	I had to	tuve que
4	I helped	ayudé
5	I answered	contesté
6	I spoke	hablé
7	I worked	trabajé
8	I wrote	escribí
9	I learned	aprendí
10	I liked	me gustó
11	I prepared	preparé
12	I served	serví

2

Answers

1 Hice mis prácticas en un supermercado.
2 Hice mis prácticas en junio de este año.
3 Era muy severo.
4 Eran agresivos y maleducados.
5 Aprendí a trabajar en equipo.
6 No me gustó trabajar allí porque fue aburrido.

Main topics and objectives

- Describing future plans
- Using a variety of verbs to refer to the future

Grammar

- Talking about the future
- Using **si** clauses

Key language

Quiero...
Voy a...
Me gustaría...
seguir estudiando
encontrar trabajo
ir a la universidad

trabajar como voluntario/a en...
vivir en el extranjero
formar una familia

Si (no) apruebo mis exámenes,...
Si trabajo mucho,...
Si tengo dinero,...
Si practico más deporte,...
Si tengo suerte,...

voy a ir a la universidad
voy a encontrar trabajo
voy a hacer un curso de formación profesional
voy a ser (médico/a)
voy a ganar mucho dinero
voy a viajar mucho
voy a jugar al fútbol en...

voy a ser famoso/a

Resources

CD 3, tracks 8–9
Cuaderno Verde, pages 50–51
Gramática 200

Starter 1

To review verb forms followed by the infinitive

Write up the following. Give students 3 minutes to identify and correct the error in each sentence.

1 *Voy a viaja mucho.*
2 *Querer ir a la universidad.*
3 *Me gustaría a trabajar como voluntaria.*
4 *Ir a ser médico.*

(*Answers:* 1 *Voy a* ***viajar***; 2 ***Quiero*** *ir*; 3 *Me gustaría* ~~*a*~~ *trabajar*; 4 ***Voy*** *a ser*)

Check answers. Ask students to give you other examples of verbs which are followed by the infinitive.

1 Lee y escribe el futuro de estos famosos.

Reading. Students read the English bubbles and write a sentence in Spanish for each famous person pictured. A language box is supplied for support.

Answers

1 Quiero formar una familia.
2 Voy a encontrar trabajo.
3 Me gustaría vivir en el extranjero.
4 Quiero ir a la universidad.
5 Voy a trabajar como voluntaria en…
6 Me gustaría seguir estudiando.

2 Listen and pick the correct letter. Can you note down any extra information about their future plans? (1–6)

Listening. Students listen to six people being interviewed about future plans. They identify the letters of the pictures mentioned (from **a–f**), and note in English the additional information given.

Audioscript *Track 8*

1 – ¿Qué vas a hacer en septiembre?
– Quiero ir a la universidad para estudiar matemáticas.
2 – Voy a seguir estudiando.
– ¡Qué bien! ¿Qué vas a hacer después del cole?
– Quiero estudiar historia o dibujo. No estoy seguro.
3 – ¿Qué vas a hacer el año que viene?
– No voy a seguir estudiando. Quiero encontrar trabajo en un hotel internacional.
– Buena idea. A mí también me gustaría encontrar un trabajo.
4 – No sé lo que voy a hacer en el futuro. ¿Y tú?
– Sí, tengo planes. Me gustaría trabajar como voluntario con gente ciega.
5 – ¿Qué vas a hacer en los próximos cinco años?
– Me gustaría casarme y formar una familia. Quiero tener una familia grande.
– ¿Y tú?
– No sé todavía.
6 – ¿Qué vas a hacer en los próximos diez años?
– Quiero vivir en el extranjero.
– ¿Dónde quieres vivir?
– Me gustaría vivir en Australia.

Answers

1 f – wants to study maths
2 a – wants to study history or art
3 b – one of them wants to find a job in an international hotel
4 d – would like to work as a volunteer with blind people
5 e – wants a large family
6 c – would like to live in Australia

Ⓖ Grammar

Use the Grammar box to review different ways of talking about the future: **querer** + infinitive; **me gustaría** + infinitive and the near future tense; **voy a** + infinitive.

R Students take it in turn to prompt with one of these expressions (**quiero**/**me gustaría**/**voy a**) and to complete the sentence with one of the phrases in exercise 1.

3 Talk about the future with your partner. Use the information in English and your own ideas.

Speaking. Students talk about their future plans, taking it in turn to ask and answer questions. A framework, including English prompts, is supplied.

Starter 2

To review ways of talking about the future

Write up the following. Give students 3 minutes to come up with a sentence about their future intentions for each of the structures. If necessary, remind students that the first two are followed by the infinitive, and how the near future tense is formed.

querer; *me gustaría*; near future tense

Hear answers. Ask students to summarise how the structures/tenses are formed.

G Grammar

Use the Grammar box to cover **si** + present tense used with the future tense to express possibilities in the future, in preparation for exercise 4.

4 Listen and write a phrase in English for each letter below. (1–4)

Listening. Students listen and complete in English the information that is missing from the table (**A–D**).

Audioscript *Track 9*

1 Si apruebo mis exámenes, voy a ser azafata y voy a viajar mucho.
2 Si practico más deporte, voy a jugar al fútbol en el Real Madrid.
3 Si no apruebo mis GCSEs, voy a hacer un curso de formación profesional.
4 Si trabajo mucho, voy a ganar mucho dinero.

> **Answers**
> **A** pass my exams
> **B** play football for Real Madrid
> **C** don't pass my GCSEs
> **D** earn a lot of money

5 Read Gabriela's text and answer the questions in English.

Reading. Students read the text and answer the comprehension questions in English.

> **Answers**
> 1 in Cali, because her family lives there
> 2 go to university to study English
> 3 she'll have to look for a job; as a sales assistant; in the shopping centre near her house
> 4 he works as a teacher; he's going to travel abroad
> 5 she would also like to travel

⭐ ResultsPlus

Tip box on using a wide range of tenses.

6 Escribe sobre tu futuro.

Writing. Students write a text about their own future, along the same lines as Gabriela's in exercise 5. A structure is supplied for support.

Plenary

Ask students to summarise how the near future tense is formed.

Go round the class to practise 'if' clauses to express possibilities in the future. Students take it in turn to prompt with a *si* clause and to conclude with a statement using the near future tense, e.g. *Si apruebo mis exámenes... voy a ser médico.*

Cuaderno Verde, pages 50–51

1

> **Answers**
> 1 ¿Qué quieres hacer el año que viene?
>   El año que viene quiero encontrar trabajo.
> 2 ¿Qué vas a hacer después del cole?
>   Después del cole voy a trabajar como voluntario en la India.
> 3 ¿Qué te gustaría hacer en los próximos cinco años?
>   En los próximos cinco años me gustaría ir a la universidad.
> 4 ¿Qué quieres hacer en el futuro?
>   En el futuro quiero vivir en el extranjero.
> 5 ¿Qué vas a ser en el futuro?
>   En el futuro voy a ser médico.

2

> **Answers**
> 1 *si hago mis deberes*
> 2 si tengo suerte
> 3 si apruebo mis exámenes
> 4 si tengo dinero
> 5 si practico más deporte
> 6 si trabajo

3

Answers

1 *Si no hago mis deberes, no voy a aprobar los exámenes.*
2 Si practico más deporte, voy a jugar al fútbol en el Real Madrid.
3 Si tengo dinero, voy a viajar mucho.
4 Si tengo suerte, voy a ser famoso/a.
5 Si apruebo mis exámenes, voy a ir a la universidad.
6 Si trabajo, voy a ganar mucho dinero.

4

Answers

1 Ana has passed her exams. **F**
2 Ana is going to learn German. **F**
3 Ana wants to work for a good company. **T**
4 Ana is going to work hard to earn lots of money. **T**
5 In her job Ana is not going to meet new people. **F**
6 Ana does not want to travel much. **F**

4 Mi currículum vitae (Student Book pages 90–91)

Main topics and objectives

- Understanding job adverts and writing a CV
- Using the preterite

Grammar

- Using the preterite

Key language

Jobs vocabulary
Adjectives used to describe people

Currículum vitae
Datos personales
Nombre
Apellidos
Dirección
Móvil
Correo electrónico
Fecha de nacimiento
Lugar de nacimiento
Educación
Experiencia laboral
Otros datos

Idiomas
Cualidades
Pasatiempos
Referencias

Resources

CD 3, tracks 10–11
Cuaderno Verde, pages 52–53

Starter 1

To review vocabulary for talking about work experience

Write up the following, leaving gaps for the underlined words and supplying them in jumbled order underneath. Give students 3 minutes to complete the text.

Me llamo Pablo. Soy una persona trabajadora. Hablo francés y español. Busco un trabajo interesante. El año pasado trabajé como profesor. Me gustaría trabajar a tiempo parcial.

1 Lee los textos. Busca las expresiones en español para estas frases.

Reading. Students read the descriptions of four people and find the Spanish for each English phrase.

Answers

a de nueve a once de la mañana
b Trabajé como profesora en un instituto mixto.
c Me interesa la naturaleza.
d Tengo tres hijos pequeños.

⭐ ResultsPlus

Tip box on reading strategies: identifying and looking for key words.

2 Read the job ads (a–e) and then match each person in exercise 1 to the appropriate job. There is one ad too many.

Reading. Students read the adverts and identify an appropriate job (from **a–e**) for each person in exercise 1. There is one distractor.

Answers

Pedro – d **Alicia** – a **Leandro** – c **Fátima** – e

R Students summarise in English what is required for each job.

+ Students translate the ads orally round the class.

3 Listen and write down the letter of a job ad from exercise 2 for each person. (1–4)

Listening. Students listen to four people talking about the kind of job they are looking for and identify a job for each one from exercise 2 (**a–e**). Give students time to read through the adverts again before you play the recording.

Audioscript *Track 10*

1 *Soy secretaria y busco trabajo. Me gustaría empezar inmediatamente. Tengo experiencia en contestar llamadas telefónicas y escribir cartas o correos electrónicos.*
2 *Tengo treinta años y tengo una familia grande. Busco un trabajo, hablo inglés y me gusta la informática.*
3 *Me gustaría encontrar un trabajo creativo y artístico. Me encantan las plantas y la naturaleza.*
4 *Busco empleo por las mañanas en el mercado. Trabajé como dependiente el año pasado.*

Answers

1 b **2** e **3** c **4** d

Starter 2

To introduce/review vocabulary for CVs

Write up the following. Give students 3 minutes to come up with appropriate details for each category.

Nombre
Apellidos
Dirección
Móvil
Educación
Experiencia laboral
Idiomas
Cualidades
Pasatiempos
Referencias

4 Lee el currículum vitae imaginario de Shakira. Lee las frases y escribe V (verdadero), F (falso) o NM (no se menciona).

Reading. Students read the invented CV for Shakira. They then read the sentences and decide whether each one is true (V), is false (F) or contains information not mentioned in the text (NM).

Answers
1 V **2** V **3** F **4** NM **5** V **6** F

5 Mira el CV de Shakira y escucha. ¿Habla Shakira? Escribe S (sí) o N (no). (1–4)

Listening. Students listen to four recorded items. Using the CV in exercise 4, they decide whether the speaker in each of the items is Shakira (S) or not (N).

Audioscript *Track 11*

1 *Soy cantante y vivo en los Estados Unidos, pero nací en Colombia. Escribí mi primera canción con diez años y hablo español, inglés y alemán.*

2 *Soy cantante y creo que soy inteligente y positiva de carácter. Me encantan la jardinería y la naturaleza y aquí en Florida paso mucho tiempo en la playa con amigos. Mi fecha de nacimiento es 2 de febrero.*

3 *Nací en Barranquilla en Colombia y me interesan los ordenadores y los deportes. Me encanta jugar con mi 'Nintendo Wii'.*

4 *Soy colombiana, pero ahora no vivo en Colombia. Mi álbum Servicio de lavandería me hizo muy famosa. Tengo muchos premios, por ejemplo dos Premios Grammy y ocho Grammy Latino.*

Answers
1 N **2** S **3** N **4** S

6 Escribe tu propio currículum vitae o un currículum vitae para un(a) famosa.

Writing. Students write their own CV in Spanish, or the CV of a celebrity. A structure is supplied.

⭐ ResultsPlus

Tip box on using the preterite to talk about past experience.

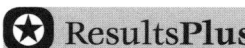 Students write their CV in Spanish on computer, using a word-processing or DTP package. They swap texts with a partner and give constructive feedback on the content and accuracy.

Plenary

Ask students to read out the *Experiencia laboral* section of their CV. Invite constructive feedback from the rest of the class on all the preterite forms used.

Cuaderno Verde, pages 52–53

1

Answers
a experienced applicants **1, 2, 4, 7**
b foreign languages **2, 4**
c immediate start **1, 5, 7,**
d weekend work only **3**
e flexible working hours **5, 6**
f part-time job only **3, 4, 7, 8**

2

Answers
a Alexa has trained as a hairdresser. **7**
b Marta is bilingual in Spanish and English. She has worked on reception for a company. **2, 4**
c Juan Carlos is a student. He has no classes at weekends and has a computer. **3, 6, 8**
d María has worked at a butcher's counter in a supermarket. **1**
e Marcos does not have a computer. He has just left school and has no work experience. **3, 6**
f Ramón has a full driving licence and he wants a job where he can drive. **5**

3

Answers
Currículum Vitae
Datos personales
Nombre: *Penélope*
Apellidos: *Cruz Sánchez*
Dirección: *Calle de las Estrellas 24, Madrid 28033*
Teléfonos: *91 809 65 65 / 06874 55 55*
Correo electrónico: *penelope@tmail.es*
Fecha de nacimiento: *28 de abril 1974*
Lugar de nacimiento: *Alcobendas, Madrid*
Educación Estudié en el Colegio de Bellas Artes, Madrid.
Experiencia laboral
Con 18 años canté con el grupo pop *Mecano*.
Trabajé como presentadora en el programa de televisión juvenil *La Quinta Marcha*.
Hice muchas películas en España.
Viajé a Estados Unidos e hice películas en Hollywood.
Gané cuatro premios Goya.
Gané un Oscar en 2009 por la película *Vicky Cristina Barcelona*.
Otros datos
Idiomas: español, inglés, francés e italiano
Cualidades: inteligente, optimista, positiva y viva
Pasatiempos: el baile y la moda
Referencias: Sr. Almodóvar, Estudios Almodóvar, Madrid

5 La entrevista (Student Book pages 92–93)

Main topics and objectives
- Conducting a job interview
- Forming the perfect tense

Grammar
- The perfect tense

Key language
¿Cómo te llamas?
Me llamo…/Mi nombre es…
¿Qué has estudiado?
He estudiado inglés, matemáticas,…
¿Por qué quieres trabajar como…?
Porque me gusta tener
responsabilidades/tener un trabajo creativo/ganar un buen sueldo.
¿Qué experiencia laboral tienes?
He trabajado en…, he servido…, he hecho…
He hablado…, he escrito…, he estudiado…
¿Has trabajado en equipo antes?
Sí, he trabajado en equipo antes.
No, nunca he trabajado en equipo.
¿Qué es importante para ti?
La gente/El dinero/La naturaleza es importante…
Los niños/Los animales son importantes para mí.
¿Cómo eres?/¿Qué cualidades tienes?
Soy amable, sincero/a, trabajador(a),…
¿Cuál es su dirección electrónica/ correo electrónico?
Mi dirección electrónica/correo electrónico es…

Resources
CD 3, tracks 12–13
Cuaderno Verde, pages 54–55
Gramática 198

Starter 1

To introduce job vocabulary

Write up the following. Give students 3 minutes, discussing in pairs, to rate each question depending on their personal response:
1 Strongly disagree 2 Disagree 3 No opinion
4 Agree 5 Strongly agree.

a *El dinero es muy importante.*
b *Prefiero trabajar en equipo.*
c *Me parece esencial tener responsabilidades en mi trabajo.*
d *No es importante tener experiencia.*
e *Me gustaría trabajar a tiempo parcial.*

Hear answers, asking students to translate the sentences into English.

1 Lee y empareja las frases con los dibujos. Escribe la letra correcta.

Reading. Students read and match the sentences in the bubbles with the correct pictures (from **a–e**).

Answers

1 e 2 a 3 d 4 b 5 c

2 Escucha y lee. Escribe las palabras. (1-8)

Listening. Students listen to a job interview and follow the gap-fill text at the same time. They then copy and complete the text.

Audioscript *Track 12*

– *¿Qué ha estudiado usted en el instituto?*
– *He estudiado asignaturas típicas como inglés, **matemáticas** y ciencias, pero he tenido clases de hechizos y trucos de magia.*
– *¿Por qué quiere ser **profesor** de magia?*

– *Quiero ser profesor de magia porque me **encanta** la magia y me interesa lo sobrenatural.*
– *¿Qué experiencia laboral tiene usted?*
– *He enseñado magia en un colegio **privado**.*
– *¿Qué es importante para usted?*
– *Los niños son muy **importantes**.*
– *¿Ha trabajado en equipo antes?*
– *Sí, he trabajo en equipo con mis **amigos**, sobre todo con mi amiga Hermione.*
– *¿Qué cualidades tiene usted?*
– *Soy amable, inocente y **sincero**.*
– *¿Cuál es su dirección electrónica?*
– *Es **h-a-r-r-y-punto-p-o-t-t-e-r-@-h-o-g-w-a-r-t-s-punto-com***

Answers

Also in bold in the audioscript.
1 matemáticas 2 profesor 3 encanta 4 privado
5 importantes 6 amigos 7 sincero
8 harry.potter@hogwarts.com

G Grammar

Use the Grammar box to introduce the perfect tense.

R Students reread the text in exercise 2 and note down the verbs in the perfect tense.

+ Give a range of prompts in English for students to practise forming the perfect tense of regular verbs, e.g. I have sent, he has lived, etc.

Starter 2

To review the perfect tense

Write up the following, omitting the words in bold. Give students 3 minutes to complete the table.

I have worked	he trabajado	trabajar
I have sent	**he mandado**	mandar
I have spoken	**he hablado**	**hablar**
I have eaten	he comido	comer
I have drunk	**he bebido**	beber
I have made	he hecho	**hacer**
I have written	he escrito	**escribir**
I have put	he puesto	**poner**

Check answers. Ask students to tell you how the perfect tense is formed.

3 Lee la conversación del ejercicio 2 y contesta a las preguntas.

Reading. Students reread the conversation in exercise 2 and answer the comprehension questions in English.

Answers

1 English, maths and science
2 because he loves magic; he is interested in the supernatural
3 he has taught magic in a private school
4 the children
5 he has worked in a team with her
6 *Any two of:* friendly, innocent, sincere

4 Look at the conversation in exercise 2 again. Write down the four phrases in which the interviewee uses the perfect tense.

Reading. Students reread the text in exercise 2 and write down the four phrases featuring the perfect tense.

Answers

He estudiado asignaturas típicas…
He tenido clases de hechizos…
He enseñado magia…
He trabajado en equipo…

5 Listen to the job interview with Yesenia and answer the questions in English.

Listening. Students listen to Yesenia's job interview and answer the comprehension questions in English.

Audioscript *Track 13*

– Hola, buenos días. ¿Cómo te llamas?
– Buenos días. Me llamo Yesenia Loredo Bernal.
– ¿Qué has estudiado en el cole, Yesenia?
– He estudiado inglés, dibujo y música.
– ¿Por qué quieres trabajar como peluquera?
– Quiero ser peluquera porque me gusta tener un trabajo creativo.
– Muy bien. Y, a ver, Yesenia, ¿qué experiencia tienes?
– He trabajado en una peluquería y también he trabajado en un salón de belleza.
– ¿Qué es importante para ti?
– Sobre todo la gente es importante para mí. Me encanta charlar y trabajar con muchas personas.
– ¿Cómo eres, Yesenia?
– Soy una persona muy alegre y también soy ambiciosa.
– ¿Cuál es tu dirección electrónica?
– Lo siento, pero en este momento no tengo correo electrónico.

Answers

1 English, art and music
2 hairdresser; she wants a creative job
3 *Any one of:* she has worked in a hairdresser's; she has worked in a beauty salon
4 people
5 very cheerful; ambitious
6 she doesn't have one (at the moment)

Zona Cultura

Use the Zona cultura box to remind students that Spanish makes a distinction between 'you' in formal and informal contexts.

- **tú** – to one person, familiar: use with a friend, family member, someone you know well
- **usted** – to one person, formal: use with a stranger, colleague, older person, someone you don't know well

Students work out which form is used in the interviews in exercises 2 and 5.

6 Look at the pictures below and create a job interview using the information. Then invent your own job interview with your partner.

Speaking. In pairs: students put together a job interview using the picture prompts supplied. They take it in turn to ask and answer questions. They then make up interviews using their own details (real or invented). A language box is supplied.

ResultsPlus

You could record the interviews, either as audio or as video, so students can watch them and identify areas in which they could improve their language and/or performance.

Plenary

Ask students to summarise when the perfect tense is used and how it is formed.

Practise the perfect tense by prompting in Spanish ('I' forms) for students to translate into English, e.g. **he usado** – I have used. Then move on to prompting in English.

Cuaderno Verde, page 54

1

Answers

j	b	t	b	e	b	i	d	o
u	p	u	e	s	t	o	s	d
g	o	u	l	t	s	h	t	a
a	q	e	a	u	o	c	f	t
d	d	g	v	d	p	e	p	i
o	i	z	a	i	e	h	r	s
m	a	n	d	a	d	o	a	i
e	m	l	o	d	h	s	m	v
o	d	i	m	o	c	v	b	s

1	yo	*he*	*puesto*	I have put
2	yo	he	comido	I have eaten
3	tú	has	mandado	you have sent
4	él/ella	ha	hecho	he/she has done/made
5	usted	ha	bebido	you have drunk
6	nosotros/as	hemos	visitado	we have visited
7	vosotros/as	habéis	lavado	you have washed
8	ellos/ellas	han	jugado	they have played
9	ustedes	han	estudiado	you have studied

2

Answers

Esta mañana he tenido mucho que hacer. Primero (**1**) *he comido* un bocadillo y (**2**) **he bebido** un café con leche. Después (**3**) **he estudiado** un poco y (**4**) **he hecho** los deberes. Más tarde (**5**) **he jugado** con mi ordenador y (**6**) **he mandado** mensajes a mis amigos. A mediodía (**7**) **he puesto** la mesa y (**8**) **he comido** con mi madre. Por la tarde (**9**) **he visitado** a mis abuelos y (**10**) **he lavado** su coche.

Cuaderno Verde, page 55

1

Answers

Alejandro – past
Luisa – future
María – past
Ana – present
Pedro – past
José – present

2

Answers

Alejandro: fui, hablé, aprendí – preterite
María: he trabajado, he tenido, he servido, he hablado – perfect
Pedro: tuve, gustó, di, pasé, fue – preterite; eran – imperfect
Luisa: voy a buscar – near future; apruebo – present; voy a ir – near future; gustaría – conditional; tengo – present; voy a encontrar – near future
Ana: hago, encanta, trabajo – present
José: prefiero, es – present

Prueba oral: Work/study placement (Student's Book pp. 94–95)

Topics revised
- Talking about work experience
- Talking about leisure activities
- Talking about future plans

Resources
CD 5, tracks 21–23

Overview

Read through the task box at the top of the page and outline for students how this section works. They will hear a Speaking controlled assessment model interaction in three parts and do exercises focused on the language used. These exercises, along with the advice/activities on how to improve speaking performance in Results Plus, will help them prepare to take part in a role-play style interaction of their own on the topic.

Before listening

As the task requires students to ask as well as answer questions, you could start with a pre-listening task on questions. Write up the following. Students working in pairs decide (a) what each one means and (b) which they think will be used in the recording by Leena (playing the job interviewee) and which will be used by the examiner (playing the job interviewer).

1 *¿Qué experiencia laboral tienes?*
2 *¿Qué haces en la tienda?*
3 *¿Por qué te interesa este trabajo?*
4 *¿Cuándo empieza el trabajo?*
5 *En tu opinión, ¿qué cualidades tienes?*
6 *¿Qué te gusta hacer en tu tiempo libre?*
7 *En este trabajo, ¿tengo que mandar correos?*
8 *¿Qué quieres hacer en el futuro?*

(*Answers:*
1 *What work experience do you have?*
2 *What do you do in the shop?*
3 *Why are you interested in this job?*
4 *When does the job start?*
5 *In your opinion, what qualities do you have?*
6 *What do you like to do in your spare time?*
7 *In this job, do I have to send emails?*
8 *What do you want to do in the future?*

Leena's/interviewee's questions: 4, 7
Examiner's/interviewer's questions:
1, 2, 3, 5, 6, 8)

1 You are going to listen to Leena, an exam candidate, playing the part of someone being interviewed for the work/study placement. Listen to part 1 and match up the two halves of Leena's answers.

Listening. Explain to the students that they will hear a sample of the kind of role-play style interaction they are expected to have in the Speaking controlled assessment.

They listen to the first part of the recording and match the sentence halves.

Audioscript *Track 21*

Part 1
– *Buenos días. ¿Qué experiencia laboral tienes?*
– *Bueno… trabajé de canguro el año pasado para una familia española con niños pequeños. Cuidé a tres niños de cinco, ocho y nueve años. Ahora trabajo los sábados en una tienda de ropa. Soy dependienta.*
– *¿Qué haces en la tienda?*
– *Empiezo a las ocho y primero tengo que limpiar la tienda. Luego, a las nueve y media, la tienda abre. Me gusta mucho ayudar a los clientes porque es interesante. Me gusta también porque mis compañeros son muy sinceros. Lo que más me gusta es organizar la ropa porque es muy fácil. Lo peor es que el trabajo no se paga bien.*

> **Answers**
> **1** c **2** a **3** f **4** d **5** b **6** e

2 Listen to part 2 of Leena's interview and note down the words that fill the gaps. What question does Leena ask?

Listening. Students now listen to the second part of Leena's interview and complete the gap-fill version of the transcript. The answers are supplied in random order for support.

Students then identify the question that Leena asks the interviewer.

With a confident class you could ask students to read the text and try to work out the answers first, then use the recording to check.

Audioscript *Track 22*

Part 2
– *¿Por qué te interesa este trabajo?*
– *Quiero este trabajo porque me **encanta** España. El año pasado fui de vacaciones a España **con** mi familia y lo pasé fenomenal. Comí paella y **nadé** en el mar. Hablo un poco de español y es mi asignatura **preferida** del cole porque es muy divertida. Me gustaría mucho trabajar y **estudiar** en España para aprender más de la cultura **española**. ¿Cuándo empieza el trabajo?*
– *Empieza en julio y termina en septiembre. En tu opinión, ¿qué cualidades tienes?*
– *Creo que **soy** responsable y organizada. También soy **trabajadora** y nunca soy pesimista **ni** tímida. Además **siempre** soy puntual.*

Answers

1 encanta **2** con **3** nadé **4** preferida **5** estudiar
6 española **7** soy **8** trabajadora **9** ni **10** siempre

Question: ¿Cuándo empieza el trabajo? *When does the job start?*

Answers

1 deportes **2** invierno **3** navegar, correos
4 exámenes **5** trabajar, hotel **6** encontrar, divertido

Question: En este trabajo, ¿tengo que mandar correos? *In this job, do I have to send emails?*

✚ Students find examples of the following in what Leena says in the audioscript for exercise 2: the preterite, the conditional, opinions, reasons, adjectives, negatives, connectives and qualifiers. Point out that including details like these will earn them extra marks in the exam.

(*Answers:*
Preterite: fui, pasé, comí, nadé
Conditional: me gustaría
Opinions: me encanta España, lo pasé fenomenal, mi asignatura preferida, me gustaría mucho
Reasons: porque me encanta España, porque es muy divertida, para aprender más de la cultura española
Adjectives: fenomenal, preferida, divertida, responsable, organizada, trabajadora, pesimista, tímida, puntual
Negatives: nunca, ni
Connectives: porque, y, para, también, además
Qualifiers: un poco de, muy, mucho)

3 Now listen to part 3 of Leena's interview and rewrite the jumbled words in bold. What is the second question that Leena asks?

Listening. Students listen to the third and final part of Leena's interview and write out the words that are given as anagrams. A confident class could attempt to work out the words first, and then use the recording to check their answers.

Audioscript *Track 23*

Part 3

– *¿Qué te gusta hacer en tu tiempo libre?*
– *Me gustan mucho los deportes. Normalmente, en verano, juego al tenis, pero en invierno me gusta hacer equitación. Los sábados mis amigos y yo vamos al cine. Lo que más me gusta es navegar por Internet y leer correos electrónicos. En este trabajo, ¿tengo que mandar correos?*
– *Sí, hay que mandar correos y contestar llamadas telefónicas. ¿Qué quieres hacer en el futuro, Leena?*
– *Si apruebo mis exámenes, voy a ir a la universidad. Quiero estudiar idiomas. Pero si no apruebo los exámenes, voy a buscar un trabajo. Me gustaría trabajar en un polideportivo o en un hotel. Voy a encontrar un trabajo variado y divertido.*

⭐ **ResultsPlus**

The Results Plus support for speaking activities is differentiated, allowing students to identify and work towards their target level: covering the basics, Grade C, increasing their marks. Encourage students to adopt the techniques in these sections in all extended speaking activities.

Read through and discuss the Results Plus section together.

4 Now it's your turn! Prepare your answers to the task and then do the interview with your partner or your teacher.

Speaking. Students take part in a role-play interview for a job in the style of a controlled assessment task. They should use all the support supplied, here and elsewhere on the spread:

- the Results Plus advice on the language to include
- Leena's responses, adapted to talk about themselves
- the English points in the task box, p. 94
- their answers to exercises 1–3.

Each student takes part in an interview as the person answering the questions. If they are working with a partner, they will take turns asking and answering.

If possible, record the interviews or have the students record themselves. They can then swap recordings with a partner, listen to each other's version and offer comments on how it might be improved. A simple marking system is suggested (one/two/three stars for listed categories). Students should then identify two or three areas which they would like to improve next time they do an extended speaking task.

Topics revised
- Writing about work experience

1 Read the text and choose the correct title for each paragraph. What words/phrases in the text support your decisions?

Reading. Students read the text and choose the correct title (from headings **a–d**) for each paragraph (**1–4**), giving reasons for their choices.

Answers

1 c **2** a **3** d **4** b

2 Find the equivalent of these expressions in Spanish in the text.

Reading. Students reread the text in exercise 1 and identify the Spanish versions of the English phrases listed.

Answers

1 El mes pasado…
2 Hice mis prácticas…
3 …durante quince días.
4 me levanté a las seis de la mañana
5 …desafortunadamente llegué tarde
6 Hice muchas cosas…
7 …salí a comprar bocadillos.
8 Mi jefe era muy simpático.
9 No me gusta nada hacer fotocopias…
10 ¡Eso me gustó mucho!

3 Find the preterite of each of these verbs in Joel's text and translate them. Now can you find two other verbs in the preterite that Joel uses to say what he did?

Reading. Students find in the text the preterite forms of the infinitives listed, then translate them into English. They then find two other verbs in the preterite that Joel uses to say what he did.

Answers

1 coger → cogí (I took)
2 hablar → hablé (I spoke)
3 mandar → mandé (I sent)
4 escribir → escribí (I wrote)
5 salir → salí (I went out)

Other preterite verbs: *Any two of:* me levanté, llegué, contesté, comí, terminé

4 Read the text again and answer the questions in English.

Reading. Students reread the text and answer the comprehension questions in English.

Answers

1 a fortnight
2 7:30
3 by train, then underground
4 *Any four of:* speak to customers, answer phone calls, send emails, write letters, go out to buy sandwiches, photocopy
5 photocopying
6 eat pizza in the canteen (on the last day)
7 didn't like it/it was a bit of a pain.
8 a creative job/one that doesn't involve using a computer every day

5 You might be asked to write about your work experience as a controlled assessment task. Use the Results Plus to help you prepare your account.

Students read through the language support material supplied in preparation for doing their own extended writing task in exercise 6.

⊛ ResultsPlus

The Results Plus section gives students the support they need to structure and improve their writing. The support is differentiated, allowing students to identify and work towards their target level: covering the basics, Grade C, increasing their marks. Encourage students to adopt the kind of approach taken in this section in all extended writing activities.

6 Now write a full account of your work experience.

Writing. Students write their own text on work experience in the style of a controlled assessment task (at least 100 words). As well as the Results Plus guidelines on the language to include, they should use all the support supplied here:

- Joel's text, adapted to refer to themselves
- advice on using reference resources
- the sample structure for the text.

7 Check carefully what you have written.

Writing. Students check their own work using the list of features supplied.

Te toca a ti (Student Book pages 180–181)

● Self-access reading and writing

A Reinforcement

1 Read the sentences and unjumble the jobs.

Reading. Students read and complete the sentences with the correct job, by unjumbling the words that are given as anagrams.

> **Answers**
>
> **1** médico **2** peluquera **3** dentista
> **4** futbolista **5** recepcionista

2 Read the emails and answer the questions below.

Reading. Students read the two emails and then identify who is being described in each question.

> **Answers**
>
> **1** Chuy **2** Leída **3** Leída **4** Leída **5** Chuy
> **6** Chuy **7** Leída **8** Chuy

3 Copy out the grid and fill in the missing verbs.

Writing. Students copy out the table and complete it with the missing verbs.

> **Answers**
>
> **A** trabajo **B** estudié **C** escribir **D** escribo
> **E** bebo **F** bebí **G** hice

B Extension

1 Match up the questions and the answers.

Reading. Students match the questions and answers.

> **Answers**
>
> **1** *b* **2** a **3** e **4** c **5** f **6** d

2 Read the word snake and write out the sentence correctly.

Reading. Students separate the word snake out into a sentence.

> **Answers**
>
> Mis prácticas laborales fueron bastante divertidas porque trabajé con niños y mi jefe era simpático.

3 Read the text and copy and complete it with the correct words.

Reading. Students copy and complete the gap-fill text, using the words supplied.

> **Answers**
>
> **1** dieciocho **2** pequeño **3** parcial **4** mando
> **5** telefónicas **6** paga **7** domingos **8** trabajé
> **9** gustó **10** gustaría

4 Copy Eugenia's text from exercise 3, changing key phrases, to write a letter from Simón. Include the information below.

Writing. Students copy and adapt the text in exercise 3 to make it a letter from Simón, whose details are supplied.

Module 6 Mi tiempo libre (Student Book pages 100–121)

Unit	Main topics and objectives	Grammar	Skills
Repaso 1 La tele (pp. 100–101)	• Revising TV programmes • Using articles and adjectives correctly	Adjective agreement Using definite/indefinite articles	Telling the time Including extra details when writing
Repaso 2 El cine (pp. 102–103)	• Revising types of films • Using a range of opinions	Verbs of opinion	
1 La paga (pp. 104–105)	• Talking about hobbies and pocket money • Using conjugated verbs and infinitives	Infinitives v. conjugated verbs Direct object pronoun **lo**	Including adverbs of frequency
2 El campeonato (pp. 106–107)	• Describing sports and sporting events • Using tenses referring to the past and the present	Present and past verbs	Using a range of tenses
3 ¿Quedamos? (pp. 108–109)	• Making arrangements to go out • Using the present continuous tense	The present continuous tense	Using expressions to buy thinking time
4 Una crítica (pp. 110–111)	• Writing a film review • Using emphatic adjectives	**Acabar de** Emphatic adjectives	Using absolute superlatives to give opinions
5 La tecnología (pp. 112–113)	• Talking about new technology • Revising comparatives	The comparative	Comparing things
Prueba oral: Leisure (pp. 114–115)	Exam speaking practice	Revision	
Prueba escrita (pp. 116–117)	Exam writing practice	Revision	
Leer y escuchar (Modules 5–6) (pp. 118–119)	Listening and reading skills	Revision	
Te toca a ti (pp. 182–183)	Self-access reading and writing		

6 Repaso 1 *La tele* (Student Book pages 100–101)

Main topics and objectives

- Revising TV programmes
- Using articles and adjectives correctly

Grammar

- Adjective agreement
- Using definite/indefinite articles

Key language

el telediario/las noticias
los programas de deportes
los documentales
los concursos
las series de policías
los programas de tele-realidad
las telenovelas

¿Qué ponen en la tele hoy/esta tarde/mañana?
¿Quieres venir a mi casa a ver (una telenovela)?
¿Quieres ver (el telediario) conmigo?

A la una...
A las dos/tres...
   ...y cuarto/veinte/media
   ...menos cuarto/veinte/media

entretenido/a(s)
educativo/a(s)
curioso/a(s)
lento/a(s)
largo/a(s)
malo/a(s)
tonto/a(s)
emocionante(s)

genial(es)
guay(s)

Me gusta mucho (Hollyoaks).
Es una telenovela/un concurso/...
Me gusta porque es muy/un poco/ bastante...
No me gusta nada (El Factor X).
Es un/una...
No me gusta porque es...

Resources

CD 3, tracks 14–16
Cuaderno Verde, page 58
Gramática 208

Starter 1

To review vocabulary for talking about TV programmes

Give students 3 minutes working in pairs to come up with an example of a programme on British television for each of the following. When they have completed their lists, hear answers. Each time they have the same correct answer in a category as another pair, they win one point. If they have a correct answer no other pair has thought of, they win two points. The pair with the most points wins.

una telenovela
un programa de deportes
un documental
un concurso
una serie de policías
un programa de tele-realidad
el telediario/las noticias

Point out that *programa* is masculine, even though it ends in -a.

1 Escucha y escribe la letra correcta. (1–5)

Listening. Students listen to five conversations and identify the type of television programme/film being described (from pictures **a–g**). There are two distractors. A language box is supplied for support.

Audioscript *Track 14*

1 – *¿Qué ponen en la tele hoy?*
   – *Hay un programa de deportes a las ocho de la tarde.*
2 – *¿Qué ponen en la televisión mañana?*
   – *Nada especial, pero hoy ponen una serie de policías muy buena. Empieza a las once menos cuarto.*
3 – *¿Qué ponen esta tarde?*

   – *Un concurso muy divertido. ¡Me encanta!*
   – *¿A qué hora?*
   – *A las tres y cuarto.*
4 – *Hola, Paco. ¿Quieres venir a mi casa hoy a ver la tele?*
   – *¿Qué ponen?*
   – *Hay un documental sobre los adolescentes y el alcohol.*
   – *¿A qué hora empieza?*
     A las nueve y cuarto.
5 – *¿Quieres ver la tele conmigo?*
   – *Vale. ¿Qué ponen?*
   – *Ponen una telenovela muy buena a las cinco y media.*
   – *¡Fenomenal!*

Answers
1 b **2** e **3** d **4** c **5** g

★ ResultsPlus

Tip box on telling the time.

2 Escucha otra vez. ¿A qué hora ponen el programa? (1–5)

Listening. Students listen to the recording in exercise 1 again and note the time given for each programme. A language box is supplied for support.

Audioscript *Track 15*

As exercise 1.

Answers
1 8:00 **2** 10:45 **3** 3:15 **4** 9:15 **5** 5:30

R In pairs, students practise times, taking it in turn to prompt with a time in English and to respond with the Spanish version.

3 Lee los textos. Copia y completa la tabla en inglés.

Reading. Students copy out the table. They then read the three texts and complete the table with the details in English.

Answers

	type of programme	opinion (P/N/P+N)	reason
1	comedy	P	very entertaining
2	reality shows	N	very boring
3	music programmes	P+N	he loves listening to rock and pop music

4 Read the texts again and try to note at least two extra details in each text.

Reading. Students reread the texts in exercise 3 and note two extra details for each text.

Answers

1 favourite is *Gavin and Stacey*; actors are excellent/ every episode is very funny/always makes her laugh
2 worst is *I'm a celebrity, get me out of here*; most of the celebrities are stupid or unpleasant
3 very slow – only one or two are good; favourite is *The X Factor*

Starter 2

To review adjective agreement; to review TV vocabulary

Write up the following. Give students 3 minutes working in pairs to complete the sentences with an appropriate adjective in the correct form.

aburrido, bueno, malo, tonto, entretenido, educativo

Me encantan las series de policías porque son...
No me gustan los programas de deporte. Son...
Prefiero el telediario. Es más...
Odio las telenovelas porque son...

Check answers. Summarise adjective endings using *tonto* as a model.

5 Escucha. Contesta a las preguntas en inglés. (1–4)

Listening. Students listen to four people talking about what they watch on TV. For each person they answer the comprehension questions in English. A language box is supplied. The names of the programmes discussed are also supplied in random order for support.

Audioscript *Track 16*

1 *Mi programa preferido es* Hospital Central *porque es muy entretenido. Es una telenovela muy buena con muchos médicos guapos. Los actores son fenomenales.*

2 *Me gustan mucho las series de policías y la mejor serie se llama* Antivicio. *Es una serie muy emocionante y nunca es aburrida.*

3 *Mi programa favorito se llama* Todo el mundo quiere a Raymond. *Me encantan las comedias y prefiero las comedias americanas. Esta comedia es muy graciosa y siempre me hace reír.*

4 *El peor programa es* El Factor X. *Odio los programas de música.* El Factor X *es muy aburrido y bastante tonto. Además la música es muy mala.*

Answers

1 a *Hospital Central*
  b soap opera
  c *Any two of:* very good, handsome doctors, fantastic actors
2 a Antivicio
  b detective series
  c *Any two of:* best detective series, very exciting, never boring
3 a *Todo el Mundo quiere a Raymond*
  b comedy
  c very funny, always makes him laugh
4 a *The X Factor*
  b music programme
  c *Any two of:* very boring, quite stupid, bad music

R Students take it in turn to prompt with an adjective from the language box (e.g. *tontas*) and to respond with a sentence (e.g. *Las telenovelas son tontas.*).

6 Con tu compañero/a, haz diálogos, cambiando los datos subrayados.

Speaking. In pairs: students discuss TV programmes. They adapt the dialogue supplied, taking it in turn to ask and answer questions.

G Grammar

Use the Grammar box to review the use of the definite and indefinite articles.

7 Write about a programme that you like and one that you don't like.

Writing. Students write about a TV programme they like and one they don't like. A language box is supplied.

★ ResultsPlus

Tip box on including extra details to make your writing more interesting.

Plenary

Ask students to summarise adjective endings, giving examples of expressions from the lesson, e.g. *Los programas de tele-realidad son tontos.*

Cuaderno Verde, page 58

1

Answers

1 el telediario
2 las telenovelas
3 *los documentales*
4 los concursos
5 las series de policías
6 los dibujos animados
7 los programas de deportes

2

Answers

1 *Me encantan los programas de deporte porque son interesantes.*
2 Odio el telediario porque es…
3 Me gustan los dibujos animados porque son…
4 Me gusta(n) la(s) telenovela(s) porque es/son..
5 No me gustan las series de policías porque son…
6 Me encantan los documentales porque son…
7 Odio los concursos porque son…

6 Repaso 2 *El cine* (Student Book pages 102–103)

Main topics and objectives

- Revising types of films
- Using a range of opinions

Grammar

- Verbs of opinion

Key language

las películas...
de ciencia-ficción
del Oeste
de guerra
románticas
de terror
de acción
de artes marciales

las comedias
los dibujos animados

porque...
son las mejores

me gustan los caballos
me interesa la historia
me hacen feliz
me dan miedo
son muy emocionantes
son muy guays
me hacen reír
son muy graciosos/as

Me gustan más...
Prefiero...
Me encantan...
Me gustan...
Me interesan...
No me gustan...
No me gustan nada...
Odio...
las películas de...
porque (no) son guays/
  aburridas/...

Quiero dos entradas para...
¿Me da dos entradas para...?

Lo siento, pero no quedan
  entradas.
¿Para qué sesión?
Para la sesión de las cuatro y
  media?
¿Cuánto cuestan las entradas?
¿Quiere palomitas de maíz/
  caramelos/refrescos?
Aquí tiene.

Resources

CD 3, tracks 17–19
Cuaderno Verde, page 59

Starter 1

To introduce the vocabulary for types of films; to use reading strategies

Use ActiveTeach to display the language box by exercise 1 on p. 102. Alternatively, write up the items. Give students 3 minutes to copy the list in their preferred order, starting with the one they like least and finishing with their favourite.

Ask students to translate the types of films into English. Then work out what the class likes and doesn't like, taking a vote by show of hands on what came bottom of their lists and what came top.

1 Escucha y escribe la letra correcta. (Sobra un dibujo.) (1–8)

Listening. Students listen to eight people talking about their favourite films and note the film mentioned each time (from pictures **a–i**). There is one distractor. A language box is supplied.

Audioscript *Track 17*

1 Me encanta ir al cine con mis amigos. Siempre bebo Coca-Cola y prefiero ver películas románticas porque me hacen feliz.

2 A mí me gusta mucho ver películas del Oeste porque son bastante emocionantes. También me gustan los caballos.

3 En mi opinión las películas de ciencia-ficción son las mejores porque son muy informativas y también son interesantes.

4 Las películas de terror siempre me dan miedo. ¡Son fenomenales!

5 Me encantan las películas de artes marciales porque me interesa mucho el deporte y son muy guays.

6 Me interesa la historia y por eso prefiero ver películas de guerra.

7 Los dibujos animados son muy divertidos y además algunos son muy graciosos.

8 Las películas de acción son buenísimas. Me gustan mucho porque son muy emocionantes.

Answers

1 *d* **2** b **3** a **4** e **5** g **6** c **7** i **8** f

➕ Students write five sentences giving their own opinion (including reasons) of different types of films.

2 Lee la conversación y luego escoge la(s) palabra(s) correcta(s).

Reading. Students read the conversation about going to the cinema and then complete the sentences about it, choosing from two options each time.

Answers

1 bien **2** A Charo le gustaría **3** acción
4 divertido **5** nueve **6** dos horas

Starter 2

To review expressing likes and dislikes; to review vocabulary for types of films

Tell students you are going to talk about your own film preferences but it's possible you might make a few mistakes. Ask them to listen out and put up their hands if they hear something that is incorrect.

Then make a series of statements along the following lines, as though you were looking at film listings in a newspaper. In some of them make errors in the type of film, e.g.

¿Qué ponen? Ah… Kung Fu Panda. Me gustan las películas de ciencia-ficción.

3 Escucha. Copia y completa la tabla. (1–4)

Listening. Students copy out the table. They then listen to four people talking about their film preferences and complete the table with the details. A language box is supplied.

Audioscript *Track 18*

1 – Juan, ¿qué tipo de películas te interesan?
   – Pues… No me interesan nada las películas de terror. Para mí son malas y me dan miedo.
2 – María, ¿te gustan las películas de guerra?
   – Sí, me gustan mucho las películas de guerra porque me interesa la historia y son bastante educativas.
3 – Miguel, ¿qué películas prefieres?
   – A ver… es difícil decir, pero a mí me gustan más las películas románticas porque me hacen feliz y además algunas son graciosas.
4 – Ana, ¿te interesan también las películas románticas?
   – Pues, no. Prefiero las películas de acción porque son muy emocionantes y no son lentas.

Answers

	tipo de película	opinión	¿Por qué?
1	terror	💔	malas, me dan miedo
2	guerra	❤	me interesa la historia, (son bastante) educativas
3	románticas	❤	me hacen feliz, (algunas son) graciosas
4	acción	❤	(muy) emocionantes, no son lentas

4 Have a conversation about films. First practise the dialogue with a partner. Then change the underlined words to match the picture prompts. Finally, make up your own conversation.

Speaking. In pairs: students discuss films. They practise the dialogue supplied, then adapt it, using the picture and text prompts supplied to change the underlined details. They then move on to making up their own conversation.

5 Escribe un párrafo sobre tus películas preferidas.

Writing. Students write a paragraph on their favourite films, using their replies to exercise 4.

6 Escucha. Copia y completa la tabla. (1–4)

Listening. Students copy out the table. They then listen to four conversations where people are buying cinema tickets and complete the table with the details. The names of the films are supplied for support.

Audioscript *Track 19*

1 – Buenas tardes.
   – Quiero dos entradas para Juno, por favor.
   – ¿Para qué sesión?
   – Para la sesión de las ocho. ¿Cuánto cuestan las entradas?
   – Son doce euros.
   – Vale.
   – ¿Algo más?
   – Sí, unas palomitas de maíz.
2 – Buenos días.
   – Buenos días. ¿Me da cinco entradas para Kung Fu Panda?
   – ¿Para qué sesión?
   – Para la sesión de las seis menos cuarto. ¿Cuánto es?
   – Son veinticinco euros en total.
   – Vale.
   – ¿Algo más?
   – No, nada más, gracias.
3 – Buenas tardes.
   – Quiero seis entradas para Narnia, por favor.
   – ¿Para qué sesión?
   – Para la sesión de las cuatro menos cuarto. ¿Cuánto cuestan?
   – Son cuarenta y ocho euros en total.
   – Vale.
   – ¿Quiere palomitas de maíz?
   – No, no quiero palomitas de maíz, pero deme unos caramelos.
   – Aquí tiene.
4 – Buenos días.
   – ¿Me da cuatro entradas para 27 Vestidos, por favor?
   – ¿Para qué sesión?
   – Para la sesión de la una y veinte. ¿Cuánto es?
   – Son veintiocho euros en total.
   – Vale.
   – ¿Quiere palomitas de maíz, caramelos o refrescos?
   – No, no quiero palomitas de maíz. ¿Me da cuatro refrescos?
   – ¿Coca-Cola o limonada?
   – Coca-Cola.

Answers

	película	número de entradas	sesión	precio de entradas en total	comida/bebida
1	*Juno*	2	*8:00*	*12€*	*palomitas de maíz*
2	Kung Fu Panda	5	5:45	25	–
3	Narnia	6	3:45	48	caramelos
4	27 Vestidos	4	1:20	28	4 refrescos (Coca-Cola)

Plenary

Review adjective agreement using types of films.

Then go round the class. Students take it in turn to give an opinion of a film and to give a reason for that opinion using **porque**.

Cuaderno Verde, page 59

1

Answers

Marco: Hola, Cristina. ¿Qué (**1**) *tal*?
Cristina: Pues…, muy (**2**) **bien**, gracias.
Marco: ¿Quieres ir (**3**) **al cine** esta noche?
Cristina: De acuerdo. ¿Qué (**4**) **ponen**?
Marco: Ponen *Una pareja de tres* con Owen Wilson y Jennifer Aniston. ¿La conoces? Es (**5**) **una película** romántica y también es una (**6**) **comedia**.
Cristina: Claro que sí, tío. Me (**7**) **gustan** mucho las películas (**8**) **románticas** porque son (**9**) **emocionantes** y las comedias son (**10**) **divertidas**.
Marco: Empieza (**11**) **a las ocho** y veinte.
Cristina: Vale. ¿A qué hora termina?
Marco: Termina a las (**12**) **once menos cuarto**.

2

Answers

a ¿Cuánto cuestan dos entradas? **3**
b ¿Quieres ir al cine? **5**
c ¿Me da dos entradas para *El Caballero Oscuro*? **1**
d ¿Para qué sesión? **2**
e ¿Te gustan las películas de terror? **4**

3

Answers

● ¿Te interesan (**1**) **las películas de ciencia ficción**?
■ No, no me interesan porque no son (**2**) **emocionantes** y algunas son (**3**) **tontas**.
● ¿(**4**) **Te gustan** las comedias?
■ Sí, me encantan (**5**) **las comedias**. Son (**6**) **graciosas/divertidas**. También (**7**) **me encantan los dibujos animados** porque me hacen reír.
● ¿Cuál es tu (**8**) **película favorita**?
■ Mi película favorita (**9**) **se llama** *Bolt*. Es una película (**10**) **guay** y genial.

6

1 La paga (Student Book pages 104–105)

Main topics and objectives

- Talking about hobbies and pocket money
- Using conjugated verbs and infinitives

Grammar

- Infinitives v. conjugated verbs
- Direct object pronoun **lo**

Key language

Me gusta...
Suelo...
hacer esquí
jugar al billar/fútbol/tenis de mesa
nadar
patinar
salir con amigos
escuchar música
leer libros/revistas
ver la tele
hago, juego, nado, patino, salgo, escucho, leo, veo

¿Cuánto dinero te dan tus padres?
¿Tus padres te dan paga?
Mis padres me dan... euros/ libras...
al día
a la semana
al mes
¿Cómo lo gastas?
¿Qué haces con tu dinero?
Lo gasto en...

Compro...
Ahorro para comprar...

caramelos
crédito para mi móvil
maquillaje
revistas
ropa
videojuegos
una moto
un iPod

Resources

CD 3, tracks 20–22
Cuaderno Verde, pages 60–61
Gramática 206

Starter 1

To practise verb forms and structures; to review sports vocabulary

Write up the following, leaving gaps for the underlined words. Supply the underlined words separately.

1 *Quiero jugar al golf.*
2 *Juego al fútbol todos los días.*
3 *Me encanta nadar.*
4 *Odio hacer esquí porque es aburrido.*
5 *Suelo salir con mis amigos.*
6 *Leo revistas.*

Check answers, asking students to translate the sentences into English.

1 Escucha y escribe las letras correctas. (1–5)

Listening. Students listen to five people talking about activities and write the correct letter (from pictures **a–j**).

Audioscript *Track 20*

1 *Me gusta hacer muchas cosas. Salgo con mis amigos dos veces a la semana. A mí me gusta ver la tele también.*
2 *Cada día hago patinaje porque quiero patinar en los próximos juegos olímpicos. A veces también hago esquí, pero no es mi pasión.*
3 *En mi tiempo libre, una vez a la semana, nado. Me encanta nadar. En casa prefiero leer libros o revistas.*
4 *Normalmente mis amigos y yo escuchamos música, pero mañana vamos a jugar al tenis de mesa en el bar.*
5 *Casi nunca juego al fútbol porque odio jugar en equipo. Suelo jugar al billar los domingos en el club de deporte.*

Answers

1 *g, j* 2 *a, b* 3 *f, i* 4 *h, e* 5 *d, c*

R Give students 3 minutes working in pairs to write down as many expressions featuring a verb + the infinitive as they can.

+ Students listen again and note down expressions of frequency.

G Grammar

Use the Grammar box to review key structures with the infinitive and conjugated verbs.

2 Con tu compañero/a, pregunta y contesta.

Speaking. In pairs: students take it in turn to ask and answer about the sports they do. A framework is supplied.

⭐ ResultsPlus

Tip box on improving speaking performance.

Starter 2

To practise listening for numbers

In pairs: ask students each to write out five amounts of money without showing the list to their partner. All amounts should be under 100€. Students then take it in turn to read out their prices for their partner to write them down. They swap their answers and check who got the most correct.

3 Lee el blog de Esther. ¿Verdadero (V), falso (F) o no se menciona (NM)?

Reading. Students read Esther's blog and the statements about it. They decide whether each statement is true (**V**) or false (**F**) or contains information not given in the text (**NM**).

Answers

1 F 2 NM 3 V 4 V 5 V

4 Escucha y lee las frases. Escribe las letras correctas.

Listening. Students listen to the five sentences, reading the text at the same time. They then match each sentence to the correct picture (from **a–e**).

Audioscript *Track 21*

1 A veces me gusta comprar algo caro como ropa.
2 Mis padres me dan diez euros a la semana y siempre lo gasto en maquillaje.
3 Mis abuelos me dan dos euros al día. Gasto mi dinero en caramelos o chocolate.
4 No gasto la paga. Ahorro mi dinero porque quiero comprarme una moto.
5 Mi padrastro me da diez euros al mes y lo gasto en crédito para mi móvil.

Answers

1 b 2 a 3 c 4 e 5 d

➕ Students translate the sentences into English.

G Grammar

Use the Grammar box to review the direct object pronoun **lo**.

5 Escucha. Copia y completa la tabla en inglés. (1–5)

Listening. Students copy out the table. They listen to five conversations about pocket money and complete the table with the details in English. A language box is supplied.

Audioscript *Track 22*

1 – ¿Cuánto dinero te dan tus padres?
  – Pues… me dan treinta euros al mes.
  – ¿Qué haces con tu dinero?
    Normalmente compro revistas de moda.
2 – ¿Recibes dinero de tus padres?
  – Sí, mis padres me dan diez euros cada semana.
  – ¿Cómo lo gastas?
  – Lo gasto en ropa o maquillaje, pero también ahorro. Quiero comprar un ordenador portátil en el futuro.
3 – ¿Tus padres te dan paga?
  – Sí, claro.
  – ¿Cuánto te dan?
  – Me dan cuarenta euros al mes.
  – ¡Eso es mucho!
  – Sí, ya lo sé. Ahorro mucho y a veces compro videojuegos o DVDs.
4 – ¿Cuánto dinero te dan tus padres?
  – Me dan cinco euros a la semana.
  – ¿Qué haces con tu dinero?
  – Compro chocolate y caramelos.

5 – ¿Recibes dinero de tus padres?
  – Si hago mis deberes todos los días, me pagan diez euros al mes.
  – ¿En qué te lo gastas?
  – Lo gasto en descargar música o comprar crédito para mi móvil.

Answers

	How much?	How often?	Buys/Saves for…?
1	30€	monthly	fashion magazines
2	10€	weekly	clothes or make-up; also saving to buy a laptop
3	40€	monthly	saves a lot; sometimes buys videogames and DVDs
4	5€	weekly	buys chocolate and sweets
5	10€	monthly	downloads music or credit for mobile phone

6 Write a paragraph about your hobbies and your pocket money.

Writing. Students write a paragraph about their hobbies and how they spend their pocket money. Sentence openings and a language box are supplied.

Plenary

Ask the class to list all the expressions of frequency they know.

Then ask students to tell you how much pocket money they get (including an expression of frequency, e.g. **al mes**). Also ask them what they do with the money.

Cuaderno Verde, pages 60–61

1

Answers

1 Todos los días me gusta **leer** un rato y suelo **escuchar** música.
2 Dos veces al mes suelo **nadar** en la piscina. Me encanta **nadar**.
3 Una vez a la semana **juego** al billar, pero prefiero **jugar** al tenis de mesa.
4 Los miércoles me encanta **salir** con mis amigos.
5 Nunca **hago** esquí porque no me interesa **hacer** deporte.

2

Answers

(**a**) *¡Hola! Me llamo Pablo y en mi tiempo* (**d**) libre me encanta jugar con (**j**) mi ordenador. Suelo chatear con mis (**g**) amigos y a veces descargo música. Siempre mando (**b**) correos electrónicos a mi (**h**) amigo en Francia. Me interesa leer (**e**) revistas de deportes y los sábados juego al (**c**) fútbol en el parque. También me (**i**) gusta la música. Toco la (**f**) guitarra y canto en un grupo de música rock.

3

Answers

1 David   **2** Vicente   **3** topping up mobile
4 Marta   **5** an iPod   **6** Juan

---

2 El campeonato (Student Book pages 106–107)

Main topics and objectives
● Describing sports and sporting events
● Using tenses referring to the past and present

Grammar
● Present and past verbs

Key language
hacer atletismo
hacer alpinismo
hacer footing
hacer gimnasia
hacer vela
montar a caballo
practicar baloncesto

jugar a la pelota vasca
ir de pesca

Me encanta...
jugar al fútbol/voleibol...
porque es divertido, etc.
En el colegio...
Los sábados...
En mi tiempo libre...
hago/practico...
juego al...
juego en el equipo de...
una vez/dos veces a la semana
Entrenamos en...
un parque
una piscina
el polideportivo
el estadio

una pista de tenis
una pista de atletismo

La semana pasada...
El mes pasado...
jugué al...
marqué... goles
practiqué...
hice...

Resources
CD 3, track 23
Cuaderno Verde, pages 62–63

Starter 1

To practise associating expressions of time with specific tenses

Write up the following. Give students 3 minutes to work out which tense would be used with each expression.

Present or Past ?
antes
mañana
todos los días
el año pasado
por lo general
el sábado pasado
los sábados
ayer

Check answers, asking students to translate the expressions into English.

1 Escucha. Copia y completa la tabla en inglés. (1–4)

Listening. Students copy out the table. They listen to four conversations about sport and complete the table with the details in English.

Before they start, read through together the Zona cultura box on the Basque sport of pelota.

Audioscript *Track 23*

1 – ¿Practicas algún deporte?
   – Sí. Normalmente hago footing todos los días, pero la semana pasada jugué a la pelota vasca con mis amigos.
2 – ¿Qué hiciste ayer?
   – Pues ayer hice gimnasia con mi hermana, pero normalmente prefiero jugar al billar. Es algo diferente.
3 – ¿Practicas algún deporte?

– Por lo general no hago mucho. A veces hago alpinismo con mis amigos. Sin embargo, el martes pasado fui de pesca con mi padre y lo pasé bomba.
4 – ¿Qué hiciste el fin de semana?
   – Hace dos semanas fui a casa de mi abuelo e hice vela con él. Es un deporte emocionante. Normalmente juego al baloncesto dos veces a la semana.

Answers

	sports they do regularly	sports done recently
1	goes jogging	Basque pelota
2	snooker	gymnastics
3	climbing	fishing
4	basketball	sailing

R Students in pairs spend 1 minute memorising the picture captions in exercise 1. They then take it in turn to prompt with a letter (e.g. 'e') and to respond, book closed, with the correct expression (e.g. *hacer vela*).

G Grammar

Use the Grammar box to review present and preterite forms and the common time expressions associated with these tenses.

Students could go on to the website of a major sporting event in their favourite sport. Ask them to summarise some of the information there, reporting back to the class with the three details of the event in English.

2 Read the email and work out what the words in red mean. Use the *Vocabulario* section to check. Then answer the questions.

Reading. Students read Sara's email and translate the words in red into English. They then answer the comprehension questions in English.

Answers

equipo titular – first team
Entrenamos – We train
golpea – hits
la pelota – the ball
hockey sobre hielo – ice hockey
hockey sobre hierba – (field) hockey

1 tennis **2** Rafael Nadal, he hits the ball well and scores points easily **3** ice hockey, she skated badly and didn't score a goal

Starter 2

To review the preterite

Write up the following. Give students 3 minutes to complete the sentence in four different ways using the preterite.

El fin de semana pasado…

Hear some answers. Ask the class to confirm whether the verb form used each time is correct.

3 Prepare a spoken presentation on sports. Answer the following questions.

Speaking. Students put together and give a presentation on sports. Questions are supplied to help them structure what they say. A language box is also supplied.

Remind students to work out what they want to say and then to create very short notes to use when they are giving the presentation.

4 Escribe un blog sobre deportes.

Writing. Students write a blog about sports, using the material they prepared for exercise 3.

5 Read about Fernando Torres. Work out the English for the words and phrases in red. Then decide if the statements are true (T) or false (F).

Reading. Students read the text on Fernando Torres. They translate the words and phrases in red into English. They then read the statements about the text and decide whether each statement is true (**V**) or false (**F**). Some vocabulary is glossed for support.

Answers

delantero – forward
(el) menor – youngest
una media de – an average of
la Copa Mundial – the World Cup
la Copa de Europa – the European Cup

1 F **2** F **3** T **4** F **5** T **6** T

➕ 🔍 Ask students to choose and research another sportsperson on the internet and note three facts about him/her in Spanish and English.

Plenary

Prompt with present tense 'I' forms of key verbs. Students respond with the correct preterite form.

Go round the class asking students to tell you what sports they did last week, sports they used to do, and sports they usually do.

Cuaderno Verde, pages 62–63

1

Answers

1 hacer atletismo **2** hacer alpinismo **3** hacer footing
4 hacer gimnasia **5** hacer vela **6** montar a caballo
7 practicar baloncesto **8** jugar a la pelota vasca
9 ir de pesca

2

Answers

1 Todos los días *voy* de pesca.
2 Los viernes **juego** al voleibol en la playa.
3 Ayer **fui** a jugar al tenis con mi hermano.
4 La semana pasada **hice** vela en el mar.
5 Normalmente **voy** al parque a jugar al fútbol.
6 El año pasado **practiqué** baloncesto.
7 Hace tres días **hice** gimnasia en el instituto.
8 Generalmente **juego** a la pelota vasca con mi tío.

3

Answers

1 His uncle was a famous footballer. **T**
2 He started playing tennis when he was five.
3 He won his first championship before he was nine years old. **T**
4 He plays tennis six days a week.
5 He has not played at Wimbledon.
6 He was first in the 2009 Gland Slam. **T**
7 He has never won any Olympic medals.
8 He has won over 50 titles. **T**

4

Answers

1 nació **2** le gustó **3** empezó a jugar **4** jugó
5 ganó un partido **6** recibió

Main topics and objectives

- Making arrangements to go out
- Using the present continuous tense

Grammar

- The present continuous tense

Key language

Lo siento, pero (Miguel) no está en casa porque...
está trabajando

está jugando al fútbol/tenis/rugby
está haciendo sus deberes en casa de (Juan)
¿Puede decirle que voy a ir...
al cine/al parque/
al polideportivo/a la bolera?

Tengo que...
hacer de canguro
limpiar mi dormitorio
hacer los deberes
salir con mis padres
lavarme el pelo
trabajar

¿Quieres ir al/a la...?
No puedo ir porque...
...no tengo dinero

Resources

CD 3, tracks 24–27
Cuaderno Verde, page 64

Starter 1

To introduce the present continuous tense

Write up the following. Give students 3 minutes to translate the sentences into English.

está jugando al fútbol
estoy escribiendo correos
está haciendo sus deberes
estoy viendo la televisión
no estoy haciendo nada
está trabajando

Check answers. Explain that this is a new tense, the present continuous, that they will be using in this unit.

1 Escucha y lee. Completa el diálogo con palabras del cuadro.

Listening. Students listen and complete the gap-fill dialogue. The answers are supplied in random order. There are two distractors.

Audioscript *Track 24*

- *¿Dígame?*
- **Hola**. *¿Está Martín?*
- *¿De parte de **quién**?*
- *Soy María del Carmen.*
- *Un momento... ¡Martín..., Martín...! Lo siento, no **está**. Está jugando al fútbol en el parque con su **hermano**. ¿Quieres dejarle algún mensaje?*
- *¿Puede decirle que voy a ir al **polideportivo** esta tarde?*
- *¿Al polideportivo? De **acuerdo**.*
- *Gracias. ¡Hasta luego!*
- *¡Hasta luego!*

Answers

Also in bold in the audioscript.
1 Hola **2** quién **3** está **4** hermano
5 polideportivo **6** acuerdo

2 Lee la conversación del ejercicio 1 y contesta a las preguntas.

Reading. Students reread the dialogue in exercise 1 and answer the comprehension questions in English.

Answers

1 at the park
2 with his brother
3 that she is going to the sports centre this afternoon

3 Escucha. Copia y completa la tabla. (1–3)

Listening. Students copy out the table. They listen to three conversations and complete the table with the details in English.

Audioscript *Track 25*

1 - *¿Diga?*
- *Hola, ¿está Eva?*
- *Lo siento. Eva está haciendo sus deberes en la casa de su abuela.*
- *¿Puedo dejarle un mensaje?*
- *¿De parte de quién?*
- *Soy Natalia. ¿Puede decirle que voy al cine mañana?*
2 - *¿Dígame?*
- *Buenas tardes. ¿Está Conchita?*
- *Lo siento, pero Conchita está trabajando.*
- *Vale. ¿Puedo dejarle un mensaje?*
- *Claro que sí. ¿De parte de quién?*
- *Soy Trinidad. ¿Puede decirle que esta noche voy a la bolera?*
3 - *¿Diga?*
- *Hola, buenos días. ¿Está Rafael?*
- *Lo siento. Rafael está jugando al tenis con su hermana.*
- *¿Puedo dejarle un mensaje?*
- *Vale. ¿De parte de quién?*
- *Soy Javier. ¿Puede decirle que no puedo ir al polideportivo mañana?*

Answers

	What is the person doing?	Message left?
1	*homework at grandmother's house*	*going to cinema tomorrow*
2	working	going bowling tonight
3	playing tennis with his sister	can't go to sports centre tomorrow

G Grammar

Use the Grammar box to introduce the present continuous tense.

✚ Students write a paragraph on what they are doing at the moment, using the present continuous tense.

Starter 2

To practise the present continuous tense

Write up the following. Give students 3 minutes working in pairs to complete the sentence opening in five different ways, each using the present continuous tense. Encourage them to be imaginative.

No puedo ir porque…

Check answers. Ask students to summarise how the present continuous is formed.

4 Read the text messages and match them to the correct picture. (There is one picture too many.) Then write out what each text says in correct Spanish.

Reading. Students read the text messages (1–4) and match each one to the correct picture (from a–e). They then write out the Spanish texts in full. There is one distractor.

Answers

1 c **2** a **3** b **4** d

1 Hola. Estoy tomando un café en el centro comercial. Te quiero. Adiós. Sofía
2 Estoy viendo una película/peli. Nos vemos mañana en la bolera. Adiós. Javier
3 Estoy en la ciudad también. ¿Quedamos en el parque? Saludos. Helena
4 Hola. Estoy descansando. ¿Quieres venir a una fiesta? Besos. Oscar

🅁 Students translate the texts into English.

5 Listen. Where do they suggest meeting? What excuse is given for saying no? Write the correct letter. (1–5)

Listening. Students listen to five conversations. For each they note the place mentioned, then identify the correct picture for the excuse given (from a–f). There is one distractor.

Audioscript *Track 26*

1 – Hola Alejandro, ¿quieres ir a la playa esta tarde?
– Lo siento, no puedo porque tengo que trabajar.
2 – Hola Tatiana, ¿quieres venir al cine conmigo?
– Lo siento pero tengo que lavarme el pelo.
3 – ¿Qué tal, tío? ¿Quieres ir a la piscina mañana?
– Lo siento, pero no puedo ir, tío, porque tengo que hacer de canguro para mi hermanito.
4 – Hola, guapa. ¿Quieres ir a la pizzería conmigo? ¿Te gusta la pizza?
– ¡Qué lástima! No puedo ir porque tengo que limpiar mi dormitorio.
5 – Hola, Felipe, ¿quieres ir al polideportivo?
– Me gustaría mucho, pero no puedo.
– ¿Por qué?
– Porque tengo que hacer mis deberes.

Answers

1 beach – f **2** cinema – e **3** swimming pool – a
4 pizzeria – b **5** sports centre – c

6 Read the conversation below aloud in pairs. Then change the underlined words to make a new conversation, using the information on the right.

Speaking. In pairs: students read the dialogue aloud. They then adapt it, changing the underlined details and using the picture prompts.

⭐ ResultsPlus

Tip box on using expressions to gain thinking time.

7 Listen and take notes in English. Where and when will they meet? (1–2)

Listening. Students listen to two conversations in which people are making arrangements to meet. They note details of where and when for each conversation.

Audioscript *Track 27*

1 – Hola, Talía. ¿Qué haces?
– Pues … estoy viendo la tele.
– ¿Quieres venir a la piscina conmigo?
– Sí, pero prefiero nadar en el mar. ¿Vamos a la playa?
– Vale, sí… hace mucho sol hoy. ¿A qué hora?
– ¿A las diez y cuarto?
– A las diez y cuarto no puedo. ¿Quedamos a las once?
– De acuerdo. ¿Dónde quedamos?
– En el colegio.
– De acuerdo. ¡Hasta pronto!
2 – Hola, Fernando. ¿Qué estás haciendo?
– Nada, estoy haciendo mis deberes.
– ¿Quieres ir al cine o a la bolera conmigo esta tarde?
– ¡Claro! Me gustaría ir a la bolera. ¿Dónde quedamos?

– *En el centro comercial.*
– *Vale, ¿a qué hora?*
– *Pues, ¿a las cuatro?*
– *No, a las cuatro no puedo. ¿A las cinco?*
– *De acuerdo, a las cinco. ¡Hasta luego!*

Answers

1 (arrange to go to the beach), meet at school at 11
2 (arrange to go to the cinema), meet in the shopping centre at 5

⊛ ResultsPlus

☞ Suggest students use the computer to help them learn and practise new language. They could type up a list of useful phrases/sentences in two columns: the Spanish and the English translation. They can then copy the text, delete one of the columns and rekey the missing text.

This is a good way to practise verb forms and also helps develop fluency and accuracy in writing. If they keep a master list, adding useful expressions to it throughout the year, this will also be a valuable revision tool before the exam.

Plenary

Ask students to summarise how the present continuous tense is formed and when it is used.

Go round the class. Students each come up with a different reason for refusing an invitation, using *No puedo ir porque…* Give a prize for the most inventive excuse.

Cuaderno Verde, page 64

1

Answers

1 ● Hola Marisa, ¿qué haces?
2 ■ Nada, estoy mandando mensajes.
3 ● ¿Quieres ir a la bolera esta tarde?
4 ■ Lo siento, pero tengo que salir con mis padres.
5 ● Pues, ¿quieres ir al cine mañana?
6 ■ ¡Sí! ¿A qué hora quedamos?
7 ● ¿A las siete y media?
8 ■ Vale, ¡hasta mañana entonces!

2

Answers

1 A ver, Pedro *está descansando* en el jardín. *e*
2 Gustavo está limp**iando** el salón. **a**
3 Caterina est**á** v**iendo** la televisión. **c**
4 Sara est**á** hac**iendo** de canguro. **b**
5 José est**á** jug**ando** al fútbol. **f**
6 ¿Y yo? Est**oy** trabaj**ando** con el ordenador. **d**

4 Una crítica (Student Book pages 110–111)

Main topics and objectives

- Writing a film review
- Using emphatic adjectives

Grammar

- Acabar de
- Emphatic adjectives

Key language

Es...
misteriosa
bonita
original
emocionante
extraña

fea
mágica
terrorífica
sorprendente
impresionante
triste
feliz

Admiro a...
Adoro a...
Odio a...
porque sus películas son...
porque sus libros son...
porque su música es...
interesantísimo/a(s)
divertidísimo/a(s)
feísimo/a(s)

bellísimo/a(s)
buenísimo/a(s)
aburridísimo/a(s)

Resources

CD 3, tracks 28–29
Cuaderno Verde, page 65

Starter 1

To introduce more vocabulary for talking about films and TV programmes; to review adjective agreement

Write up the following, omitting the words in italics. Give students 3 minutes to complete the grid.

un programa...	una película...	English
emocionante	emocionante	exciting
misterioso	misteriosa	mysterious
aburrido	aburrida	boring
original	original	original
deprimente	deprimente	depressing
fascinante	fascinante	fascinating
extraño	extraña	strange
bonito	bonita	lovely

Check answers. Review adjective agreement.

1 Look at this image from the film *Pan's Labyrinth*. Which adjectives would you use to describe the scene? Look up any you don't know in the *Vocabulario* section and then write a few sentences in Spanish.

Writing. Students look at the film still from *Pan's Labyrinth* and write a few sentences in Spanish to describe it. A language box is supplied. They can look up any words they don't know after trying to work them out.

2 Listen and read the text about *El laberinto del fauno*. Look for these phrases in Spanish in the text. (They are all in bold type.)

Listening. Students listen to the review of *El laberinto del fauno/Pan's Labyrinth*, following the

text at the same time. They then match the English expressions (**1–12**) to the correct Spanish versions, which are shown in bold within the text.

Audioscript *Track 28*

Acabo de ver una película increíble que se llama El laberinto del fauno. *Trata de una niña de trece años que se llama Ofelia. La película tiene lugar cinco años después de la Guerra Civil en España.*

La película cuenta la historia de Ofelia. Vive con su madre y su cruel padrastro en un pequeño pueblo. Una noche Ofelia descubre un laberinto donde vive un fauno mágico. El fauno dice que Ofelia es la princesa de un mundo mágico.

Lo que más me gusta de la película son los personajes fantásticos del mundo mágico. Ivana Baquero actúa en el papel de Ofelia y es una actriz excelente. Los efectos sonoros y los efectos especiales son excelentes y la fotografía es espectacular. El final de la película es muy triste pero también es alegre.

La película fue dirigida por Guillermo Del Toro, el famoso director de Blade 2 *y* Hellboy. *No es una película de aventuras tipo* Narnia. *Es una historia muy seria. La recomendaría porque es emocionante y bonita.*

Answers

1 los personajes
2 los efectos sonoros
3 cuenta la historia de
4 los efectos especiales
5 lo que más me gusta
6 la recomendaría porque
7 dirigida por
8 trata de
9 actúa en el papel de...
10 tiene lugar
11 acabo de ver
12 el final

G Grammar

Use the Grammar box to introduce **acabar de**.

R Students produce sentences of their own using **acabo de**.

Starter 2

To review vocabulary for discussing a film in detail

Write up the following, jumbling the order of **a–f**. Give students 3 minutes to match the sentence halves.

1 *Acabo de ver*
2 *La película trata de*
3 *Lo que más me gusta son*
4 *Los efectos sonoros*
5 *Mi actor preferido*
6 *La recomendaría porque*

a *una película increíble.*
b *la historia de un anillo mágico.*
c *los efectos especiales.*
d *consiguen crear un ambiente misterioso.*
e *actúa en el papel del rey.*
f *no sólo es emocionante, sino que también es divertida.*

Check answers, asking students to translate the sentences into English and identify the film described (*The Lord of the Rings*).

3 Lee el texto y escoge las tres frases correctas.

Reading. Students reread the text in exercise 2 and identify the three correct sentences in English about it.

Answers
1, 3, 6

G Grammar

Use the Grammar box to introduce emphatic adjectives.

R Students choose six other adjectives and write out their emphatic forms.

4 Lee las frases. ¿A quién admiran?

Reading. Students read the texts and identify who is being described in each. The answers are supplied in jumbled order.

Answers
1 JK Rowling   **2** Daniel Craig   **3** Madonna
4 Penélope Cruz

5 Habla de artistas, autores, actores o músicos.

Speaking. In pairs: students discuss artists, authors, actors and/or musicians, taking it in turn to ask and give their opinion. A language box is supplied along with a sample exchange.

6 Escucha. Copia y completa la tabla en inglés. (1–6)

Listening. Students copy out the table. They listen to six conversations and complete the table with the details in English. A language box is supplied for support.

Audioscript *Track 29*

1 – *¿Te gustó la película?*
  – *Sí, sí. Los efectos sonoros son buenísimos.*
2 – *¿Qué tal tu libro? ¿Te gusta?*
  – *Lo odio. Se trata de una familia muy rica en Estados Unidos. Es aburridísimo.*
3 – *¿Cómo es la telenovela?*
  – *Es muy buena porque cuenta una historia interesantísima.*
4 – *¿Qué tal fue la película ayer?*
  – *¡Fenomenal! Los efectos especiales fueron buenísimos.*
5 – *¿Te gusta el nuevo programa de la tele?*
  – *Sí, me encanta. Los actores son divertidísimos.*
6 – *¿Qué tal la película?*
  – *No me gusta nada porque el actor es feísimo.*

Answers

	What is discussed?	opinion (✓/✗) + detail (really…)
1	*film*	✓ *sound effects are really good*
2	book	✗ really boring (about a very rich family in the US)
3	soap opera	✓ really interesting story
4	film	✓ special effects really good
5	television programme	✓ really fun actors
6	film	✗ really ugly actor

7 Escribe sobre una película que te interese.

Writing. Students write a review of a film they are interested in. A framework is supplied for support.

Students could do this on computer. Encourage them to check their texts for accuracy and to produce a second draft.

Plenary

Ask students to summarise how emphatic adjectives are formed.

Go round the class. Students take it in turn to prompt in English and to respond with the appropriate absolute superlative in Spanish, e.g. 'really/so/very difficult' – **dificilísimo.**

Cuaderno Verde, page 65

1

Answers

Acabo de ver una película **divertidísima** que se llama *Volver*. Está dirigida por el **famosísimo** director español Pedro Almodóvar. Me encanta porque es un director muy original. La película trata de una familia de mujeres – una chica, Paula, y su madre, su tía y su abuela. Penélope Cruz actúa en el papel de la madre y aparece **bellísima**. En la película, Paula mata a su padrastro, un hombre **cruelísimo**. Después, la situación para Paula es **dificilísima** y tiene que encontrar trabajo. En la película no hay efectos especiales, pero la música y la fotografía son **buenísimas**. Lo que más me gusta es la historia, que es **interesantísima**. El final de la película es muy alegre. La recomendaría porque es emocionante y todos los personajes son excelentes.

2

Answers

1 film – *really fun*
2 director – extremely famous
3 mother – really beautiful
4 stepfather – really cruel
5 photography – really good
6 story – incredibly interesting
7 end of film – very happy
8 characters – great

3

Answers

1 The extremely famous Spanish film director, Pedro Almodóvar.
2 A girl called Paula, her mother, her aunt and her grandmother.
3 Penélope Cruz plays the role of the mother.
4 She kills her stepfather.
5 The story, which is incredibly interesting.
6 Because it's exciting/moving and all the characters are great.

5 La tecnología (Student Book pages 112–113)

Main topics and objectives

- Talking about new technology
- Revising comparatives

Grammar

- The comparative

Key language

descargo música
navego por Internet
hago compras por Internet
mando correos electrónicos
uso Facebook
veo vídeos
chateo
juego con videojuegos del PC

siempre
de vez en cuando/a veces
todos los días
una vez a la semana
dos veces a la semana
los fines de semana
por las noches

descargar música...
comprar discos...
las compras en el centro
   comercial...
las compras por Internet...
los correos electrónicos...
las cartas tradicionales...

es más... que...
son más... que...

barato/a(s), caro/a(s)
fácil(es), difícil(es)
peligroso/a(s), seguro/a(s)
rápido/a(s), lento/a(s)

En el futuro creo que la gente (no)
   va a...
leer libros electrónicos
ir a los centros comerciales
hacer muchas compras por
   Internet
mandar cartas tradicionales

Resources

CD 3, tracks 30–31
Cuaderno Verde, pages 66–67
Gramática 212

Starter 1

To review the comparative (regular forms)

Write up the following as models. Give students 3 minutes to write two sentences of their own using the comparative structures shown. The statements can be about celebrities, fictional characters and/or themselves and their friends. (You could write up a list of adjectives for support.)

Mi hermano es más perezoso que mi hermana.
Mi hermana es menos inteligente que mi hermano.

1 Listen and choose the correct letters. Write in English how often they do each activity. (1–4)

Listening. Students listen and identify the correct activity pictures (from **a–h**). For each activity they also write in English how often the speaker does it.

Audioscript *Track 30*

1 En mi casa navego por Internet por lo menos dos veces a la semana. Tengo mi propia página web sobre mi vida y mis pasatiempos. También uso Facebook todos los días.

2 Siempre hago compras en eBay, por ejemplo ropa, zapatos o libros. En mi opinión, las compras por Internet son bastante seguras. También descargo música de vez en cuando.

3 Me encanta usar mi ordenador y mando correos electrónicos a mis amigos los fines de semana. El problema es que recibo mucho correo basura. Por las noches chateo en los chats con mi novia.

4 Prefiero jugar a videojuegos de PC que ver la tele porque es mucho más divertido. Normalmente juego una vez a la semana. A veces veo vídeos en YouTube. Es guay.

Answers

1 b – twice a week, e – every day
2 c – always, a – sometimes
3 d – weekends, g – evenings
4 h – once a week, f – sometimes

2 Con tu compañero/a, mira los dibujos y haz los diálogos.

Speaking. In pairs: students make up exchanges using the prompts supplied.

3 Lee los textos. Copia y completa la tabla en inglés.

Reading. Students copy out the tables. They then read the texts and complete the tables with the details in English.

Answers

	comparing...	with...	opinion
1	shopping online	shopping in city	online is cheaper
2	emails	traditional letters	emails easier/quicker
3	chat rooms	telephone calls	chat rooms more dangerous
4	PC games	chess	PC games better/more variety

Starter 2

To review the comparative

Write up the following. Give students 3 minutes to write three sentences, each on one of the topics listed below and using a comparative. If necessary, give an example for support.

barato, caro, fácil, difícil, peligroso, seguro, rápido, lento

los correos electrónicos
las compras por Internet
las cartas tradicionales
las compras en el centro comercial

Check answers, asking students to translate their sentences into English.

4 Escucha. Copia y completa la tabla del ejercicio 3 en inglés. (1–3)

Listening. Students copy out the table. They listen to three conversations about shopping options and complete the table with the details in English.

Audioscript *Track 31*

1 – *¿Cómo te llamas?*
  – *Me llamo Tomás.*
  – *¿Te gusta recibir y mandar correos electrónicos, Tomás?*
  – *Sí, me encantan los correos electrónicos porque son más rápidos que las cartas tradicionales.*

2 – *¿Qué opinas de las compras por Internet?*
  – *¡No me gustan nada! Odio eBay y otros sitios parecidos. Creo que los centros comerciales son mucho más fáciles.*
  – *¿Por qué?*
  – *Porque hay más variedad.*

3 – *¿Prefieres descargar música o te gusta ir a una tienda de discos?*
  – *Siempre descargo música por Internet porque es mucho más barato que comprar discos compactos en una tienda.*

Answers

	comparing…	with…	opinion
1	emails	traditional letters	emails quicker
2	internet shopping	shopping centres	shopping centres much easier
3	downloading music	buying CDs	downloading much cheaper

5 Lee los textos y escribe M (María) o J (Juan).

Reading. Students read the texts and then answer each of the 'Who…?' questions. Some vocabulary is glossed for support.

+ Students reread the texts in exercise 5 and find examples of the following:

- adverbs of frequency
- phrases for giving opinions
- reasons for opinions
- comparatives
- direct object pronouns

6 Write about using the internet. Try to include the points below.

Writing. Students write a text on their own use of and attitude towards the internet. A framework and a language box are supplied for support.

Plenary

Ask students to summarise how the comparative is formed, giving you examples using **más… que**, **menos… que** and **tan… como**.

Give a range of statements in Spanish about the things discussed in the unit, e.g. *Los chats son menos divertidos que los correos electrónicos.* Ask students to say whether they agree or disagree with each statement, using the opinion expressions from the lesson and the appropriate form of the comparative.

Cuaderno Verde, page 66

1

Answers

1 Los fines de semana uso Internet porque es **más fácil que** ir a la biblioteca. *Paco*
2 Siempre descargo música porque es **menos caro que** comprar discos. *Miguel*
3 Todos los días mando correos electrónicos porque es **mejor que** escribir cartas tradicionales. *Rosa*
4 Pienso que en el futuro leer libros electrónicos va a ser **tan cómodo como** leer libros tradicionales. *Nuria*
5 En Internet de vez en cuando hay precios **más baratos que** en las tiendas. *Javier*
6 Mis padres piensan que hacer compras por Internet es **tan difícil como** usar Facebook. *Charo*
7 Nunca hago compras por Internet porque es **menos seguro que** ir a las tiendas. *Victoria*
8 A veces veo vídeos, pero es **peor que** jugar con videojuegos. *Inma*

2

Answers

1 Hacer compras por Internet es mejor que ir a las tiendas.
2 Escribir cartas es más caro que mandar correos electrónicos.
3 Comprar CD es peor que descargar música.

Cuaderno Verde, page 67

1

Answers

guapísimo/facilísima/buenísima/dificilísimos/carísimo/
lentísimo/baratísimas/guapísimo/hermosísima/
famosísimos

2

Answers

1 *No me gustan **las** telenovelas porque son más tont**as** que **los** concursos.*
2 Me encantan las series de policías porque **son** tan buen**as** como **las** películas de acción.
3 Odio **los** dibujos animados porque **son** menos divertid**os** que las telenovelas.
4 A veces veo **el** telediario porque **es** más educativ**o** que jugar con el ordenador.
5 Creo que **el** programa *El Factor X* **es** tan entretenid**o** como *Gran Hermano*.
6 Pienso que ir al cine **es** mejor **que** ver un**a** película en Internet.
7 **El** telediario no es peor que **un** documental porque es muy informativ**o**.

3

Answers

1 Todos los días *me gusta navegar* por Internet.
   Every day I like to surf the internet.
2 Ayer no <u>practiqué</u> natación porque <u>hizo</u> frío.
   Yesterday I didn't swim because it was cold.
3 Hace tres semanas <u>fui</u> a Barcelona y <u>visité</u> el museo de Picasso.
   Three weeks ago I went to Barcelona and I visited the Picasso museum.
4 Normalmente <u>juego</u> al tenis, pero en este momento <u>estoy haciendo</u> los deberes.
   Normally I play tennis but at the moment I am doing my homework.

Topics revised	**Resources**
● Talking about leisure activities	CD 5, tracks 24–26

Overview

Read through the task box at the top of the page and outline for students how this section works. They will hear a Speaking controlled assessment model presentation in three parts and do exercises focused on the language used. These exercises, along with the advice/activities on how to improve speaking performance in Results Plus, will help them prepare to give a presentation of their own on the topic.

1 You are going to listen to Jamar, an exam candidate, giving a presentation on leisure. Listen to part 1 and choose the correct option to complete each sentence.

Listening. Explain to the students that they will hear a sample of the kind of presentation they are expected to have in the Speaking controlled assessment.

They listen to the first part of the recording and complete the multiple-choice sentences.

Audioscript *Track 24*

Part 1

Buenos días, voy a hablar de mis pasatiempos. Me encantan todos los deportes, pero mi deporte preferido es el tenis. Empecé a jugar a los ocho años y suelo jugar en un club cerca de mi casa. También soy miembro del equipo titular del cole. En el cole entrenamos los martes y los jueves. Tenemos dos partidos cada sábado. Los domingos prefiero jugar al fútbol en el parque con mis amigos. Si estoy en casa, me encanta ver la Fórmula 1 en la tele con mi hermano. A mi hermana no le gustan los coches. Prefiere hacer patinaje con sus amigas. En verano mis hermanos y yo jugamos al bádminton. Creo que el bádminton es más fácil que el fútbol.

> **Answers**
>
> **1** el tenis **2** casa **3** los martes y los jueves
> **4** fútbol **5** mi hermano **6** patinaje

✚ Students listen again and note the opinion verbs and phrases that Jamal uses. He uses some in the third person singular so draw pupils' attention to the differences: **prefiero/prefiere**, etc.

(*Answers:* me encantan, mi deporte preferido, prefiero, me encanta, no le gustan, prefiere)

2 Listen to part 2 of Jamar's presentation and note down the words that fill the gaps.

Listening. Students now listen to the second part of Jamal's presentation and complete the gap-fill version of the transcript. The answers are supplied in random order for support.

With a confident class you could ask students to read the text and try to work out plausible answers first, then use the recording to check.

Audioscript *Track 25*

Part 2

– *¿Eres fan de algún deportista famoso?*
– *Sí, sí. **Soy** fan del campeón de Fórmula 1 Lewis Hamilton. Admiro a Hamilton porque es simpático y muy **ambicioso**. Hamilton empezó su carrera en karts **y** fue el campeón europeo de karts **en** el año 2000. Ahora es el campeón de Fórmula 1 **más** joven del mundo.*
– *¿Qué deporte o actividad te gustaría hacer en el futuro?*
– *A ver, me **gustaría** hacer alpinismo o hacer esquí porque me **encantan** las montañas. El invierno pasado **fui** a Francia con mi familia y mi hermano **mayor** hizo alpinismo. ¡Fue genial! El año que viene voy a hacer un curso de alpinismo en el polideportivo cerca de mi casa **durante** seis semanas.*

> **Answers**
>
> *Also in bold in the audioscript.*
> **1** Soy **2** ambicioso **3** y **4** en **5** más **6** gustaría
> **7** encantan **8** fui **9** mayor **10** durante

✚ Students find examples of the following in what Jamal says in exercise 2: use of the preterite, the near future and the conditional, opinions, reasons, adjectives, time expressions, connectives and qualifiers. Point out that including details like these will earn them extra marks in the exam.

(*Answers:*
Preterite: empezó, fue, fui, hizo
Near future: voy a hacer
Conditional: te gustaría, me gustaría
Opinions: soy fan del, admiro, me encantan, ¡Fue genial!
Reasons: porque es simpático y muy ambicioso, porque me encantan las montañas
Adjectives: famoso, simpático, ambicioso, joven, pasado, mayor, genial
Time expressions: en el año 2000, ahora, en el futuro, el invierno pasado, durante seis semanas, el año que viene
Connectives: porque, y, o
Qualifiers: muy, más)

3 Now listen to part 3 of Jamar's assessment and put these statements into the correct order. Can you note down the two questions that Jamar is asked?

Listening. Students listen to the third and final part of Jamal's presentation and answer the questions, then identify the two questions that he is asked. These questions focus on linguistic detail. You may need to play the recording more than once.

Audioscript *Track 26*

Part 3

– *¿Qué deportes o actividades no te gustan?*

– *Bueno, no me gusta ir de pesca porque es muy pesado. Fui de pesca con mi padre el mes pasado, pero fue fatal y por eso no quiero ir de pesca nunca más. Además, tengo miedo al agua porque no puedo nadar. También odio los videojuegos porque son aburridísimos. No suelo usar el ordenador en casa porque no me interesa.*

– *Y ¿qué vas a hacer en el futuro en tu tiempo libre?*

– *Pues, siempre voy a practicar deportes porque los deportes son muy importantes para mí. El año que viene me gustaría estudiar educación física en el instituto. Si apruebo mis exámenes, voy a estudiar ciencias del deporte en la universidad.*

Answers

f, c, a, g, d, b, e

Questions:

¿Qué deportes o actividades no te gustan? *What sports or activities do you not like?*

Y ¿qué vas a hacer en el futuro en tu tiempo libre? *And what are you going to do in the future in your spare time?*

⭐ ResultsPlus

The Results Plus support for speaking activities is differentiated, allowing students to identify and work towards their target level: covering the basics, Grade C, increasing their marks. Encourage students to adopt the techniques in these sections in all extended speaking activities.

Read through and discuss the Results Plus section together.

---

4 Now it's your turn! Prepare a presentation on your leisure time and then present it to your partner or your teacher.

Speaking. Students do a presentation on leisure time in the style of a controlled assessment task. They should use all the support supplied, here and elsewhere on the spread:

- the Results Plus advice on the language to include
- Jamar's responses, adapted to talk about themselves
- the English points in the task box, p. 114
- their answers to exercises 1–3.

Each student gives a presentation as the person answering the questions. If they are working with a partner, they will take turns asking and answering.

If possible, record the presentations or have the students record themselves. They can then swap recordings with a partner, listen to each other's version and offer comments on how it might be improved. A simple marking system is suggested (one/two/three stars for listed categories). Students should then identify two or three areas which they would like to improve next time they do an extended speaking task.

6 Prueba escrita (Student Book pages 116–117)

Topics revised
● Writing a review

1 Read the text and choose the correct title for each paragraph. Which words/phrases in the text support your decisions?

Reading. Students read the text and choose the correct title (from headings **a–d**) for each paragraph (**1–4**), giving reasons for their choices.

Answers

1 c **2** a **3** d **4** b

2 Find the equivalent of these expressions in Spanish in the text.

Reading. The students find in the text the Spanish versions of the English phrases listed.

Answers

1 Voy mucho al cine…
2 Las películas que más me gustan son…
3 …algunas son un poco graciosas.
4 Sin embargo, mi película preferida del momento…
5 La película cuenta la historia de…
6 La película está dirigida por…
7 Matt Damon actúa en el papel de…
8 Fuimos al cine…
9 …venden palomitas de maíz que están riquísimas
10 Estoy ahorrando para comprar…

3 Which phrase from exercise 2 uses the preterite? Now find three more phrases from the text which use a verb in the preterite.

Reading. Students identify the preterite verb used in the answers to exercise 2, then identify three more preterite verbs in the text.

Answers

8 Fuimos al cine; Fui, fuimos (de compras), compré

4 Read the text again and answer the questions in English.

Reading. Students reread the text and answer the comprehension questions in English.

Answers

1 horror films **2** they're exciting and sometimes a bit funny **3** spy/action film; *El ultimátum de Bourne*
4 he's quite good-looking and an exceptional actor
5 in the shopping centre **6** they always sell delicious popcorn **7** went shopping **8** she's saving up to buy some new DVDs

5 You might be asked to write about films as a controlled assessment task. Use the Results Plus to help you prepare your account.

Students read through the language support material supplied in preparation for doing their own extended writing task in exercise 6.

⊛ ResultsPlus

The Results Plus section gives students the support they need to structure and improve their writing. The support is differentiated, allowing students to identify and work towards their target level: covering the basics, Grade C, increasing their marks. Encourage students to adopt the kind of approach taken in this section in all extended writing activities.

6 Now write about films and going to the cinema.

Writing. Students write their own text about films, including a review, in the style of a controlled assessment task (at least 100 words). As well as the Results Plus guidelines on the language to include, they should use all the support supplied here:

● Eva's text, adapted to refer to themselves
● advice on using reference resources
● the sample structure for the text.

7 Check carefully what you have written.

Writing. Students check their own work using the list of features supplied.

● This section helps students develop their listening and reading skills in preparation for the exam.

Resources

CD 5, tracks 27–29

LEER

1 Look at this extract from a Spanish TV guide. Write down the letter of the programme each person will watch. *(1 mark for each person)*

Reading. Students read the Spanish TV guide text and the statements from five people. For each person they identify the correct programme.

This is a straightforward test of TV vocabulary. There is one additional item to prevent consequential errors. All questions approximate to Grade F.

> **Answers**
>
> **1** f **2** a **3** e **4** c **5** d

⭐ **ResultsPlus**

Tip box on distractors and not using the same option twice.

2 Read these two CVs and answer the questions below. Write A (Alfonso) or B (Bárbara). *(6 marks)*

Reading. Students read the two CVs and answer the questions on them using A (Alfonso) or B (Bárbara).

This task requires careful reading of both CVs: there are a number of clues in the questions and the headings, for example. Questions 1 and 4–6 are vocabulary specific and approximate to Grade E; questions 2 and 3 require a certain amount of linking of vocabulary and they approximate to Grade D.

> **Answers**
>
> **1** B **2** A **3** B **4** B **5** B **6** A

⭐ **ResultsPlus**

Tip box on reading both texts in detail, to check whether both are correct for a particular question, and on using headings to locate the relevant information.

3 Read the report on Miguel's work experience written by his boss. Select the 5 correct sentences. Write the correct letters [5 only]. *(5 marks)*

Reading. Students read the report and identify the five correct sentences from those listed (**a–k**).

This question contains a wide range of opinions with qualifiers and perhaps a little unfamiliar vocabulary that may also be cognates. The unfamiliar vocabulary as such is not tested and may give additional support to the answer. This question approximates to Grade C.

> **Answers**
>
> a, c, g, h, k

⭐ **ResultsPlus**

Tip box on qualifiers.

ESCUCHAR

4 Listen to this telephone conversation between Jorge and Marisol arranging to go out and answer the questions. *(5 marks)*

Listening. Students listen to two people making arrangements to go out and answer the comprehension questions in English.

This dialogue is divided into five parts. The vocabulary is fairly straightforward and the answers are quite accessible. The first two questions approximate to Grade F; the last three approximate to Grade E.

Audioscript *Track 27*

1 – *¿Quieres jugar al tenis conmigo el sábado por la mañana?*
 [Repeated as above]

2 – *Lo siento, pero no puedo. Tengo que visitar a mis abuelos.*
 [Repeated as above]

3 – *¿Qué quieres hacer por la noche, entonces?*
 – *Me gustaría ir a la bolera.*
 – *Vale, de acuerdo.*
 [Repeated as above]

4 – *¿Dónde y a qué hora quedamos?*
 – *¿En la estación a las nueve?*
 – *Pues sí, a las nueve.*
 [Repeated as above]

5 – *¿Y cuánto cuesta? Sólo tengo diez euros.*
 – *Sin problema. Cuesta seis euros por persona.*
 – *Perfecto.*
 [Repeated as above]

> **Answers**
>
> **1** morning **2** (she has to) visit (her) grandparents
> **3** go to the bowling alley/go bowling **4** station
> **5** 6€

 ResultsPlus

Tip box on listening to the whole dialogue before beginning to answer the questions.

5 During a job interview, Daniel is asked about his previous job as a waiter. Write the letters of the topics discussed. *(3 marks)*

Listening. Students listen to Daniel being interviewed for a job and note the letters of the topics being discussed (from **a–f**).

Both the interviewer's questions and the applicant's answers provide clues to the topics discussed. The exact words of the answer options, however, may not always be used. It is a slightly longer item that is heard without pauses. Although the interview is in the past tense, it doesn't test time frames. The answers can be given in any order. This task approximates to Grade D.

Audioscript *Track 28*

Example:
– *Hábleme de su lugar de trabajo.*
– *Trabajé en la cafetería de un hotel.*
  [Repeated as above]
1 – *¿Qué hizo usted exactamente?*
  – *Serví la comida y las bebidas.*
  [Repeated as above]
2 – *¿Y cuánto dinero ganó usted?*
  – *Diez euros a la hora.*
  [Repeated as above]
3 – *¿Y qué tal el jefe y los otros camareros?*
  – *Todos eran muy simpáticos.*
  [Repeated as above]

Answers

In any order: d, f, a

6 When does Silvia most enjoy doing these activities? Write the correct letter for each one. *(4 marks)*

Listening. Students listen to Silvia talking about the activities she likes (**1–4**) and identify when she does each one (from **a–e**).

Each item is heard separately and some association of vocabulary is necessary (e.g. *cumpleaños* with 'special occasion'). There is also language in the answer options that is negated by the speaker and this could be distracting. This question approximates to Grade C.

Audioscript *Track 29*

1 *Me encantan las fiestas cuando es mi cumpleaños, por ejemplo. No es tan divertido cuando no celebramos nada.*
  [Repeated as above]
2 *Escucho música todos los días. Tengo un estéreo fenomenal en mi habitación en casa.*
  [Repeated as above]
3 *Ir de tiendas es mi pasatiempo favorito. Es genial en fin de semana, pero no me interesa durante las vacaciones.*
  [Repeated as above]
4 *Veo mucho atletismo y tenis cuando hace buen tiempo. Prefiero ir al estadio porque el ambiente es aburrido en la televisión.*
  [Repeated as above]

Answers

1 e **2** d **3** a **4** b

A Reinforcement

1 A computer virus has jumbled up the letters in these adjectives. Use the English meanings to help you sort them out.

Reading. Students unjumble the anagrams to find the Spanish versions of the English adjectives listed.

> **Answers**
>
> **1** *malo* **2** lento **3** emocionante **4** educativo
> **5** entretenido **6** informativo

2 Read the text and answer the questions below.

Reading. Students read the text and answer the comprehension questions in English.

> **Answers**
>
> **1** action films because the special effects are usually very good
> **2** they're silly and boring
> **3** Westerns
> **4** no – she says they're very slow and quite violent
> **5** twice a week
> **6** going to the cinema

3 Copy out the sentences and complete them with your opinions about films and television programmes.

Writing. Students copy and complete the gap-fill sentences by supplying details of their own opinions of films and TV programmes.

B Extension

1 Find the odd one out in each list of sports.

Reading. Students identify the odd one out in each group of four sports.

> **Answers (sample)**
>
> *Accept any answer which is plausibly argued.*
> **1** equitación **2** fútbol **3** pesca
> **4** footing **5** gimnasia

2 Read the text. Copy and complete the English sentences below with the correct information.

Reading. Students read and complete the sentences using the correct form of the verbs shown in brackets.

> **Answers**
>
> **1** Jaime's favourite sport is **sailing**.
> **2** He does this sport with **his family**.
> **3** He describes his favourite sport as **quite exciting**.
> **4** His father has **lots of experience**.
> **5** His boat is called *Felicidad*.
> **6** His boat has **a radio-CD**.
> **7** In the future he would like to **work on a boat**.
> **8** He learnt a lot when he **did a sailing course (on a 7-metre sailing boat)**.

3 Copy out these sentences about Jaime's text, choosing the correct ending.

Writing. Students copy and complete the sentences, choosing from the two options given each time.

> **Answers**
>
> **1** El deporte preferido de Jaime es **la vela**.
> **2** Practica este deporte con **su familia**.
> **2** La música preferida de Jaime es **el rock**.
> **3** En el futuro Jaime quiere **trabajar**.
> **4** El verano pasado Jaime hizo **un curso de vela**.

4 Now change the information given in bold in each of the exercise 3 sentences (and the name!) to write about a friend or family member.

Writing. Students rewrite the sentences in exercise 3 replacing the phrases in bold with the details of a friend or family member of their own.

Module 7 ¡Viva mi barrio! (Student Book pages 122–137)

Unit	Main topics and objectives	Grammar	Skills
Repaso Mi casa (pp. 122–123)	• Talking about your home • Using prepositions	Prepositions	Identifying question words Using relative clauses
1 ¿Cómo es tu casa? (pp. 124–125)	• Talking about different types of houses • Expressing opinions and points of view	Using a variety of phrases to express opinions	Understanding and using adjectives Using a variety of opinion phrases
2 Mi barrio (pp. 126–127)	• Talking about your neighbourhood • Using different expressions to talk about the future	Talking about the future	Identifying positive and negative opinions Using different structures to talk about the future
3 El centro comercial (pp. 128–129)	• Shopping for clothing • Using direct object pronouns	Demonstrative adjectives (**este**) Direct object pronouns	Using appropriate verb forms Using varied language
4 Compras y quejas (pp. 130–131)	• Shopping and making complaints • Using the preterite	Preterite verb endings	
Prueba oral: Celebrity homes (pp. 132–133)	Exam speaking practice	Revision	
Prueba escrita (pp. 134–135)	Exam writing practice	Revision	
Te toca a ti (pp. 184–185)	Self-access reading and writing		

Main topics and objectives

- Talking about your home
- Using prepositions

Grammar

- Prepositions

Key language

Vivo en...
un piso
un apartamento
un chalé
una casa

Abajo/Arriba/Fuera hay...
un aseo
un comedor
un cuarto de baño
un dormitorio

un estudio/despacho
un garaje
un jardín
un salón
una cocina
una habitación
una terraza

un armario
un equipo de música
un espejo
un lavaplatos
un ordenador
un sofá
un televisor
una alfombra
una butaca
una cama
una cocina eléctrica
una estantería

una lámpara
una lavadora
una moqueta
una nevera
una puerta
una ventana

delante de
detrás de
encima de
debajo de
al lado de
a la derecha de
a la izquierda de
entre

Resources

CD 4, tracks 2–4
Cuaderno Verde, page 70

Starter 1

To review house vocabulary

Write up the following, jumbling the order of the second column. Give students 2 minutes to identify the room or place in a house where you would do each of the following. With a confident class, you could omit the second column and let students supply the answers.

sleep	*un dormitorio*
have a shower	*un cuarto de baño*
cook	*una cocina*
watch TV with your family	*un salón*
park the car	*un garaje*
eat outdoors	*una terraza*

Can they name any other rooms or other places around the house? Prompt as necessary to review *un aseo, un jardín, un comedor, un estudio*.

1 Escucha la descripción y escribe la letra de la casa correcta.

Listening. Students listen to a description of a house and identify the picture of the house being described.

Audioscript *Track 2*

Vivo en una casa. Abajo en la planta baja hay un aseo, una cocina, un salón y un comedor.

Arriba en la primera planta tenemos dos dormitorios, un estudio y un cuarto de baño.

Fuera hay un garaje y tenemos un jardín.

Answers

b

---

2 Con tu compañero/a, describe la otra casa del ejercicio 1.

Speaking. In pairs: students look at the picture of the other house in exercise 1 and describe what rooms it has in it. A language box is supplied.

3 Lee las frases y escribe el nombre de la habitación en inglés.

Reading. Students read the six sentences and identify in English the room described each time.

Answers

1 bedroom **2** kitchen **3** bathroom **4** living room
5 dining room **6** garage

⭐ ResultsPlus

Tip box on recognising question words and the forms of these words when used in a relative clause.

Starter 2

To review prepositions; to review house vocabulary

Write up the following. Give students 3 minutes to draw a small, simple illustration for each sentence. If necessary, supply the English translations for the prepositions in random order.

El gato está...
1 ...*encima del ordenador.*
2 ...*a la izquierda del equipo de música.*
3 ...*detrás de la televisión.*
4 ...*debajo de la cama.*
5 ...*entre el sofá y la ventana.*

Check answers. Ask students what kind of words **encima de, entre**, etc., are. Ask them what **delante de, al lado de** and **a la derecha de** mean.

You could also review what happens when prepositions like **delante de** are followed by **el** (**de** + **el** becomes **del**).

4 Listen. Which item is missing from each description? (1–3)

Listening. Students listen to three descriptions of rooms and read the lists of furniture items supplied for each. They identify the missing item in each case.

Audioscript *Track 3*

1 En el dormitorio hay una cama, un ordenador y un equipo de música.
2 En el salón hay un sofá, una lámpara y una estantería.
3 En la cocina hay una lavadora, una puerta y una ventana.

> **Answers**
> 1 un armario   2 un televisor   3 una nevera

G Grammar

Use the Grammar box to review prepositions and **de** + **el** = **del**.

5 Look at the picture. Choose the correct preposition in the sentences below.

Reading. Using the pictures, students complete the multiple-choice sentences by selecting the correct preposition in each case.

> **Answers**
> 1 Hay un equipo de música **encima de** la mesa.
> 2 Hay una silla **delante de** la mesa.
> 3 Hay un armario **a la izquierda de** la mesa.
> 4 Hay un sombrero **encima del** armario.
> 5 Hay zapatos **debajo del** armario.
> 6 Las revistas están **debajo de** la cama.
> 7 La cama está **debajo de** la ventana.
> 8 La pizza está **encima de** la cama.

6 Listen and look at the picture of the bedroom. Which object is being described? Write the correct word in Spanish. (1–6)

Listening. Students listen to six sentences describing the location of different items. Using the picture in exercise 5, they identify the item each time.

Audioscript *Track 4*

1 Está delante de la mesa.
2 Está encima del armario.
3 Están debajo de la cama.
4 Está al lado de la puerta.
5 Está entre la alfombra y la ventana.
6 Está detrás de los discos compactos.

> **Answers**
> 1 la silla   2 el sombrero   3 las revistas   4 el armario
> 5 la cama   6 el equipo de música

7 Describe tu dormitorio.

Writing. Students write a description of their own bedroom. A list of points to include is supplied.

Plenary

Use a soft ball or a soft toy to review prepositions. Place it in various places in the classroom to prompt students to respond, e.g., *Está al lado del ordenador*, etc.

Once you have covered all the prepositions, give the ball/toy to a student, who supplies the next prompt. Students then take it in turn to prompt for the rest of the class.

Cuaderno Verde, page 70

1

> **Answers**
> *salón/armario*/dormitorio/jardín/lavadora/cama/televisor/ equipodemúsica/garaje/cocina/patio/nevera/sofá/ lavaplatos/puerta/ordenador/mesa/estantería/lámpara/ terraza/ventana/alfombra

kitchen cocina	garden jardín	bedroom dormitorio	living-room *salón*
armario lavadora nevera lavaplatos puerta mesa ventana estantería	garaje patio mesa terraza puerta	*armario* cama televisor equipo de música puerta ordenador mesa lámpara alfombra ventana estantería	equipo de música sofá puerta ordenador mesa estantería lámpara alfombra ventana televisor

2

Answers

1 Hay un equipo de música al lado del ordenador. **T**
2 La mesa está encima de la estantería. **F** – *La mesa está debajo de la estantería.*
3 El sombrero está a la izquierda del armario. **F** – *El sombrero está encima del armario.*
4 Hay revistas detrás de la cama. **F** – *Hay revistas debajo de la cama.*
5 Los pósters están debajo de la ventana. **F** – *Los pósters están al lado/a la izquierda de la ventana.*
6 La silla está delante de la mesa. **T**

1 ¿Cómo es tu casa? (Student Book pages 124–125)

Main topics and objectives
- Talking about different types of houses
- Expressing opinions and points of view

Grammar
- Using a variety of phrases to express opinions

Key language
¿En qué tipo de casa vives?
Vivo en...
un apartamento
un chalé
una casa
un piso
una granja
un bloque de pisos
un edificio
un rascacielos

adosado/a
antiguo/a

bonito/a
cómodo/a
feo/a
moderno/a
nuevo/a
pequeño/a
viejo/a
grande

Está...
en un pueblo
en la ciudad
en las afueras
en el campo
en la costa
en la playa
en la montaña

Lo bueno es que...
Lo malo es que...
Lo que más me gusta es que...
Lo que menos me gusta es que...
...(no) hay/(no) tenemos...
(un) aparcamiento
(un) ático

(un) garaje
(un) jardín (con césped)
(un) sótano
(una) terraza
calefacción
habitaciones grandes

Pienso que...
Creo que...
En mi opinión...
Me encanta vivir en...
Odio vivir en...
...porque...

Resources
CD 4, tracks 5–7
Cuaderno Verde, page 71

Starter 1

To review adjective agreement; to review/introduce adjectives for talking about houses

Write up the following, omitting the words in italics. Give students 3 minutes to complete the table.

Vivo en un piso...	Vivo en una casa...	English
moderno	*moderna*	*modern*
bonito	bonita	*nice*
pequeño	*pequeña*	small
cómodo	cómoda	comfortable
grande	*grande*	*big*
viejo	vieja	old
feo	fea	*ugly*

Check answers. Ask students to summarise how adjective endings change.

⭐ ResultsPlus
Tip box on the importance of learning adjectives and adjective endings well.

1 Escucha y escribe la letra de la foto correcta. (1–5)

Listening. Students listen to five people talking about where they live and identify the letter of the correct picture (from **a–e**). A language box is supplied.

Audioscript *Track 5*

1 – ¿En qué tipo de casa vives?
 – Vivo en una casa.
 – ¿Dónde está?
 – En las montañas.
 – ¿Cómo es?
 – Es un poco pequeña, pero eso no es un problema porque es muy cómoda.

2 – ¿En qué tipo de casa vives?
 – Vivo en un piso en un edificio moderno.
 – ¿Dónde está?
 – En las afueras.
 – ¿Cómo es?
 – Es nuevo y muy cómodo.

3 – ¿En qué tipo de casa vives?
 – Vivo en una granja.
 – ¿Dónde está?
 – Está en el campo.
 – ¿Cómo es?
 – Es muy grande y muy vieja.

4 – ¿En qué tipo de casa vives?
 – Vivo en un chalé adosado.
 – ¿Cómo es?
 – Es un poco feo.
 – ¿Dónde está?
 – Está en la costa.

5 – Vivo en un apartamento en un bloque de pisos antiguo en la ciudad. Mi apartamento es muy cómodo.

Answers

1 e **2** b **3** a **4** d **5** c

2 Listen again and write down the adjectives you hear in Spanish. Then translate them into English. (1–5)

Listening. Students listen to the recording in exercise 1 again. They note the adjectives they hear, then translate them into English.

Audioscript *Track 6*

As exercise 1.

Answers

1 pequeña – small; cómoda – comfortable
2 moderno – modern; nuevo – new; cómodo – comfortable
3 grande – big; vieja – old
4 adosado – semi-detached; feo – ugly
5 antiguo – old; cómodo – comfortable

3 Con tu compañero/a, haz tres diálogos.

Speaking. In pairs: students discuss where they live. A framework and picture prompts are supplied.

Starter 2

To review language for giving opinions

Write up the following. (You could make it more challenging by omitting the capital letters and punctuation.) Give students 3 minutes to unscramble the sentences.

1 *Lo enorme. piscina es que una tenemos mejor*
2 *gusta mi pequeño piso, pero es. Me muy*
3 *que jardín malo es no Lo tenemos.*
4 *mi porque casa Odio no nada cerca. hay*

Check answers, asking students to translate each sentence into English.

(*Answers:*
1 *Lo mejor es que tenemos una piscina enorme.*
2 *Me gusta mi piso, pero es muy pequeño.*
3 *Lo malo es que no tenemos jardín.*
4 *Odio mi casa porque no hay nada cerca.*)

4 Listen. Are the people's opinions of their houses positive (P), negative (N) or both (P+N)? Listen again and write down what facilities each person has or doesn't have. (1–4)

Listening. Students listen to four people talking about their houses. They note whether each person's opinion is positive (P), negative (N) or a mixture of both (P + N). They then listen again and write down in English the facilities mentioned by each speaker. A language box is supplied.

Audioscript *Track 7*

1 *Lo bueno es que tenemos un jardín con césped, y también una terraza.*
2 *Lo malo es que no tenemos aparcamiento o garaje, ¡qué pena!*
3 *Nuestra granja es espaciosa; lo bueno es que tenemos un ático y un sótano. Lo que menos me gusta es que no hay calefacción, por eso hace frío en invierno.*
4 *Tenemos habitaciones grandes y mucho espacio incluso un sótano y un garaje. Por desgracia no hay jardín.*

Answers

1 P – garden (with lawn), terrace
2 N – no parking space or garage
3 P+N – attic and basement; no heating
4 P+N – big rooms, basement and garage; no garden

5 Mira la casa de Shakira y la casa de Rosa. Lee los textos. Copia y completa la tabla. (1–6)

Reading. Students copy out the table. They look at the pictures of two different houses and read the texts. They then complete the table with the details in English. Some vocabulary is glossed for support.

Answers

	Whose house?	opinion	reason
1	*Shakira's*	*beautiful house*	*likes the swimming pool*
2	Rosa's	modest, comfortable	great for pets
3	Shakira's	classic elegant	beautiful views of swimming pool and river
4	Shakira's	perfect for her	she's a good person
5	Rosa's	likes the small house	money can't buy happiness
6	Shakira's	doesn't like rich people's houses	people should live in small houses if they care about the environment

6 Write about your house. Answer the questions in Spanish below.

Writing. Students write a text about their own house. Questions are supplied so that they know what details to include.

⭐ ResultsPlus

Tip box on including a variety of opinion phrases when speaking or writing.

Plenary

Go round the class. Each student tells you whether he/she lives in a house/flat, etc., and says something about his/her house using one of the following openings:

Lo bueno es que...
Lo malo es que...
Lo que más me gusta es que...
Lo que menos me gusta es que...

2

Answers

(**a**) *Vivo en un piso moderno* (**f**) en las afueras. Lo bueno es (**b**) que tenemos habitaciones (**h**) grandes y una terraza. Creo que es (**c**) importante tener una terraza porque no (**d**) tenemos jardín. Sin embargo, me (**e**) encanta mi piso porque es bueno (**g**) vivir cerca de una ciudad.

Cuaderno Verde, page 71

1

Answers

s	g	q	m	o	d	e	r	n	o	p
g	r	a	n	d	e	d	s	b	k	i
r	a	s	c	a	c	i	e	l	o	s
x	n	n	a	n	h	f	f	o	c	o
r	j	u	s	t	a	i	g	q	ó	n
v	a	e	a	i	l	c	x	u	m	m
i	h	v	l	é	i	g	e	o	v
e	l	o	p	u	z	o	s	a	d	f
j	a	a	d	o	s	a	d	o	o	e
o	z	f	s	p	e	q	u	e	ñ	o
o	b	o	n	i	t	o	h	c	d	j

place	adjective
bloque	moderno
granja	grande
rascacielos	viejo
piso	nuevo
edificio	cómodo
chalé	antiguo
casa	adosado
	pequeño
	bonito
	feo

2 Mi barrio (Student Book pages 126–127)

Main topics and objectives

- Talking about your neighbourhood
- Using different expressions to talk about the future

Grammar

- Talking about the future

Key language

En mi barrio (no) hay...
muchos turistas

mucho tráfico
muchos habitantes
muchas tiendas
una zona peatonal
muchos museos y muchas galerías de arte
muchos árboles
muchos espacios verdes
muchas áreas de ocio
red de transporte público

Lo bueno es que...
Lo mejor es que...
Me gusta...

Me encanta...
Lo malo es que...
Lo peor es que...
No me gusta...
Odio...
Por desgracia...

Resources

CD 4, tracks 8–9
Cuaderno Verde, page 72

Starter 1

To review vocabulary for talking about a town/city/area

Use ActiveTeach to show the language box by exercise 1 on p. 126. Alternatively, write up the statements. Give students 3 minutes to identify what kind of opinion each statement expresses: positive/negative/could be positive or negative.

Check answers, asking students to translate the sentences into English.

1 Empareja los dibujos con las frases.

Reading. Students match the statements (**1–10**) with the correct pictures (from **a–j**).

```
Answers
1 c   2 d   3 g   4 b   5 h
6 f   7 a   8 e   9 j   10 i
```

2 Escucha. ¿Positivo (P), negativo (N) o positivo y negativo (P+N)? (1–4)

Listening. Students listen to four conversations in which people talk about their town. For each they note whether the opinion expressed is positive (P), negative (N) or a mixture of both (P + N).

Audioscript *Track 8*

1 – *¿Qué opinas de tu ciudad?*
– *Me gusta mucho mi ciudad, lo bueno es que hay muchas tiendas bonitas y tenemos una zona peatonal muy grande. Por desgracia también hay mucho ruido.*
2 – *¿Qué opinas de tu pueblo?*
– *Odio mi pueblo. No hay nada que hacer. ¡Qué aburrido! No hay muchos habitantes y lo peor es que no hay red de transporte público.*
3 – *¿Qué opinas de tu ciudad?*
– *Mi ciudad es interesante, y lo mejor es que hay muchos museos y muchas galerías de arte, pero lo malo es que hay muchos turistas.*

4 – *¿Qué opinas de tu ciudad?*
– *No me gusta mi ciudad... lo malo es que no hay muchas áreas de ocio. No hay muchos árboles, tampoco espacios verdes y lo peor es que hay mucho tráfico. ¡Qué fea!*

```
Answers
1 P+N   2 N   3 P+N   4 N
```

R In pairs, students write lists of other Spanish adjectives that fall into the positive and negative categories.

★ ResultsPlus

Tip box on recognising positive/negative/mixed opinions.

3 Write some positive and negative opinions about where you live. Use as many of the expressions above as possible.

Writing. Students write sentences about where they live, expressing positive and negative opinions and using as many of the expressions in the tip box as they can.

4 Escucha la entrevista. Escribe los datos siguientes en inglés.

Listening. Students listen to the interview and note in English the details requested.

Audioscript *Track 9*

– *¿Dónde vives?*
– *Vivo en Granada. Es una ciudad histórica e importante. También es grande y turística.*
– *¿Dónde está?*
– *Está en Andalucía, en el sur de España.*
– *¿Cómo es tu ciudad?*
– *Es muy bonita, pero a veces es ruidosa.*
– *¿Qué hay allí?*
– *A ver... hay muchos monumentos. Hay parques, restaurantes y bares.*
– *¿Qué opinas de tu ciudad?*

– *Me gusta... lo bueno es que hay muchos turistas y muchas tiendas, pero lo malo es que hay demasiado tráfico y mucha basura.*
– *¿Dónde te gustaría vivir?*
– *Me gustaría vivir en Madrid porque hay buenas discotecas y galerías de arte allí.*

Answers

1 Granada
2 historical, important, big, touristy, very nice but noisy sometimes
3 lots of monuments, parks, restaurants and bars
4 positive: lots of tourists and shops; negative: too much traffic and a lot of rubbish
5 Madrid, because there are lots of discos and art galleries there

Starter 2

To review different ways of talking about the future

Write up the following. Give students 3 minutes to write out the sentences in the correct chronological order.

1 *Voy a ir a la piscina mañana.*
2 *Me gustaría salir con mis amigos el sábado.*
3 *Quiero ver el telediario contigo esta tarde.*

Check answers (**3, 1, 2**), asking students to translate each phrase into English. Ask them to summarise what all the verb expressions used in these sentences have in common (they are followed by the infinitive).

5 With your partner, talk about the two places shown below. Use your imagination.

Speaking. In pairs: students talk about the two places pictured. A framework is supplied.

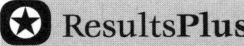 ResultsPlus

Tip box on verb + infinitive structures used to talk about the future.

6 Lee y contesta a las preguntas.

Reading. Students read the text and answer the comprehension questions in English.

Answers

1 touristy, (very) big
2 in the north of Spain
3 *Any six of:* bars, discos, restaurants, shopping centre, museums, art galleries, sports centre, (nice) parks
4 very noisy, too many people (lots of inhabitants and tourists)
6 in a quiet farm, in the countryside, near a small village

7 Write about where you live and where you would like to live. Use the questions in exercise 5 to help you structure your text.

Writing. Students write a description of the area in which they live and an area where they would like to live. They should use the questions in exercise 5 to structure their text.

Students could prepare their texts on computer. Encourage them to check their texts for accuracy and to produce a second draft.

Read out some examples of students' texts, focusing particularly on the places they would like to live. Have a class discussion on which places students prefer. Encourage students to justify their own opinions and to consider possible reasons for their classmates' preferences.

Plenary

Ask students to give you the three verb + infinitive structures used in the lesson to talk about the future (**me gustaría...**, **quiero...** and **voy a...**).

Then ask them to tell you all about where they live and say where they would like to live in the future.

Cuaderno Verde, page 72

1

Answers

1 Me gusta mi barrio porque hay *muchas* tiendas.
2 Quiero vivir en una ciudad **histórica**.
3 Lo mejor del centro comercial es que es **barato**.
4 Lo bueno es que los parques son **grandes**.
5 Odio mi pueblo porque es **feo** y **aburrido**.
6 Lo malo es que no hay muchos espacios **verdes**.
7 Me encantan las galerías de arte porque son **interesantes**.

2

Answers

1 In the east.
2 It is quite big. There is an art museum/gallery and a modern sports centre. It is a very pretty town. There is a big park. It's a very quiet place.
3 In summer it is noisy, because of (too many) tourists.
4 In a city/big town. Because there is much more to do there. She wants to live near restaurants, cinemas and shops or near a shopping centre.

7

3 El centro comercial (Student Book pages 128–129)

Main topics and objectives
- Shopping for clothing
- Using direct object pronouns

Grammar
- Demonstrative adjectives (**este**)
- Direct object pronouns

Key language
(No) Me gusta mucho ir de compras.
Voy de compras…
una vez a la semana/al mes
dos veces a la semana/al mes

Voy con…
mis amigos/padres
mi hermana

Prefiero comprar…
Me gusta más comprar…
en los centros comerciales
por Internet
de segunda mano
cosas nuevas

(No) Me gustan…
* los grandes almacenes*
* las tiendas pequeñas*
…porque son…
baratos/as
caros/as
interesantes
aburridos/as
tranquilos/as
ruidosos/as

este abrigo
esta corbata

estos guantes
estas gafas de sol

de cuero
de seda
de algodón
de lana

el abrigo
el sombrero
la corbata
la gorra
las gafas de sol

Resources
CD 4, tracks 10–12
Cuaderno Verde, page 73

Starter 1

To review key verbs in the present tense

Write up the following, omitting the words in italics. Give students 3 minutes to copy and complete the table.

| *prefiero* | quiero | *voy* | me gusta |
| prefieres | *quieres* | vas | *te gusta* |

Check answers.

1 Escucha y escribe la letra correcta. (1–4)

Listening. Students listen to someone talking about their shopping habits and answer the multiple-choice questions.

Audioscript *Track 10*

1 – *¿Prefieres comprar en los centros comerciales o por Internet?*
  – *A ver, a mí me gusta comprar en los centros comerciales.*
2 – *Y ¿prefieres las tiendas pequeñas o los grandes almacenes?*
  – *Me encantan los grandes almacenes porque hay mucha variedad.*
3 – *¿Prefieres pagar más y recibir las cosas inmediatamente o pagar menos y esperar?*
  – *Tengo que recibir mis cosas inmediatamente. No soy muy paciente.*
4 – *¿Prefieres comprar cosas nuevas o de segunda mano?*
  – *Prefiero comprar cosas de segunda mano. Es más barato y más ecológico.*

Answers
1 a **2** b **3** a **4** b

2 Con tu compañero/a, haz el sondeo del ejercicio 1.

Speaking. In pairs: students do the quiz in exercise 1.

 **ResultsPlus**

Tip box on answering questions.

3 Read the messages. Then copy the English summaries, correcting the four errors in each.

Reading. Students read the texts and then copy out the English summaries, correcting the three errors in each.

Answers
a Simón goes shopping once a week with his **sister**. He likes buying new things in **small shops** because they are **quiet**. He **hates** internet shopping.
b Julia goes shopping with her mother **once** a week. She likes department stores because they are **cheap**. She **doesn't like** small shops because they are **too expensive**.

Starter 2

To review expressions of frequency

Write up the following, jumbling the order. Give students 3 minutes to put them in order, starting with the least frequent and finishing with the most frequent.

una vez a la semana
dos veces a la semana
dos veces al mes
doce veces al año
cada día

Check answers, asking students to translate the expressions into English.

4 Write a paragraph about your shopping preferences. Answer these questions...

Writing. Students write a paragraph about their own shopping preferences, using the questions supplied to structure their writing. A language box is supplied.

5 Escucha y lee.

Listening. Students listen to a conversation in a shop and follow the text at the same time.

Audioscript *Track 11*

– *Buenas tardes. ¿En qué puedo servirle?*
– *Me gusta este abrigo. ¿Me lo puedo probar?*

– *¿Qué tal le queda?*
– *¿Lo tiene en rojo?*
– *Aquí lo tiene.*
– *Perfecto. Lo voy a comprar.*

G Grammar

Use the Grammar box to review demonstrative adjectives and direct object pronouns.

R Write up: *la gorra, el vestido, los guantes, las zapatillas.* Students complete the sentence ___ *tengo*, using the appropriate direct object pronoun for each item in the gap. They then translate the four sentences into English.

+ Students in pairs prompt with an item of clothing (e.g. *las botas*) and respond with the correct form of 'this'/'these' and 'it'/'them' (e.g. *estas botas – las tengo*).

6 Escucha. Copia y completa la tabla en inglés. (1–2)

Listening. Students copy out the table. They then listen to two conversations and complete the table with the details in English.

Audioscript *Track 12*

1 – *Buenas tardes. ¿En qué puedo servirle?*
– *Estoy buscando una gorra para mi hijo. Aquí tiene las gorras.*
– *Me gusta esta gorra, pero no me gusta el color.*
– *¿La tiene en rojo?*
– *Aquí la tiene.*
– *Perfecto. La voy a comprar.*
2 – *Buenas tardes. ¿En qué puedo servirle?*
– *¿Tiene estas gafas de sol en otro color?*
– *Sí, las tengo en amarillo, verde y naranja.*
– *¿Me las puedo probar?*
– *Por supuesto... ¿Qué tal le quedan?*
– *Me gustan mucho, pero son demasiado caras.*

Answers

	item	problem	Bought? ✓/✗
1	cap	doesn't like colour, wants a red one	(red one) ✓
2	sunglasses	wrong colour, too expensive	✗

7 Practise the dialogue in exercise 5 with your partner, changing the underlined words. Use the clothes vocabulary in exercise 6 to help you.

Speaking. In pairs: students adapt the dialogue in exercise 5, changing the underlined words.

+ Choose pairs of students to perform their dialogue in front of the class and ask the others to give constructive feedback.

Plenary

Ask students to summarise the different forms of 'this'/'these' and 'it'/'them'. Test them on these using prompts in English, e.g. 'this tie – I'm going to buy it'.

Cuaderno Verde, page 73

1

Answers

1 ¿Tiene *este* bolso en negro? Sí, *lo* tengo en negro.
2 ¿Tiene *estas* gafas en otro color? Sí, *las* tengo en marrón.
3 ¿Tiene *estos* calcetines en otra talla? Sí, *los* tengo más grandes.
4 ¿Tiene *esta* gorra en azul? No, *la* tengo en verde.
5 ¿Tiene *estos* guantes en cuero? Sí, *los* tengo en cuero.
6 ¿Tiene *esta* corbata en seda? Sí, *la* tengo en seda.

2

Answers

1 *Prefiero comprar en tiendas pequeñas **porque son interesantes y tranquilas**.*
2 Prefiero comprar cosas nuevas **porque no me gusta comprar cosas de segunda mano**.
3 Prefiero las tiendas pequeñas **porque los grandes almacenes son caros**.
4 Prefiero comprar por Internet **porque me gusta pagar menos**.

3

Answers

Dependiente: Buenas tardes, ¿en que puedo servirle? *1*
Clienta: Mmm, no me gusta en verde. ¿La tiene en negro? **6/4**
Dependiente: Sí… ¿Que tal le queda? **3**
Dependiente: Sí. Aquí la tiene. **7/5**
Clienta: Me gusta esta falda. ¿Me la puedo probar? **2**
Dependiente: Sí. Aquí tiene una más grande. **5/7**
Clienta: Perfecta. La voy a comprar. **8**
Clienta: Es demasiado pequeña. ¿Tiene una más grande? **4/6**

4 Compras y quejas (Student Book pages 130–131)

Main topics and objectives

- Shopping and making complaints
- Using the preterite

Grammar

- Preterite verb endings

Key language

Rebajas
Grandes ofertas y descuentos

Electrónica
DVD y fotografía
Telefonía

Hogar
Electrodomésticos
Textil
Muebles

Ocio y cultura
Librería y papelería
Música

Moda
Ropa y zapatería
Joyería y relojería

Salud y belleza
Peluquería
Perfumería
Maquillaje

Deportes
Ropa deportiva
Calzado deportivo

Regalos
Flores
Cestas de fruta

Ayer…
El fin de semana pasado…
La semana pasada…
fui de compras con…
fuimos a…
vi…
compré…
gasté…
lo pasamos…

Quisiera un reembolso.
Quisiera cambiar…
esta camiseta/esta maleta/esta sudadera/este reloj.
Es demasiado grande/pequeño/a.
Está roto/a.
No funciona.
Quiero hablar con el director.

¿Tiene el recibo?
Sí, aquí lo tiene.
Le voy a dar otro/a…
Lo siento. No puedo cambiar el/la…
Muy bien. Aquí tiene su reembolso.

Resources

CD 4, tracks 13–14
Cuaderno Verde, pages 74–76
Gramática 196

Starter 1

To review the preterite

Write up the following, omitting the underline. Give students 3 minutes to complete the sentences by selecting the correct verb each time.

1 *Fui/Vi al centro comercial.*
2 *Gasté/Vi un DVD.*
3 *No vimos/gastamos la televisión.*
4 *Gastamos/Compramos veinte euros.*
5 *Compré/Gasté unos zapatos.*
6 *Fuimos/Compramos a la tienda de ropa.*
7 *No gasté/fui mucho dinero.*
8 *Compramos/Fuimos un libro.*

Check answers, asking students to translate them into English. Remind students as necessary that the 'we' form of **-ar** verbs is the same in the present tense and the preterite.

1 In which department would you buy the items shown in the pictures?

Reading. Students identify the correct store department for each of the items pictured.

Answers

a Hogar – electrodomésticos
b Moda – Joyería y relojería
c Electrónica – DVD y fotografía
d Salud y belleza – Perfumería
e Hogar – muebles
f Regalos – Flores
g Moda – Joyería y relojería
h Deportes – Calzado deportivo

2 Escucha y contesta a las preguntas en inglés. (1–2)

Listening. Students listen to two conversations about shopping and for each conversation answer the comprehension questions in English.

Audioscript *Track 13*

1 *Fui de compras ayer con mi hermano. Fuimos al centro comercial juntos. Me gusta mucho comprar en los centros comerciales porque hay mucha variedad. Compré unos pendientes de plata porque me encantan las joyas. También compré el nuevo libro de Philip Pullman. Gasté cuarenta euros. ¡Ay!*

2 *El fin de semana pasado fui a una tienda que me gusta mucho porque siempre hay cosas baratas de segunda mano. Compré un abrigo de cuero y una corbata para mi padre. Vi unas gafas de sol muy bonitas, pero no las compré. Gasté diez euros.*

Answers

1 **a** yesterday **b** shopping centre **c** silver earrings, a new book by Philip Pullman **d** 40€
2 **a** last weekend **b** a second-hand shop **c** a leather coat and a tie (for his father) **d** 10€

G Grammar

Use the Grammar box on p. 131 to review the preterite forms of verbs used to talk about shopping.

R Students translate the following sentences into Spanish.

I went to the shopping centre.
We saw a film.
I spent 20 euros.
We bought some presents.

3 Lee y termina las frases en inglés.

Reading. Students read the text and complete the sentences in English.

Answers

1 Generally Rodrigo goes shopping with **his friends**.
2 He is very lucky because **he lives in quite a big town**.
3 What he likes best about his town is that **there's a very good shopping centre and also lots of small, interesting shops**.
4 Last weekend he went shopping with **his friend Anita**.
5 Anita bought **a pair of second-hand Gucci sunglasses**.
6 Rodrigo bought **a hat**.

Starter 2

To review language for talking about shopping

Write up the following, jumbling the order of the words in each sentence. Give students 3 minutes to write out the sentences in the correct order. You can include capitals and closing punctuation if necessary for support.

1 *me gusta mucho ir de compras*
2 *lo que más me gusta es que hay muchas tiendas*
3 *mi amiga compró unas gafas de sol*
4 *fuimos a una cafetería y tomamos un café*

Check answers, asking students to translate them into English.

4 Busca estas palabras en español en el texto del ejercicio 3.

Reading. Students reread Rodrigo's text in exercise 3 and find in it the Spanish versions of the four English verbs listed.

Answers

I went – fui
we saw – vimos
she bought – compró
I didn't spend – no gasté

5 Write a paragraph about shopping. Answer the following questions…

Writing. Students write a paragraph about shopping. A list of questions shows them what information to include. Sample answer openings are also given.

6 Escucha los diálogos y escribe la letra correcta. Listen again and note what happens: exchange, refund or nothing? (1–4)

Listening. Students listen to four conversations about shopping problems and identify the correct picture for each one (from **a–e**). They then listen again and note the outcome in each case.

Audioscript *Track 14*

1 – *Buenos días. ¿Qué quería?*
  – *Quisiera cambiar esta maleta. Está rota.*
  – *¿Tiene el recibo?*
  – *Sí, aquí lo tiene.*
  – *Muy bien. Aquí tiene otra maleta.*
2 – *Quisiera cambiar esta camiseta. Es demasiado pequeña.*
  – *¿Tiene el recibo?*
  – *Sí, aquí lo tiene.*
  – *Muy bien. Le voy a dar otra camiseta. ¿En qué talla entonces?*
  – *No sé, pero una mucho más grande, por favor.*
3 – *Buenos días. ¿Qué desea?*
  – *Mi madre me compró esta sudadera y no me gusta.*
  – *Bueno… ¿Tiene el recibo?*
  – *Sí, aquí está. Quisiera un reembolso.*
  – *Muy bien. Aquí tiene su reembolso.*
4 – *Buenos días, señora.*
  – *Compré este reloj ayer y no funciona. Está roto.*
  – *Lo siento, señora. ¿Tiene el recibo?*
  – *¿El recibo? No, no tengo el recibo.*
  – *Lo siento, pero sin recibo no puedo cambiar el reloj.*
  – *Me parece inaceptable. Quiero hablar con el director.*

Answers

1 d – exchange **2** a – exchange
3 c – refund **4** b – nothing

7 Con tu compañero/a, haz diálogos, cambiando los datos subrayados.

Speaking. In pairs: students make up dialogues, using the prompts to replace the underlined details in the dialogue supplied.

+ Choose some pairs to perform their dialogue in front of the class and ask the other students to give constructive feedback.

Plenary

Play a team game to review the preterite forms used in the unit. Use the English versions of the verbs in the Grammar box and the corresponding forms of **gastar** as prompts. Keep a note of the order in which you give them. Read the prompts out quickly so that the teams have to work together to keep up. Have the teams swap and check each other's lists. The team with the most correct answers wins.

Cuaderno Verde, pages 74–75

1

Answers

1 Last weekend they went to look at designer clothes. **3**
2 They went to a bar for snacks. **9**
3 Olivia bought some trousers. **7**
4 The designer shops are very expensive. **4**
5 Rosa would like to buy something from one of the designer shops. **10**
6 Rosa goes shopping with her sister. *1*
7 There are lots of small shops in the old part of Madrid. **5**
8 They were pleased not to have spent a lot of money. **8**
9 Rosa bought a second-hand belt. **6**
10 Rosa and Olivia usually go to the shopping centre nearby. **2**

2

Answers

1 we went – fuimos
2 I loved – me encantó
3 I bought – compré
4 she bought – compró
5 we did not spend – no gastamos
6 we drank – bebimos
7 we ate – comimos
8 I would like to buy – me gustaría comprar

3

Answers

Dependienta: *Buenos días, ¿qué quería?*
Clienta: Ayer compré este reloj. No funciona.
Dependienta: Lo siento. ¿Tiene el recibo?
Clienta: Sí, aquí lo tiene.
Dependienta: Muy bien. Le voy a dar otro reloj.
Clienta: No, gracias. Quisiera un reembolso.
Dependienta: Aquí lo tiene. Gracias.

4

Answers

1 The customer bought a watch last week. **F**
2 The watch is too big. **F**
3 The customer has the receipt. **T**
4 The shop will not change the watch. **F**
5 The customer asks for a refund. **T**
6 The shop gives the customer a refund. **T**

5

Answers

– *Buenas tardes. ¿Qué quería?*
– Ayer/Compré una camiseta ayer. Es demasiado pequeña.
– ¿Tiene el recibo?
– No, no tengo el recibo.
– Lo siento, no puedo cambiar la camiseta/cambiarla.
– Quisiera hablar con el director.

Cuaderno Verde, page 76

1

Answers

bebí/vimos/fui/ir/comprar/gasté/bebimos/estar/comer/
gusta/fuimos/ver/beber/vivo/vio/fue/ser/voy/compré/es/
hay/gastó/pasar/vi

	gastar	comprar	beber
I	gasté	compré	*bebí*
he/she	gastó	✗	✗
we	✗	✗	bebimos

ver	ir
vi	fui
vio	fue
vimos	fuimos

2

Answers

(1) **Fuera** hay un jardín (2) **a la izquierda** de la casa. Está (3) **delante del** garaje. En la casa hay una cocina (4) **abajo** y (5) **al lado** está el comedor. (6) **Arriba**, (7) **entre** los dos dormitorios, está el cuarto de baño.

3a

Answers

☺	☹
On coast	No garage
Parking on street	Too quiet/boring in winter
Garden	Too many cars in summer
Very nice swimming pool	Difficult to park on street in summer
Great views of the beach	

3b

> **Answers**
>
> He **would** like to live in a bigger house. He **is going** to **live** on the coast because he **wants** to live near to the beach.

7 Prueba oral: Celebrity homes (Student Book pp. 132–133)

Topics revised

● Talking about where you live

Resources

CD 5, tracks 30–32

Overview

Read through the task box at the top of the page and outline for students how this section works. They will hear a Speaking controlled assessment model interaction in three parts and do exercises focused on the language used. These exercises, along with the advice/activities on how to improve speaking performance in the Results Plus, will help them prepare to take part in a role-play style interaction of their own on the topic.

1 You are going to listen to Anna, an exam candidate, playing the part of a celebrity. Listen to part 1 and choose the correct word to complete each sentence.

Listening. Explain to the students that they will hear a sample of the kind of role-play style interaction they are expected to have in the Speaking controlled assessment.

They listen to the first part of the interview and complete the multiple-choice sentences.

Audioscript *Track 30*

Part 1

– *Tienes casas en Nueva York y Málaga. ¿Cómo es tu casa en Nueva York?*
– *Es un apartamento antiguo. Hay cuatro dormitorios grandes, tres cuartos de baño, dos salones, una sala de cine donde veo películas y una cocina. También tiene una terraza preciosa.*
– *¿Prefieres tu casa en Málaga o en Nueva York?*
– *A ver… Creo que prefiero mi chalé en Málaga porque es muy grande, pero muy tranquilo. Está en la costa y me encanta descansar y nadar en el mar. En la planta baja hay una cocina muy moderna, tres salones y una sala de juegos. En la primera planta, hay cinco dormitorios y cinco cuartos de baño. Fuera hay una piscina climatizada. Cuando hace frío, nado en la piscina. ¿Te gusta nadar?*
– *Claro, en una piscina climatizada.*

> **Answers**
>
> **1** antiguo **2** tres **3** terraza **4** chalé
> **5** la costa **6** la primera planta

✚ Remind students that the task says they should ask at least two questions. What question did Anna ask the journalist in Part 1?

(Answer: ¿Te gusta nadar? Do you like to swim?)

2 Listen to part 2 of Anna's interview and note down the words that fill the gaps.

Listening. Students now listen to the second part of Anna's interview and complete the gap-fill version of the transcript.

With a confident class you could ask students to read the text and try to work out plausible answers first, then use the recording to check. Discuss whether alternative answers the students came up with could also be correct in the context.

Audioscript *Track 31*

Part 2

– *¿Qué opinas de Nueva York?*
– *Me gusta **mucho** Nueva York. Lo **mejor** es que hay parques muy bonitos. En Central Park por ejemplo hay muchos árboles **pero** lo malo es que hay muchos **turistas** y hay demasiado tráfico. **También** hay mucho ruido, y lo **peor** es que hay mucha basura. ¡Qué feo!*
– *¿Qué te gusta hacer en Nueva York?*
– *Me gusta mucho **ir** de paseo por el parque. Tengo una piscina en mi edificio y hago natación todos los días. **Además** en Nueva York hay museos y galerías de arte **interesantes**. Me encantan las galerías **porque** me gusta mucho el dibujo.*

> **Answers**
>
> **1** mucho **2** mejor **3** pero **4** turistas **5** También
> **6** peor **7** ir **8** Además **9** interesantes
> **10** porque

3 Now listen to part 3 of Anna's interview. In which order does she use these sentences? What does Anna ask her interviewer?

Listening. Students listen to the third and final part of Anna's interview and reorder the sentences as she mentions them. They then identify the question Anna asks the interviewer.

Audioscript *Track 32*

Part 3

– *¿Qué hiciste en Málaga durante tu última visita?*
– *A ver, fui a la playa, descansé y tomé el sol. Un día fui de compras. Compré una camisa y luego visité una galería de arte. Después cené en un restaurante con mis amigos. Prefiero la comida mexicana. ¿Qué tipo de comida prefieres?*
– *Prefiero la comida italiana. ¡Mmm! ¿Cuándo vas a volver a Nueva York?*

– *Creo que voy a volver en invierno. Voy a celebrar la Navidad en mi piso. Cuando nieva en Nueva York, me encanta porque hay buen ambiente.*

– *¿Te gustaría vivir en otra parte del mundo?*

– *Bueno… pienso que me gustaría vivir en una casa antigua en el campo lejos de todo. Me encantaría hacer equitación todos los días. A mí me gusta mucho la tranquilidad.*

Answers

c, e, a, d, b, f

Question: ¿Qué tipo de comida prefieres? *What type of food do you like?*

⭐ ResultsPlus

The Results Plus support for speaking activities is differentiated, allowing students to identify and work towards their target level: covering the basics, Grade C, increasing their marks. Encourage students to adopt the techniques in these sections in all extended speaking activities.

Read through and discuss the Results Plus section together.

---

4 Now it's your turn! Prepare yourself for your interview then do it with your partner or your teacher.

Speaking. Students take part in a role-play interview about where they live in the style of a controlled assessment task. They should use all the support supplied, here and elsewhere on the spread:

- the Results Plus advice on the language to include
- Anna's responses, adapted to talk about themselves
- the English points in the task box, p. 132
- their answers to exercises 1–3.

Each student takes part in an interview as the person answering the questions. If they are working with a partner, they will take turns asking and answering.

If possible, record the interviews or have the students record themselves. They can then swap recordings with a partner, listen to each other's version and offer comments on how it might be improved. A simple marking system is suggested (one/two/three stars for listed categories). Students should then identify two or three areas which they would like to improve next time they do an extended speaking task.

Topics revised

● Writing about where you live

1 Read the text and put these topics in the order of the text.

Reading. Students read the text on Isabel's neighbourhood and then reorder the topics according to when she mentions them.

Answers

d, a, e, b, c

2 Find the equivalent of these expressions in Spanish in the text.

Reading. Students reread the text in exercise 1 and find in it the Spanish versions of the ten English phrases listed.

Answers

1 Me gusta mucho vivir aquí.
2 Lo bueno es que…
3 …pero lo malo es que…
4 …hay mucho que hacer.
5 Lo mejor es que…
6 Ayer, por ejemplo…
7 Pasé el día entero…
8 Sin embargo, me encanta vivir en la ciudad.
9 No me gustaría nada vivir en el campo.
10 Es la mejor ciudad del mundo.

3 Look at the text again. Make a list of nine words and phrases used to give opinions.

Reading. Students reread the text and list nine words and phrases used to give opinions.

Answers

Give opinions: me gusta mucho, me gusta bastante, lo bueno es que, lo malo es que, lo mejor es que, ¡Lo pasé genial!, lo peor es que, me encanta, es la mejor

4 Read the text and answer the questions in English.

Reading. Students reread the text, then answer the comprehension questions in English.

Answers

1 a historic city
2 in the south of Spain
3 *Either of:* there's lots of space, the rooms are quite big
4 there's no garden
5 it has lots of very pretty green spaces
6 *Any three of:* went on a bike ride, visited the Little Island of Birds, read, sent messages, enjoyed the peace and quiet
7 it can sometimes be noisy, there is a lot of traffic
8 it's boring

5 You might be asked to write about your local area as a controlled assessment task. Use the Results Plus to help you prepare your account.

Students read through the language support material supplied in preparation for doing their own extended writing task in exercise 6.

✪ ResultsPlus

The Results Plus section gives students the support they need to structure and improve their writing. The support is differentiated, allowing students to identify and work towards their target level: covering the basics, Grade C, increasing their marks. Encourage students to adopt the kind of approach taken in this section in all extended writing activities.

6 Now write a full account of your local area.

Writing. Students write their own text on where they live in the style of a controlled assessment task (at least 100 words). As well as the Results Plus guidelines on the language to include, they should use all the support supplied here:

- Isabel's text, adapted to refer to themselves
- relevant language from throughout the module
- the sample structure for the text.

7 Check carefully what you have written.

Writing. Students check their own work using the list of features supplied.

● Self-access reading and writing

A Reinforcement

1 Read the description and choose the correct bedroom. Then write a description of the other bedroom.

Reading. Students read the text and identify the bedroom being described. They then write a description of the other bedroom pictured.

Answers

b

2 Unjumble these questions and then use the phrases in the panel to write answers to them.

Reading. Students rewrite the questions, putting the words in the correct order. They then answer the questions, supported by the phrases in the panel.

Answers

¿En qué tipo de casa vives?
¿Dónde está?
¿Cómo es?
¿Cuántos dormitorios hay?
¿Qué hay fuera de tu casa?
¿Qué opinas de tu casa?

3 Put this conversation into the correct order.

Writing. Students reorder the sentences to make a conversation in a clothes shop.

Answers

b, f, c, e, a, d

B Extension

1 Unjumble the words in bold, and then match them up to the correct symbol.

Reading. Students unjumble the anagrams to complete the sentences, then match each completed sentence (**1–10**) to the appropriate picture (from **a–j**).

Answers

1 árboles – a **2** habitantes – g **3** transporte – i
4 tráfico – d **5** peatonal – h **6** espacios –e
7 turistas – c **8** tiendas – b **9** ocio – j
10 galerías – f

2 Write a description of these two places.

Reading. Students write descriptions of two places, using the English prompts. A language box is supplied.

3 Read the text. Choose the correct information.

Writing. Students read the text and answer the multiple-choice questions.

Answers

1 a **2** c **3** b

Module 8 La salud   (Student Book pp. 138–155)

Unit	Main topics and objectives	Grammar	Skills
Repaso 1 Pasándolo mal (pp. 138–139)	• Talking about the body and illnesses • Using doler to say what hurts	The verb **doler**	Making adjectives agree
Repaso 2 ¿Cuánto es? (pp. 140–141)	• Buying food • Number practice	Larger numbers	Memorising vocabulary Learning numbers and prices
1 Estar en forma (pp. 142–143)	• Talking about how to stay in good shape • Using the preterite and near future tense	The preterite and the near future tense	Using a variety of verbs to talk about mealtimes
2 ¿Llevas una vida sana? (pp. 144–145)	• Giving advice on lifestyle • Using the conditional of **deber**	The conditional of **deber**	Using text layout to help comprehension
3 Los jóvenes (pp. 146–147)	• Talking about issues facing young people • Using the near future tense	The near future tense	Using a range of expressions to introduce a point of view
Prueba oral: Sport photograph (pp. 148–149)	Exam speaking practice	Revision	
Prueba escrita (pp. 150–151)	Exam writing practice	Revision	
Leer y escuchar (Modules 7–8) (pp. 152–153)	Listening and reading skills	Revision	
Te toca a ti (pp. 186–187)	Self-access reading and writing		

Main topics and objectives

- Talking about the body and illnesses
- Using **doler** to say what hurts

Grammar

- The verb **doler**

Key language

el brazo
el estómago
el pie
la boca
la cabeza
la espalda
la garganta
la mano
la nariz
la pierna
las muelas/los dientes

los oídos
los ojos

Me duele (el brazo/la cabeza).
Me duelen (los ojos/las muelas).
Tengo/Tiene dolor de (espalda/
  oídos).

No me encuentro bien.
Me siento mal.
¿Desde hace cuánto tiempo?
Desde hace…
una hora
un día
una semana
quince días
un mes
dos horas/días/semanas/meses

Tienes que…
beber mucha agua
ponerte esta crema

descansar en casa
tomar este jarabe
tomar una aspirina
ir al hospital inmediatamente

Estoy enfermo/a.
Estoy cansado/a. Tengo sueño.
Tengo un resfriado.
Tengo gripe.
Tengo fiebre. Tengo frío/calor.
Tengo tos.
Tengo una insolación.

Resources

CD 4, tracks 15–17
Cuaderno Verde, page 79

Starter 1

To review *me duele/me duelen*; to review vocabulary for parts of the body

Write up the following. Give students 3 minutes to translate the sentences into Spanish. If necessary, give a model sentence for support.

me duele…	*me duelen…*
la garganta	*los pies*	*los oídos*	*la cabeza*

1 My head hurts.
2 My ears hurt.
3 My throat hurts.
4 My feet hurt.

Check answers. Ask students to summarise how **me duele/me duelen** are used. Can they give you examples of other verbs which behave in this way? (e.g. *gustar, encantar, interesar*)

1 Escucha y escribe la(s) letra(s) correcta(s). (1–7)

Listening. Students listen to seven people complaining about symptoms and write the letters of the correct body parts for each person (from **a–m**). A language box summarises the structures **me** (etc.) **duele(n)** and **tengo** (etc.) **dolor de…**

Audioscript *Track 15*

1 *Me duelen el brazo y la pierna. Es terrible.*
2 *Ay… me duelen las muelas… y también me duele la boca.*
3 *Me duelen mucho los oídos. No puedo escuchar música.*
4 *Me duele mucho el estómago y tengo dolor de cabeza.*
5 *¡Me duele todo! Me duelen mucho los pies y la espalda.*
6 *Me duelen los ojos y la nariz. Es fatal.*
7 *Me duele un poco la garganta y me duelen las manos.*

Answers

1 e, h **2** c, k **3** l **4** f, m
5 g, i **6** a, b **7** j, d

R Students work in pairs to practise the body vocabulary. They take it in turn to point to a part of the body and to name it in Spanish.

G Grammar

Use the Grammar box to review **doler**.

+ Students work in pairs to practise saying 'My… hurt(s)' and the body vocabulary. They take it in turn to point to a part of the body and to describe the relevant ailment, e.g. *Me duelen las orejas.*

2 Listen and write down what hurts and how long it has been hurting. (1–6)

Listening. Students listen to six conversations and note down for each what part of the body hurts and how long the person has been suffering. A language box is supplied.

Audioscript *Track 16*

1 – *¿Qué te pasa?*
  – *Me duelen los ojos.*
  – *¿Desde hace cuánto tiempo?*
  – *Desde hace dos semanas.*
2 – *¿Qué le pasa?*
  – *No me siento bien. Me duele mucho la mano.*
  – *¿Desde hace cuánto tiempo?*
  – *Desde hace cinco días.*
3 – *¿Qué te pasa, María?*
  – *Ay, no me encuentro bien.*
  – *¿Por qué?*
  – *Porque me duele mucho el estómago.*

– *¿Desde hace cuánto tiempo?*
– *Desde hace un día.*

4 – *¿Qué le pasa, señor?*
– *Pues… me duele mucho el brazo.*
– *¿Desde hace cuánto tiempo?*
– *Desde hace cuatro horas.*

5 – *¿Qué te pasa, Santiago?*
– *No me encuentro bien. Me duele mucho la garganta.*
– *Pobrecito. ¿Desde hace cuánto tiempo?*
– *Desde hace una semana.*

6 – *¿Qué le pasa, señora?*
– *No lo sé, pero me duelen las piernas.*
– *¿Desde hace cuánto tiempo?*
– *Pues… mucho tiempo. Desde hace un mes.*

Answers

1 *eyes, 2 weeks* **2** hand, 5 days **3** stomach, a day
4 arm, 4 hours **5** throat, a week **6** legs, a month

As body parts can be hard vocabulary to learn, you could encourage students to think up an association for each that will help them, e.g. *la garganta* – sounds like 'gargle'; *la cabeza* – think of a cab driver using his head to remember where roads are.

3 Escribe los mensajes.

Writing. Using the picture prompts, students write text messages saying what is wrong with them and for how long, using **me duele** with **desde hace**. A model text is supplied.

Answers

1 No puedo salir porque me duele la cabeza desde hace tres semanas.
2 No puedo salir porque me duele la pierna desde hace cinco horas.
3 No puedo salir porque me duele el brazo desde hace un mes.

Starter 2

To review language for talking about symptoms

Write up the following. Give students 3 minutes working in pairs to translate the expressions into English. If necessary, supply the English versions in random order for support.

Estoy enfermo/a.
Estoy cansado/a.
Tengo un resfriado.
Tengo gripe.
Tengo fiebre.
Tengo frío.
Tengo calor.
Tengo tos.
Tengo una insolación.

Check answers. Ask students to give the full present tense of **tener**.

4 Lee y escribe la letra correcta.

Reading. Students match the sentences on remedies to the correct pictures.

Answers

1 a **2** f **3** b **4** d **5** e **6** c

---

5 Escucha y completa la tabla en inglés. (1–3)

Listening. Students copy out the table. They listen to three conversations and complete the table with the details in English. A language box is supplied. You could suggest students listen for the ailments the first time the recording is played and the suggested treatments on the second playing.

Before playing the recording, ask students to read the ailments aloud and translate them into English, to check pronunciation and comprehension.

Audioscript *Track 17*

1 – *Hola, ¿qué te pasa, amigo?*
– *Estoy enfermo.*
– *Pobrecito. ¿Qué te duele?*
– *Pues estoy muy cansado y tengo frío. Creo que tengo un resfriado.*
– *Tienes que tomar una aspirina y descansar en casa.*

2 – *Hola, Antonia, ¿qué te pasa?*
– *Ay, me duele todo el cuerpo. Tengo mucho calor.*
– *Pobrecita. ¿Qué hiciste?*
– *Jugué al voleibol en la playa y ahora tengo una insolación.*
– *Mira. Tienes que beber mucha agua y ponerte esta crema. ¿Vale?*
– *De acuerdo.*

3 – *¿Qué te pasa, Miguel?*
– *Me siento muy mal, mamá.*
– *¿Por qué?*
– *No sé, pero tengo sueño. Y creo que tengo fiebre.*
– *¿Tienes tos?*
– *Sí, tengo tos.*
– *Tienes gripe. Pobrecito. Tienes que tomar una aspirina y tomar este jarabe.*

Answers

	problems	suggested treatment
1	*tired*, feels cold, has a cold	take an aspirin, rest at home
2	aches all over, very hot, sunstroke	drink lots of water, put on cream
3	feels very bad, fever, cough	take an aspirin, take cough syrup

⭐ ResultsPlus

Tip box on checking agreement when talking about ailments using **estar**.

6 Con tu compañero/a, haz diálogos, cambiando los datos subrayados.

Speaking. In pairs: using the two series of picture prompts (**a** and **b**), students put together two dialogues about being ill, taking it in turn to ask the questions/give advice and to answer. A sample dialogue is supplied, with the details to change underlined.

Plenary

Challenge the class to come up with as many sentences for ailments as they can. As a target, tell them that there are 13 parts of the body mentioned in the unit, plus ten further expressions used to talk about ailments.

2

Answers

- ¿Qué te (**1**) *pasa*?
- Me (**2**) **siento** mal. Tengo una (**3**) **insolación** y me (**4**) **duele** la cabeza.
- ¿Desde (**5**) **hace** cuánto (**6**) **tiempo**?
- Desde hace dos (**7**) **horas**.
- (**8**) **Tienes** que (**9**) **tomar** una aspirina y ponerte esta (**10**) **crema** en la (**11**) **espalda**.

Cuaderno Verde, page 79

1

Answers

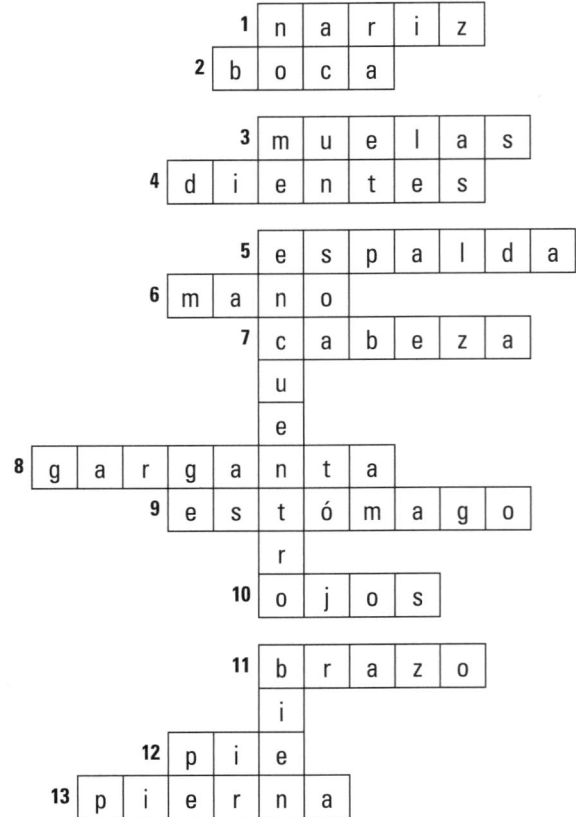

Repaso 2 *¿Cuánto es?* (Student Book pp. 140–141)

Main topics and objectives
● Buying food
● Number practice

Grammar
● Larger numbers

Key language
las cebollas
las manzanas
las naranjas
las peras
las zanahorias
los champiñones
los guisantes
los huevos
los limones
los melocotones

los melones
los pepinos
los pimientos rojos
los plátanos
los tomates

quinientos gramos de queso
medio kilo de melocotones
un kilo de tomates
una bolsa de patatas
una barra de pan
un paquete de mantequilla
un paquete de azúcar
un paquete de arroz
una botella de aceite
una lata de atún
un cartón de leche
una docena de huevos
una caja de pasteles

¿En qué puedo servirle?
Deme..., por favor
Lo siento, no queda(n)...
Aquí tiene. ¿Algo más?
No, nada más.
¿Cuánto es?
Son... euros con...

cien/doscientos/trescientos/
  cuatrocientos/quinientos gramos
  de...
Medio kilo/Un kilo/Dos kilos de...
Media/Una docena de huevos

Resources
CD 4, tracks 18–19
Cuaderno Verde, page 80

Starter 1

To review vocabulary for fruit and vegetables

Write up the following, omitting the words in bold. Give students 3 minutes to copy and complete the grid.

las	cebollas	onions
las	manzanas	**apples**
las	naranjas	**oranges**
las	peras	**pears**
las	zanahorias	**carrots**
los	champiñones	**mushrooms**
los	guisantes	**peas**
los	huevos	**eggs**
los	limones	**lemons**
los	melocotones	**peaches**
los	melones	**melons**
los	pepinos	**cucumbers**
los	pimientos rojos	**red peppers**
los	plátanos	**bananas**
los	tomates	**tomatoes**

Check answers.

1 Escucha. Escribe la(s) letra(s) correcta(s). (1–10)

Listening. Students listen to the list of items. They note each item and identify the correct picture for it (from **a–o**). A language box is supplied.

Audioscript *Track 18*

1 los huevos
2 los guisantes
3 los limones
4 los tomates y los plátanos
5 los melones y los pepinos
6 los champiñones
7 las manzanas y las naranjas
8 los melocotones y las peras
9 las zanahorias y las cebollas
10 los pimientos rojos

Answers
1 m **2** j **3** a **4** o,g **5** c,k **6** i
7 f,b **8** e,d **9** h,n **10** l

2 Match each picture to an item on the shopping list. Then look up any words on the list that you still don't understand. Finally, copy the phrases into the correct column of the grid.

Reading. Students match the pictures to the shopping list, looking up any items on the list that they are not able to work out. They then copy out the table and complete it by writing the items in the correct column.

Answers
1 j **2** h **3** f **4** i **5** g **6** e

frutas	verduras y legumbres	bebidas	otros alimentos
medio kilo de melocotones	un kilo de tomates una bolsa de patatas	un cartón de leche	quinientos gramos de queso una barra de pan una paquete de mantequilla un paquete de azúcar un paquete de arroz una botella de aceite una lata de atún una docena de huevos una caja de pasteles

R Students work in pairs. They take it in turn to prompt with a quantity (e.g. *medio kilo* or *una botella*) and to complete the item (e.g *de naranjas* or... *de aceite de oliva*).

⊛ ResultsPlus

Tip box on finding strategies to remember words: categorising. Point out to students that the categories can be topic related (e.g. fruit/vegetables/other foods) or grammatical (masculine/feminine), etc.

Students go on to the website of a Spanish supermarket chain such as Alcampo. Ask them to note down six new items of vocabulary, in Spanish and English, that they have been able to work out without using a dictionary or the *Vocabulario* section at the back of the book. Ask them how they managed to work them out, e.g. from the context, pictures, cognates, etc.

Starter 2

To practise listening for numbers

In pairs: ask students each to write out eight prices in euros (e.g. 84€) without showing the list to their partner. All prices should be under 100€. Students then take it in turn to read out their prices for their partner to write them down. They swap their answers and check who has the most correct answers.

3 Lee los precios y escribe los números correctos.

Reading. Students read the prices and write down the correct numbers.

Answers
1 – *9,50€*   **2** – 8,25€   **3** – 10,75€
4 – 11,60€   **5** – 14,40€   **6** – 15,85€

⊛ ResultsPlus

Tip box on learning numbers and giving prices.

4 Escucha. ¿Qué compran? Copia y completa la tabla. (1–6)

Listening. Students copy out the table. They listen to six conversations and complete the table with the details of what the people actually buy. A language box is supplied.

Audioscript *Track 19*

1 – *Hola. ¿En qué puedo servirle?*
 – *Quiero una caja de pasteles.*
 – *Lo siento, señora, pero no quedan más pasteles.*
 – *Bueno, tres barras de pan.*
 – *De acuerdo. Es un euro con veinte.*

2 – *Buenos días.*
 – *Deme medio kilo de cebollas y dos kilos de zanahorias.*
 – *Lo siento, pero no quedan cebollas. Aquí tiene las zanahorias.*
 – *Gracias. ¿Cuánto es?*
 – *Son dos euros con ochenta.*

3 – *Buenas tardes, ¿en qué puedo servirle?*
 – *Me gustaría comprar aquellos tomates.*
 – *Son dos euros por kilo.*
 – *Vale. Deme tres kilos.*
 – *¿Algo más?*
 – *Nada más.*
 – *Entonces son seis euros en total.*

4 – *Buenas tardes.*
 – *Deme trescientos gramos de champiñones.*
 – *Lo siento, pero no quedan champiñones.*
 – *¿Hay patatas?*
 – *Sí, una bolsa de patatas cuesta tres euros con cincuenta.*
 – *Quiero dos bolsas.*
 – *Vale, son siete euros.*

5 – *Buenos días.*
 – *Deme media docena de huevos.*
 – *¿Algo más?*
 – *No, nada más.*
 – *Vale, aquí tiene, señora.*
 – *¿Cuánto es?*
 – *Son noventa céntimos.*

6 – *Buenos días.*
 – *Deme medio kilo de plátanos.*
 – *No quedan plátanos, pero las manzanas están buenas.*
 – *Vale, deme quinientos gramos de manzanas.*
 – *¿Algo más?*
 – *No. ¿Cuánto es?*
 – *Son un euro con setenta y cinco.*

Answers

	comida y bebida	cantidad	precio
1	*pan*	*3 barras*	*1,20€*
2	zanahorias	2 kilos	2,80€
3	tomates	3 kilos	6,00€
4	patatas	2 bolsas	7,00€
5	huevos	media docena	0,90€
6	manzanas	500g	1,75€

5 Lee la conversación. Escribe la letra correcta.

Reading. Students read the conversation and identify the correct series of pictures (from **a–d**).

Answers

b

---

6 With your partner, practise the conversation from exercise 5. Then create new conversations in a grocery shop, using the pictures in exercise 5 and changing the underlined phrases.

Speaking. In pairs: students practise the dialogue in exercise 5, taking it in turn to ask and answer. They then make up new dialogues along the same lines, using the picture prompts in exercise 5 and changing the underlined details.

Plenary

Put the class into teams, with a piece of paper and a pen at the front for each team. One person from each team comes to the front and stands by the piece of paper and pen for their team. Read out a price in Spanish. The student at the front writes down the answer in numerals, then takes the pen to the next person in the team, who goes to the paper and writes the next number that you give. Read out the prices so that the fastest team never has to wait to hear the next question. Slower teams will need to remember the prompt and try to catch up.

The team with the most correct answers when you stop the game is the winner.

Cuaderno Verde, page 80

1

Answers

a *los limones* **b** las naranjas **c** los melones
d las peras **e** los melocotones **f** las manzanas
g los plátanos **h** las zanahorias **i** los champiñones
j los guisantes **k** los pepinos **l** los pimientos rojos
m los huevos **n** las cebollas **o** los tomates

2

Answers

a ocho euros con ***cincuenta*** = **8**,50€
b **veinte** euros con setenta y cinco = 20,**75**€
c catorce euros con **treinta** = **14**,30€
d **dieciséis** euros con cinco = 16,**05**€
e **doce** euros con **sesenta** = 12,60€

3

Answers

una botella de pasteles ✗
una barra de leche ✗
un kilo de patatas
un cartón de zumo
una lata de leche ✗
una botella de queso ✗
una bolsa de aceite ✗
un paquete de arroz

1 Estar en forma (Student Book pp. 142–143)

Main topics and objectives

- Talking about how to stay in good shape
- Using the preterite and near future tense

Grammar

- The preterite and the near future tense

Key language

Para estar en forma...
siempre
a menudo
normalmente
frecuentemente

de vez en cuando
rara vez
nunca
no

como
bebo
desayuno
ceno

agua, Coca-Cola, limonada
zumo, leche, café, té,
lechuga
filete/bistec
chuletas de cordero
carne de cerdo
huevos, yogur, queso
pan, patatas fritas

hamburguesas
pasteles, galletas

Contiene(n)...
muchas vitaminas
muchas proteínas
mucha grasa

Resources

CD 4, track 20
Cuaderno Verde, page 81

Starter 1

To review vocabulary for items of food and drink in the context of keeping fit

Write up the following. Give students 3 minutes to complete the table with as many examples of appropriate food and drink as they can. If necessary, they can use the language box in exercise 2 for support.

Para estar en forma...

como	no como	bebo	no bebo
leche,			

Check answers.

1 Are these food items healthy (✓) or unhealthy? (✗) How often do you eat them? Write a sentence about each one.

Writing. Students identify whether each of the food items pictures is healthy (using a tick) or unhealthy (using a cross). They then write a sentence featuring a frequency expression for each item.

Answers

1 ✓ 2 ✗ 3 ✓ 4 ✓ 5 ✓ 6 ✓ 7 ✓ 8 ✓

2 Look at the shopping baskets and write a sentence about each. Use the fruit and veg on page 140 as well as the vocabulary on this page.

Writing. Students write a sentence for each of the pictures. A language box is supplied.

Answers

a Bebo agua y como zanahorias, pescado, plátanos y manzanas.
b Bebo zumo y como pollo, lechuga y tomates.
c Bebo leche y como yogur, plátanos, huevos y chuletas de cordero.
d Bebo Coca-Cola y como patatas fritas, pan y bistec.

3 Escucha a los famosos. Escribe la letra correcta del ejercicio 2. (1–3)

Listening. Students listen to three celebrities talking about what they eat and drink, and identify the correct shopping basket from exercise 2 for each one. There is one distractor.

Audioscript *Track 20*

1 *Me llamo Sara Baras y soy bailadora de flamenco. Para estar en forma siempre bebo agua y como pescado y verduras. El desayuno es muy importante y desayuno fruta cada día. Las frutas contienen vitaminas que son muy importantes.*

2 *Me llamo Gabriel García Bernal y soy actor. Como actor, tengo una vida muy activa y es importante estar en forma. El problema es que me encanta el pan y las patatas fritas, que contienen mucha grasa. Frecuentemente bebo Coca-Cola. A veces como bistecs.*

3 *Me llamo Salma Hayek y soy actriz, por eso tengo que estar en forma. Suelo comer pollo, que contiene muchas proteínas y también ceno ensalada cada día. Me encantan la lechuga y los tomates. Normalmente prefiero beber zumo.*

Answers

1 a 2 d 3 b

Starter 2

To review language for talking about eating and drinking; to review time expressions

Write up the following. Give students 3 minutes to make up five sentences starting *Para estar en forma...*, each using a different item from both columns and an appropriate food or drink.

siempre	*ceno*
a menudo	*como*
de vez en cuando	*bebo*
nunca	*desayuno*

Hear answers.

⭐ ResultsPlus

Tip box on the different verbs used in Spanish to talk about mealtimes.

R Go round the class. Each student takes it in turn to say what he/she eats at a particular mealtime, using the appropriate verb.

4 Habla de tu estilo de vida. Contesta a las preguntas.

Speaking. In pairs: students discuss their lifestyles, taking it in turn to ask and answer. The questions and answer openings are supplied.

⭐ ResultsPlus

Tip box on recognising whether someone is talking about the past or the future.

5 Lee los textos. Copia y completa la tabla en inglés.

Reading. Students copy out the table. They read the texts, in which four people talk about their previous and current lifestyles, and then complete the table with the details in English.

Answers

name	in the past	in the future
Nico	*ate (a lot of) meat*, drank *(a lot of)* lemonade and orangeade	*drink water*, sleep 8 hours, play basketball
Benjamín	drank (a lot of) Coca-Cola, ate (two) cakes and (a packet of) biscuits	eat more good food, eat (fried) chicken, drink apple juice
Nerea	ate fish and vegetables, drank water	eat (a lot of) hamburgers or crisps, watch TV

6 ¿Qué haces para estar en forma? ¿Qué comes normalmente? Escribe un párrafo.

Writing. Students write a paragraph on what they do to stay healthy, including details of what they did last week and are going to do next week. A structure and sample sentence openings are supplied for support.

💽 Students could prepare their texts on computer. Encourage them to check their texts for accuracy and to produce a second draft.

Plenary

Ask students to summarise the structures used in the unit to talk about lifestyle.

Then go round the class. Each student in turn gives a statement relating to food/drink or exercise, either about what they did last week or what they are going to do next week, using the appropriate tense and including an appropriate time expression.

Cuaderno Verde page 81

1

Answers

1 *Cada día bebo mucho zumo porque contiene muchas vitaminas.*
2 A veces me gusta merendar fruta.
3 El sábado pasado cené mucha ensalada.
4 Rara vez como patatas fritas porque contienen mucha grasa.
5 El fin de semana pasado comí perritos calientes y bebí limonada/bebí limonada y comí perritos calientes.
6 Este fin de semana voy a desayunar fruta y voy a beber leche/voy a beber leche y voy a desayunar fruta.
7 Esta semana quiero comer más pescado porque contiene muchas proteínas.

2

Answers

Present	Future	Past
bebo	voy a desayunar	cené
contiene	voy a beber	comí
gusta	quiero comer	bebí
como		
contienen		

2 ¿Llevas una vida sana? (Student Book pp. 144–145)

Main topics and objectives
● Giving advice on lifestyle
● Using the conditional of **deber**

Grammar
● The conditional of **deber**

Key language
Language from earlier in the module
¿Qué debería hacer?

Debería/Deberías...
beber más agua, leche o zumo
ir al instituto en bicicleta.
comer bien/menos pizza
hacer más ejercicio
No deberías...
comer todos esos perritos calientes
y hamburguesas
comprar cigarrillos

Resources
CD 4, track 21
Cuaderno Verde, pages 82–83
Gramática 204

Starter 1

To review the infinitive

Write up the following. Give students 2 minutes to write out the infinitive forms of the verbs shown.

hago	*debes*
tiene	*puedo*
soy	*escuchamos*
salen	*va*

Check answers. Ask students to give you examples of structures in which the infinitive is used (e.g. with **me gusta**, with modal verbs, etc.).

1 Read the problems and match each one with a piece of advice. Write the correct letter.

Reading. Students read the problems sent to a website giving advice on healthy living and match each problem to the correct response.

Answers
1 c 2 e 3 d 4 a 5 b

2 Escribe las frases **en negrita** del ejercicio 1 en inglés.

Writing. Students reread the text in exercise 1 and translate the sentences in bold into English.

Answers
Deberías beber más agua, leche o zumo. You should drink more water, milk or juice.
Deberías ir al instituto en bicicleta. You should go to school by bike.
Deberías comer bien… You should eat well…
No deberías comer todos esos perritos calientes y hamburguesas. You shouldn't eat all those hotdogs and hamburgers.
No deberías comprar cigarrillos. You shouldn't buy cigarettes.

✚ Translate the text in exercise 1 into English, with each student translating a sentence.

G Grammar
Use the Grammar box to review the conditional of the verb **deber**.

3 Identify who is speaking and write down the advice they are given in English. (1–3)

Listening. Students listen to three conversations and note in English the advice each person is given.

Audioscript *Track 21*

1 – *No llevo una vida muy sana porque no me gusta jugar al fútbol, ni hacer natación. Prefiero quedarme en casa y usar mi ordenador. Ahora estoy un poco gordo. ¿Qué debería hacer?*
– *Pues, si quieres perder peso, deberías hacer más ejercicio. Si no te gusta practicar deportes, puedes ir al cole a pie o en bicicleta.*
2 – *¿Qué te pasa?*
– *No estoy en forma y no estoy contento. El problema es que fumo demasiado, pero me encantan los cigarrillos. ¿Qué debería hacer?*
– *No deberías comprar cigarrillos. Si quieres estar en forma, no puedes fumar. Deberías beber más agua y practicar algún deporte.*
3 – *Creo que llevo una vida sana porque estoy delgada y me gustan los deportes. El problema es que siempre tengo sueño. ¿Qué debería hacer?*
– *¿Qué te gusta comer normalmente?*
– *Pues, como comida basura, pero como fruta también.*
– *Si quieres tener más energía, deberías comer más comida con proteínas y vitaminas. Por ejemplo, deberías comer más pescado y más verduras.*

Answers
1 Jorge – do more exercise/go to school on foot or by bike
2 Alejandro – not buy cigarettes, drink more water and take up sport
3 Nadia – eat food more with protein and vitamins, e.g. more fish and vegetables

Starter 2

To review using the conditional of *deber*

Write up the following. Give students 3 minutes to write a sentence giving advice in Spanish in response to each, using the conditional of **deber**. If necessary, remind them that **deber** is followed by an infinitive.

1 *I'm a bit fat.*
2 *I'm not very fit.*
3 *I smoke.*
4 *I eat too many hotdogs.*

Check answers.

4 Con tu compañero/a, haz diálogos.

Speaking. In pairs: students take part in conversations about lifestyle problems. Student A asks what he/she should do; Student B gives appropriate advice. Picture prompts are supplied, along with a sample exchange. A language box is also supplied.

➕ Students make the dialogues longer, by having Student A first describe what his/her problem is, and then after receiving advice, also respond with a statement of what he/she is going to do in future.

5 Write out the pieces of advice you gave in exercise 4.

Writing. Students write out the advice they gave for each of the picture prompts in exercise 4.

Answers
1 Deberías comer más fruta, verduras y pescado.
2 Deberías ir al cole en bicicleta.
3 No deberías fumar. Deberías jugar al fútbol.

6 Busca estas frases en español en el texto.

Reading. Students read the two letters and identify the Spanish versions of the seven English sentences listed. Some vocabulary is glossed for support.

Answers
1 Estoy muy preocupado porque estoy un poco gordo.
2 Me gustaría perder peso.
3 Ellas están delgadísimas.
4 Evito la comida rápida pero no puedo perder peso.
5 ¿Qué debería hacer para no engordar?
6 Estar delgadísimo no es bueno.
7 No deberías pasar tanto tiempo en casa.

7 Lee otra vez las cartas del ejercicio 6. Contesta a las preguntas en inglés.

Reading. Students reread the problem page letters in exercise 6 and answer the comprehension questions in English.

Answers
1 because he is a bit fat
2 because the girls at school don't want to go out with him
3 because he hates sport
4 playing chess, surfing the net
5 he shouldn't spend so much time at home, he should walk or cycle to school

⭐ ResultsPlus
Tip box on using text layout to help comprehension.

Plenary

Ask students to summarise how **deber** is used, asking them to give you examples of advice from the unit featuring **deberías**.

To review the structure, prompt in English, e.g. 'you should do more sport'. Make it more challenging by bringing in infinitives not covered in the unit.

Cuaderno Verde pages 82–83

1a

Answers
1 *Deberías comer* mucha fruta.
2 **Deberías hacer** más deporte.
3 **Deberías beber** más agua.
4 **Deberías perder** peso.
5 No **deberías fumar** cigarrillos.
6 No **deberías comer** hamburguesas.
7 **Deberías ir** en bici.

1b

Answers
a You should **drink** more water. **3**
b You should **go** by bike. **7**
c You should **eat** lots of fruit. **1**
d You should not eat **hamburgers**. **6**
e You should **lose** weight. **4**
f You should **do** more sport. **2**
g You should not **smoke** cigarettes. **5**

2

Answers
1 Para perder peso, no deberías comer **patatas fritas**.
2 Para estar en forma, deberías ir en **bici**.
3 Para tomar más vitaminas, deberías comer **fruta**.
4 Para no tener problemas con los dientes, no deberías comer **caramelos**.

3

Answers

deberíasbebermuchaagua/deberíascomermenosgrasa/
nodeberíaspasartantotiempoencasa/
deberíashacermuchoejercicio/
nodeberíascomerchocolate/nodeberíascomprarcigarrillos

1 *No deberías comer chocolate.*
2 Deberías comer menos grasa.
3 No deberías comprar cigarrillos.
4 Deberías hacer mucho ejercicio.
5 Deberías beber mucha agua.
6 No deberías pasar tanto tiempo en casa.

4

Answers

1 *Debería comer menos chocolate.*
2 *Debería* comer más fruta.
3 *Deberías* perder peso.
4 No deberías comer hamburguesas.
5 No debería fumar.
6 Debería hacer más ejercicio.
7 Debería beber más agua.

3 Los jóvenes (Student Book pp. 146–147)

Main topics and objectives

- Talking about issues facing young people
- Using the near future tense

Grammar

- The near future tense

Key language

Creo que (no)...
Pienso que (no)...
Sé que...
En mi opinión...
El problema es que...
Por un lado... por otro lado...

No...
A veces...
Nunca...
fumo cigarrillos...
tomo drogas blandas/duras...
bebo alcohol...
llevo navajas...
porque es...
una pérdida de tiempo/una tontería
peligroso/perjudicial para la salud/caro
divertido/fácil/relajante

Resources

CD 4, tracks 22–23
Cuaderno Verde, pages 84–85

Starter 1

To introduce language for talking about problems facing young people; to review expressions used to introduce an opinion

Do exercise 1 on p. 146 as the Starter.

1 Lee las frases y escribe el nombre y la letra correcta.

Reading. Students match the speech bubbles with the correct pictures.

> **Answers**
>
> **David** b   **Ignacio** a   **Marisa** d   **Natalia** c   **Pablo** e

 Students translate the speech bubbles into English.

⭐ ResultsPlus

Tip box on using a range of expressions to introduce a point of view.

2 Busca estas frases en español en los textos.

Reading. Students read the text and identify the Spanish versions of the seven English sentences listed.

> **Answers**
>
> 1 Pienso que tomar drogas duras es muy peligroso.
> 2 Sé que fumar es tonto.
> 3 El tabaco mata a mucha gente.
> 4 El problema es que los cigarrillos son muy caros.
> 5 ...por otro lado el alcohol es perjudicial para la salud.
> 6 Las navajas están prohibidas.
> 7 ...porque es una pérdida de tiempo.

Starter 2

To review language for giving opinions; to use grammar to work out connections

Write up the following, jumbling the order of a–e. Give students 3 minutes to match the sentence halves and translate the completed sentences into English.

1 *Creo que fumar*
2 *En mi opinión tomar*
3 *Pienso que tomar drogas*
4 *Sé que beber alcohol es*
5 *No llevo navajas*

a *es peligroso.*
b *drogas blandas no es una cosa muy seria.*
c *duras es muy peligroso.*
d *perjudicial para la salud.*
e *nunca.*

Check answers, asking students how they worked out how the halves matched.

3 Read the website in exercise 2 again and write P (positive), N (negative) or P+N (positive and negative) for each opinion. Justify your answer.

Reading. Students reread the text in exercise 2. They identify whether each opinion expressed is positive (P), negative (N) or a mixture of both (P + N), each time giving a reason in English for their answer.

Answers

a N – it's dangerous/stupid, young people have serious problems with hard drugs

b P+N – loves cigarettes; knows it's stupid and kills lots of people, cigarettes are expensive

c P+N – likes drinking beer with friends; alcohol is bad for your health

d N – it's stupid, doesn't like violence, knives are illegal

e N – all drugs are bad, a waste of time

4 Escucha. Copia y completa la tabla en inglés. (1–4)

Listening. Students copy out the table. They then listen to four conversations in which young people talk about what they do/don't do and complete the table with the details in English.

Audioscript *Track 22*

1 – ¿Tomas drogas?
  – No, nunca. Las drogas duras son muy peligrosas. Es una tontería tomarlas.
  – ¿Fumas?
  – Sí, fumo de vez en cuando, como todos mis amigos.
2 – ¿Tienes algún vicio?
  – Sí, bebo alcohol.
  – ¿Cuánto bebes?
  – Bueno… voy a la disco todos los viernes y bebo cinco o seis botellas de cerveza.
  – ¿Llevas navajas?
  – ¡Qué va! Yo nunca llevo navajas.
3 – ¿Tomas drogas duras?
  – No, nunca tomo drogas duras, pero me gusta el tabaco.
  – ¿Fumas mucho?
  – Pues… depende. Durante la semana sólo fumo dos o tres cigarrillos al día, pero los fines de semana fumo mucho más.
4 – ¿Tomas drogas duras?
  – Claro que no. ¿Estás loco? Es muy peligroso. Pero a veces tomo drogas blandas.
  – ¿Qué tomas?
  – Fumo porros.
  – ¿Marihuana?
  – Sí, sí, hachís.
  – Pero el hachís también es una droga peligrosa.

Answers

	things they do	things they don't do
1	smoke	take drugs
2	drink alcohol	carry knives
3	smoke	take hard drugs
4	take soft drugs/hashish	take hard drugs

5 Escribe tu opinión sobre cada dibujo del ejercicio 1.

Writing. Students write their opinion on each of the issues pictured in exercise 1. A language box is supplied for support.

This would be an ideal topic for an email exchange with students in a Spanish school.

6 Escucha y lee el poema. Rellena los espacios en blanco con palabras del cuadro.

Listening. Students listen to the poem, and read and complete the gap-fill version of the text. The answers are supplied in random order.

Audioscript *Track 23*

*Fumo, porque me **gusta**.*
Cuando estoy con mis amigos
*Con **cigarrillo** y copa en mano*
*Me siento bien y **estoy** contento.*
Pero en casa después de fumar
*O después de **beber**,*
No me gusto a mí mismo.
*Me **duele** el cuerpo,*
Odio estas adicciones.

*En el **futuro** no voy a fumar más.*
Voy a respirar aire limpio,
*Voy a **hacer** deporte,*
*Voy a levantarme por las **mañanas***
Sin pensar en cigarrillos.
Voy a ser libre.

Answers

Also shown in bold in the audioscript.
1 gusta   2 cigarrillo   3 estoy   4 beber
5 duele   6 futuro   7 hacer   8 mañanas

In pairs or groups: students discuss their opinions of the issues raised in the unit and their own lifestyles.

Plenary

Ask the class to name all the issues affecting young people which came up in the unit. Then ask students at random their opinion of each issue. Encourage them to include the expressions to introduce opinions that they have been practising (e.g. **Creo que…**, etc.).

Cuaderno Verde page 84

1a

Answers

Pablo B   **Sara** A   **Gustavo** F
Luisa A   **Ana** B   **Ramón** A

1b

Answers

1 smoking   2 alcohol   3 smoking
4 violence   5 knives   6 drug taking

Cuaderno Verde page 85

1

Answers

		Present	Past	Future
1	to go	voy	**fui**	**voy a ir**
2	to eat	**como**	**comí**	**voy a comer**
3	to want	**quiero**	quise	**voy a querer**
4	to drink	bebo	**bebió**	voy a beber
5	to smoke	fumo	**fumé**	voy a fumar
6	to hurt	**duele**	**dolió**	va a doler
7	to feel	me siento	**me sentí**	**me voy a sentir**
8	to be	**es**	**fue**	va a ser

2

Answers

1 No se debe beber alcohol porque *es* malo para la salud.

2 En el futuro nunca **voy a comer** hamburguesas porque tienen mucha grasa.

3 Todos los días **como** ensalada porque **quiero** llevar una dieta más sana.

4 La semana que viene **voy a ir** al insti en bici porque quiero estar en forma.

5 Mañana **voy a beber** mucha agua y ¡no **voy a fumar** ni un cigarrillo!

6 Ayer **comí** mucha comida basura y por la noche me **dolió** el estómago.

7 El sábado pasado **fumé** un cigarrillo por primera vez y **me sentí** fatal.

8 Anoche mi hermano **fue** a una fiesta, **bebió** demasiada cerveza y ahora le **duele** la cabeza.

Prueba oral: Sport photograph (Student Book pp. 148–149)

Topics revised

- Talking about lifestyle

Resources

CD 5, tracks 33–35

Overview

Read through the task box at the top of the page and outline for students how this section works. They will hear a Speaking controlled assessment model discussion in three parts and do exercises focused on the language used. These exercises, along with the advice/activities on how to improve speaking performance in ResultsPlus, will help them prepare to take part in a discussion of their own on the topic.

Before playing part 1, encourage pupils to look at the photo and the notes in the task box (asking them to cover up the rest of the page) and then make a list of some of the questions that they could be asked about it in Spanish.

1 You are going to listen to Alex, an exam candidate, being interviewed by his teacher. Listen to part 1 of Alex's interview and match the two halves of each statement correctly.

Listening. Explain to the students that they will hear a sample of the kind of discussion they are expected to have in the Speaking controlled assessment.

Students listen to the first part of the recording and match the sentence halves.

Once they have completed the task, ask them whether they predicted the questions correctly and how Alex might have answered any of the other questions they came up with.

Audioscript *Track 33*

Part 1

– *¿Por qué has escogido esta foto?*
– *He escogido esta foto porque me encanta jugar al baloncesto. Normalmente juego al baloncesto después del cole, pero también juego los fines de semana. Me encanta hacer deporte porque es genial.*
– *¿Dónde estás en esta foto?*
– *Aquí estoy en el patio de mi instituto. Es grande y tiene una pista de baloncesto y un campo de fútbol.*
– *¿Quiénes son las personas en esta foto?*
– *En esta foto estoy yo y mi mejor amigo James. James es el chico con el pelo negro y el jersey azul. A veces James y yo jugamos al fútbol los viernes, pero prefiero el baloncesto. En mi opinión, es mucho más fácil.*

Answers

1 f **2** c **3** a **4** g **5** b **6** d **7** e

2 Listen to part 2 of Alex's interview and note down the words that fill the gaps.

Listening. Students now listen to the second part of Alex's discussion and complete the gap-fill version of the transcript. The answers are supplied in random order for support.

With a confident class you could ask students to read the text and try to work out plausible answers first, then use the recording to check.

Audioscript *Track 34*

Part 2

– *¿Qué más haces para llevar una vida sana?*
– *Bueno, hago **mucho** ejercicio por lo menos **tres** veces a la semana. Generalmente **hago** footing. Ayer hice footing **antes** del colegio y luego a las cuatro **jugué** en el equipo de fútbol. Normalmente **prefiero** hacer deporte en equipo porque es más interesante. Mañana voy a hacer natación con mi padre.*
– *¿Qué comes o bebes normalmente?*
– *Siempre como bien porque me gusta **estar** en forma. Ceno pasta o arroz **con** carne y verduras. Y como mucha fruta. Odio la comida basura porque contiene mucha grasa. **Nunca** como caramelos porque el azúcar es **muy** malo para la salud. Siempre bebo agua, leche o zumo de manzana.*

Answers

Also in bold in the audioscript.
1 mucho **2** tres **3** hago **4** antes **5** jugué
6 prefiero **7** estar **8** con **9** Nunca **10** muy

➕ Students find examples of the following in what Alex says in exercise 2: preterite and near future verbs, negatives, opinions, reasons, adverbs, time, frequency and sequencing expressions, connectives, comparatives, qualifiers. Point out that including details like these will earn them extra marks in the exam.

(*Answers:*
Preterite: hice, jugué
Near future verbs: voy a hacer
Negatives: nunca
Opinions: prefiero hacer deporte, me gusta estar, odio la comida basura
Reasons: porque es más interesante, porque me gusta estar en forma, porque contiene mucha grasa, porque el azúcar es muy malo para la salud
Time, frequency and sequencing expressions: generalmente, ayer, antes, luego, Normalmente, mañana, siempre, nunca
Connectives: y, porque, o

Comparatives: más interesante
Qualifiers: por lo menos, más, muy)

3 Here are the questions Alex will be asked in part 3. What do they mean?

Students read the questions they will hear in part 3 of the recording and say what they mean.

Answers

¿Qué consejos tienes para llevar una vida sana? *What advice do you have for a healthy lifestyle?*
¿Fumas o tomas drogas? *Do you smoke or take drugs?*

---

4 Now listen to part 3 of Alex's interview and put these statements into the correct order.

Listening. Students listen to the third and final part of Alex's discussion and reorder the statements as they are mentioned.

Audioscript *Track 35*

Part 3

– ¿Qué consejos tienes para llevar una vida sana?
– Bueno, deberías hacer ejercicio y no deberías comer hamburguesas ni patatas fritas. También deberías comer pescado o pollo con verduras. No deberías beber refrescos porque contienen demasiado azúcar.
– Y tú, Alex, ¿fumas o tomas drogas?
– Nunca fumo, pero a veces bebo alcohol si voy a una discoteca. Nunca voy a tomar drogas. Es una tontería.

Answers

e, c, a, b, f, d

⭐ ResultsPlus

The Results Plus support for speaking activities is differentiated, allowing students to identify and work towards their target level: covering the basics, Grade C, increasing their marks. Encourage students to adopt the techniques in these sections in all extended speaking activities.

Read through and discuss the Results Plus section together.

5 Now it's your turn! Choose your own photo and then prepare to talk about it with your partner or your teacher.

Speaking. Students take part in a discussion in the style of a controlled assessment task, based on a photo showing an aspect of their lifestyle. They should use all the support supplied, here and elsewhere on the spread:

- the Results Plus advice on the language to include
- Alex's responses, adapted to talk about themselves
- the English notes in the task box, p. 149
- their answers to exercises 1–4.

Each student takes part in a discussion as the person answering the questions. If they are working with a partner, they will take turns asking and answering.

If possible, record the discussions or have the students record themselves. They can then swap recordings with a partner, listen to each other's version and offer comments on how it might be improved. A simple marking system is suggested (one/two/three stars for listed categories). Students should then identify two or three areas which they would like to improve next time they do an extended speaking task.

Topics revised
● Writing about your lifestyle

1 Read the text and choose the correct title for each paragraph. What words/phrases support your decisions?

Reading. Students read James's text on his lifestyle and match the paragraphs (1–4) to the correct titles (a–d), identifying words/phrases which justify their decisions.

Answers
1 c   2 d   3 a   4 b

2 Find these expressions in Spanish in the text.

Reading. Students reread the text in exercise 1 and find in it the Spanish versions of the ten English phrases listed.

Answers
1 Siempre como mucha fruta…
2 …porque es muy buena para la salud
3 Para mantenerme en forma…
4 …me gusta practicar deporte…
5 Para el almuerzo o la cena como…
6 El problema es que también me gusta…
7 …a veces no quiero comer ni pescado ni verduras.
8 Lo peor es que…
9 No voy a comer comida basura.
10 …es perjudicial para la salud.

3 Which paragraphs of the text are not completely in the present tense? Give three examples from each of these paragraphs of verbs which do not refer to the present.

Reading. Students identify the paragraphs in the text which are not completely in the present tense. They then give three examples in each of those paragraphs of verb forms other than the present.

Answers
Paragraphs 3 and 4

- *Any three:* fui, comí, pedí, bebí (preterite)
- voy a hacer (near future), me gustaría (hacer equitación o jugar al golf) (conditional), no voy a comer (ni a beber alcohol) (near future)

4 Read the text again and answer the questions in English.

Reading. Students reread the text and answer the comprehension questions in English.

Answers
1 quite healthy   2 water   3 goes to the gym (twice a week), does sport   4 takes drugs   5 cereal   6 meat or fish with salad   7 pizza, chocolate cake (with ice cream and cream)   8 *Any two:* do more sport (horse-riding or golf), not eat junk food, not drink alcohol

5 You might be asked to write about healthy lifestyles as a controlled assessment task. Use the Results Plus to help you prepare your account.

Students read through the language support material supplied in preparation for doing their own extended writing task in exercise 6.

✪ ResultsPlus
The Results Plus section gives students the support they need to structure and improve their writing. The support is differentiated, allowing students to identify and work towards their target level: covering the basics, Grade C, increasing their marks. Encourage students to adopt the kind of approach taken in this section in all extended writing activities.

6 Now write a full account of your lifestyle.

Writing. Students write their own text on their lifestyle in the style of a controlled assessment task (at least 100 words). As well as the Results Plus guidelines on the language to include, they should use all the support supplied here:

- James's text, adapted to refer to themselves
- relevant language from throughout the module
- the sample structure for the text.

7 Check carefully what you have written.

Writing. Students check their own work using the list of features supplied.

 # Leer y escuchar (Modules 7–8) (Student Book pp. 152–153)

● This section helps students develop their listening and reading skills in preparation for the exam.

Resources

CD 5, tracks 36–39

LEER

1 Read Carmen's supermarket receipt and answer the questions. *(4 marks)*

Reading. Students read the receipt and answer the comprehension questions in English.

The first two questions test straightforward food vocabulary and approximate to Grade G; the last two questions require a little more detail and approximate to Grade F.

> **Answers**
>
> **1** oranges   **2** potatoes   **3** 12/a dozen eggs
> **4** large packet

⊛ **ResultsPlus**

Tip box on questions with the word 'exactly'.

2 Read Antonio's description of his house and answer the questions. *(2 marks)*

Reading. Students read the text and answer the comprehension questions in English.

There are short lists of vocabulary to read through to find the phrases necessary for the answer. This question approximates to Grade E.

> **Answers**
>
> **1** beside/next to the study   **2** behind the dining room

⊛ **ResultsPlus**

Tip box on recognising prepositions.

3 Read what Elena writes about her home town and choose the word that summarises each section of her description. Write the correct letter. *(5 marks)*

Reading. Students read the text and identify the correct topic (from **a–f**) for each paragraph (**1–5**). There is one distractor.

Each individual paragraph includes a number of vocabulary items which help to identify the topic area. This question approximates to Grade C.

> **Answers**
>
> **1** c **2** f **3** e **4** b **5** d

⊛ **ResultsPlus**

Tip box on finding answers in longer texts.

ESCUCHAR

4 Listen to Ernesto talking to his mum. Answer the questions in English. *(4 marks)*

Listening. Students listen to Ernesto and answer the comprehension questions in English.

Questions 1 and 4 require simple comprehension of individual words and approximate to Grade G; questions 2 and 3 require a composite answer and approximate to Grade F.

Audioscript *Track 36*

1 – *¿Dónde estás, mamá?*
  – *Estoy en la cocina.*
  [Repeated as above]
2 – *¿Qué estás haciendo?*
  – *Lavo los platos.*
  [Repeated as above]
3 – *Mis zapatillas son demasiado pequeñas.*
  [Repeated as above]
4 – *Vamos a comprar unas zapatillas para tu cumpleaños.*
  [Repeated as above]

> **Answers**
>
> **1** in the kitchen   **2** washing up/washing dishes
> **3** (too) small   **4** (on/for his) birthday

⊛ **ResultsPlus**

Tip box on giving answers in English whenever the questions are in English.

5 Marisol's local area. Which 3 places does she like? Write the number and the correct letter. *(3 marks)*

Listening. Students listen to Marisol and identify the pictures of the three things she likes (from **a–d**). There is one distractor.

This question is a test of simple positive and negative opinions. It approximates to Grade E.

Audioscript *Track 37*

1 *Me gusta mi barrio. El polideportivo es fenomenal, pero el cine es fatal.*
  [Repeated as above]
2 *El parque es feo y sucio, pero las tiendas son estupendas.*
  [Repeated as above]

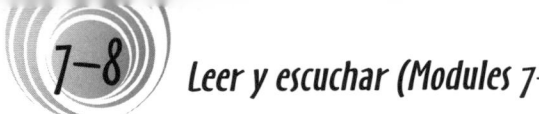
3 *Lo mejor es la discoteca en mi opinión.*
[Repeated as above]

Answers

1 c **2** d **3** a

⭐ ResultsPlus

Tip box on listening for the specific details.

6 Listen to these customers buying clothes and answer the questions in English. *(4 marks)*

Listening. Students listen to four conversations in a shop and answer the comprehension questions in English.

Each section includes more than one potential answer. This question approximates to Grade D.

Audioscript *Track 38*

1 – *¿En qué puedo servirle, señor?*
   – *Me gusta este abrigo marrón. ¿Lo tiene en negro, por favor?*
2 – *Buenos días, señora.*
   – *Este sombrero no es muy cómodo. Lo quiero en talla más grande si hay.*
3 – *El color de estos calcetines es ideal, pero no los quiero de lana.*
   – *¿Qué le parecen aquellos de algodón?*
   – *Muy bien, gracias. Prefiero el algodón.*
4 – *Este bolso de cuero vale trescientos euros y ese bolso de plástico vale ciento veinte euros.*
   – *El bolso de cuero es bonito, pero voy a comprar el bolso de plástico de ciento veinte euros.*

Answers

1 black **2** large **3** cotton **4** 120€

⭐ ResultsPlus

Tip box on distinguishing distractors.

7 Healthy lifestyles. Write the name and the correct letter. *(4 marks)*

Listening. Students listen to four conversations and note the letter of the correct sentence ending for each person.

This exercise approximates to Grade C.

Audioscript *Track 39*

1 *Ramón*
   – *¿Llevas una vida sana, Ramón?*
   – *Pues voy andando al colegio todos los días y hago mucho ciclismo. Siempre bebo mucha agua y nunca tomo comida basura.*
[Repeated as above]

2 *Teresa*
   – *¿Qué dices tú, Teresa?*
   – *Yo evito el ejercicio porque siempre me duele la espalda. Como muchas patatas fritas y me encanta la naranjada.*
[Repeated as above]

3 *Nacho*
   – *¿Y tú, Nacho, estás en forma?*
   – *Estoy un poco gordo, pero estoy perdiendo peso. Suelo comer mucha fruta y ensalada. A menudo como demasiado chocolate.*
[Repeated as above]

4 *Gloria*
   – *¿Y qué dices tú, Gloria?*
   – *No estoy preocupada por mi salud. Como bien, duermo bastante, pero también fumo cigarrillos y bebo mucho alcohol los fines de semana.*
[Repeated as above]

Answers

1 Ramón a **2** Teresa d **3** Nacho e **4** Gloria b

⭐ ResultsPlus

Tip box on listening for confirmation of an answer and on using qualifiers as clues.

La salud

8 Te toca a ti (Student Book pp. 186–187)

- Self-access reading and writing

A Reinforcement

1 Unjumble the words in **bold** and write out the phrases correctly.

Reading. Students complete the phrases by unjumbling the anagram for each one.

Answers

1 atún **2** cerveza **3** tomates **4** azúcar **5** pasteles
6 café **7** patatas **8** leche **9** pan **10** huevos

2 Match the sentences to the pictures. Then note down what each person doesn't eat.

Reading. Students match the speech bubbles (**1–4**) to the correct pictures (**a–d**). They then note in English what each person doesn't eat or drink.

Answers

1 c – red meat **2** a – tea **3** d – lemonade
4 b – junk food, fruit

3 Read the postcard. Are the statements true (T), false (F) or not mentioned (NM).

Reading. Students read the postcard and the statements about it and decide whether each is true (**T**), is false (**F**) or contains information not mentioned in the text (**NM**).

Answers

1 T **2** NM **3** F **4** T **5** T **6** NM

B Extension

1 Read the sentences halves and match them up correctly. Then translate them into English.

Reading. Students match the sentence halves, then translate the completed sentences into English.

Answers

1 c – You have to drink lots of water.
2 d – You have to rest at home.
3 a – You have to take this syrup.
4 e – You have to apply/use this cream.
5 f – You have to take an aspirin.
6 b – You have to go to hospital immediately.

2 Copy out the text and complete it with words from the box.

Reading. Students copy and complete the gap-fill text. The answers are supplied in random order.

Answers

1 cigarrillos **2** alcohol **3** cerveza
4 duras **5** malas **6** navajas

3 Read the text and answer the questions in English.

Reading. Students read the text and answer the comprehension questions in English.

Answers

1 she thinks it is quite healthy
2 riding and jogging
3 carrots and peas
4 fruit
5 it contains lots of vitamins
6 eat more fish, drink less Coca-Cola

4 Write a paragraph like Nadia's. Try to use the verbs in **bold** in her text, but with your own information or opinions. Remember to write about what you are going to eat and drink to lead a healthier life.

Writing. Students write about their own eating habits and lifestyle, using the language highlighted in bold in the exercise 3 text.

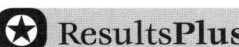 ResultsPlus

Tip box on **me gusta(n)** and **me encanta(n)**.

Module 9 Nuestro planeta (Student Book pp. 156–171)

Unit	Main topics and objectives	Grammar	Skills
Repaso Cambios medioambientales (pp. 156–157)	• Talking about the environment • Using **se debe/es necesario** + infinitive	**Se debe/Es necesario** + infinitive	Adapting and customising model texts
1 Piensa globalmente (pp. 158–159)	• Discussing local solutions • Using **para** + infinitive (in order to…)	**Para** + infinitive (in order to…)	Listening for detail Using expressions to gain thinking time Extending sentences
2 Voluntarios (pp. 160–161)	• Talking about global citizenship • Using the future tense	The future tense Using **si** + present + future	Extending sentences
3 Sin techo, sin derecho (pp. 162–163)	• Talking about homelessness • Recognising different time frames	Recognising preterite, present and future tenses	Using different time frames Reading questions carefully and responding appropriately
Prueba oral: Environment (pp. 164–165)	Exam speaking practice	Revision	
Prueba escrita (pp. 166–167)	Exam writing practice	Revision	
Leer y escuchar (Module 9) (pp. 168–169)	Listening and reading skills	Revision	
Te toca a ti (pp. 188–189)	Self-access reading and writing		

Main topics and objectives

- Talking about the environment
- Using **se debe/es necesario +** infinitive

Grammar

- **se debe/es necesario +** infinitive

Key language

Se debe…
Es necesario…
comprar productos ecológicos
consumir menos energía
proteger la naturaleza

reciclar papel y vidrio
reducir la contaminación
usar el transporte público
plantar árboles

No se debe…
malgastar agua
tirar basura al suelo

Vivo en…
un barrio industrial
en el centro de…
una ciudad turística
una ciudad histórica

una manzana
una botella de plástico vacía

una bolsa de plástico
un periódico
los restos de una hamburguesa
un tetrabrik de leche vacío
una botella de cristal vacía
un bote de champú vacío

Resources

CD 4, tracks 24–25
Cuaderno Verde, page 88
Gramática 204

Starter 1

To review modal verbs + infinitive; to review language for talking about the environment

Write up the following, omitting the underlined words and supplying them separately in random order. Give students 3 minutes to complete the sentences and translate them into English.

Se debe…
<u>consumir</u> *menos energía.*
<u>reciclar</u> *papel y vidrio.*
<u>comprar</u> *productos ecológicos.*
<u>proteger</u> *la naturaleza.*
<u>reducir</u> *la contaminación.*
<u>plantar</u> *árboles.*
<u>usar</u> *el transporte público.*

1 Empareja las frases con la fota correcta.

Reading. Students match the sentences to the correct pictures (from **a–g**).

> **Answers**
>
> **1** d **2** f **3** e **4** c **5** b **6** g **7** a

2 Busca estas frases en español en el ejercicio 1.

Reading. Students reread the sentences in exercise 1 and identify the Spanish versions of the six English phrases listed.

> **Answers**
>
> **a** demasiado tráfico **b** muchos atascos
> **c** mucha contaminación **d** espacios verdes
> **e** fábricas **f** mucha basura

⭐ Results**Plus**

Tip box on **gastar/malgastar.**

3 Escucha y escribe la(s) letra(s) correcta(s). (1–6)

Listening. Students listen to six conversations and identify the letter(s) of the recommendation(s) each person gives (from **a–i**). A language box is supplied. Some vocabulary is also glossed in the tip box for support.

Audioscript *Track 24*

1 – *¿Qué se debe hacer para proteger el medio ambiente, Lilia?*
– *Se debe usar el transporte público.*
2 – *¿Qué se debe hacer para proteger el medio ambiente, Carlos?*
– *Se debe reciclar papel y vidrio.*
3 – *¿Y tú, Pepita? ¿Qué piensas? ¿Qué se debe hacer para proteger el medio ambiente?*
– *Es necesario comprar productos ecológicos.*
4 – *Para proteger el medio ambiente, se debe reducir la contaminación y plantar árboles.*
5 – *Ana, ¿qué se debe hacer para proteger el medio ambiente?*
– *A ver… no se debe malgastar agua… y no se debe tirar basura al suelo.*
6 – *Y Juan, ¿qué piensas? ¿Qué se debe hacer?*
– *Se debe proteger la naturaleza y es necesario consumir menos energía.*

> **Answers**
>
> **1** f **2** d **3** a **4** e, g **5** h, i **6** c, b

Starter 2

To review *(no) se debe/es necesario* + infinitive; to review language for talking about the local environment

Write up the following. Give students 3 minutes to identify the correct form of the verb each time and to translate the sentences into English.

1 *Se debe compramos/comprar productos ecológicos.*
2 *Es necesario reciclar/recicla papel y vidrio.*
3 *Se deber/debe reducir la contaminación.*
4 *No se debe gastar/malgastar agua.*

Check answers. Ask students to summarise how **(no) se debe** and **es necesario** are used.

G Grammar

Use the Grammar box to review **(no) se debe/es necesario** + infinitive.

✚ Students take it in turn to prompt in English (e.g. 'we should consume less energy') and to respond in Spanish (e.g. *se debe consumir menos energía*).

4 Escucha. Copia y completa la tabla en inglés. (1–3)

Listening. Students copy out the table. They listen to three conversations and complete the table with the details in English. A language box is supplied.

Before playing the recording, introduce the structure *El mayor problema es que...* for support.

Audioscript *Track 25*

1 – *¿Dónde vives?*
  – *Vivo en un barrio industrial cerca de Gijón.*
  – *¿Qué problemas hay en tu región?*
  – *El mayor problema es que hay mucha contaminación del aire por el tráfico y las fábricas.*
  – *¿Qué se debe hacer para proteger el medio ambiente?*
  – *Creo que se debe mejorar la red de transporte y reducir la contaminación.*
2 – *¿Dónde vives?*
  – *Vivo en el centro de Madrid.*
  – *¿Qué problemas hay en tu región?*
  – *El mayor problema es que no hay espacios verdes y también a veces hay mucha basura en el centro.*
  – *¿Qué se debe hacer para proteger el medio ambiente?*
  – *Creo que es necesario plantar árboles y no tirar basura en el suelo.*
3 – *¿Dónde vives?*
  – *Vivo en Málaga. Es una ciudad turística e histórica.*
  – *¿Qué problemas hay en tu región?*
  – *El mayor problema es que en verano hay sequía. No tenemos mucha agua y el turismo causa un enorme consumo de agua.*

– *¿Qué se debe hacer?*
– *Pues... no se debe malgastar agua y hay que proteger la naturaleza. Eso es muy importante.*

Answers

	area lived in	environmental problems	possible solutions
1	*industrial area*	*pollution* (from traffic and factories)	*improve public transport*, reduce pollution
2	centre of Madrid/city centre	no green spaces, rubbish	plant trees, not throw rubbish on the ground
3	touristy, historic city	drought, tourists use a lot of water	not waste water, protect nature

5 Con tu compañero/a, pregunta y contesta, cambiando los datos subrayados.

Speaking. In pairs: students discuss environmental problems in their areas (these can be imaginary). They take it in turn to ask and answer questions. A sample exchange is supplied, with the language to change underlined.

✪ ResultsPlus

Tip box on adapting model answers and on using a variety of expressions to introduce opinions.

6 Everything in its place. Where would you put each object? Write the correct number.

Reading. Students look at the pictures + captions (1–5), which represent different kinds of recycling container. They then identify the correct container for the items of rubbish pictured (a–h).

Answers
a 4 b 3 c 3 d 1 e 5 f 3 g 2 h 3

7 Escribe un artículo sobre el medio ambiente. Contesta a las preguntas del ejercicio 5.

Writing. Students write an article on the environment, using the language of the unit.

Plenary

Ask the class what structures were used in the unit to say what we should do/have to do.

Ask a student to give an environmental problem in Spanish, then a second student to respond with a sentence on what we should do to resolve it. Continue in this way to review the language and structures of the unit.

Cuaderno Verde, page 88

1

Answers

m	c	o	n	s	u	m	i	r
a	t	f	p	m	s	p	v	e
l	u	d	l	u	a	r	c	c
g	s	c	a	j	r	o	o	i
a	a	r	n	l	h	t	m	c
s	r	s	t	f	c	e	p	l
t	i	r	a	r	v	g	r	a
a	p	o	r	o	p	e	a	r
r	e	d	u	c	i	r	r	o

1 Pienso que se debe *usar* más el transporte público. *a*
2 Creo que es necesario **reducir** la contaminación. **c**
3 Es necesario **proteger** la naturaleza. **g**
4 Opino que no se debe **tirar** basura al suelo. **i**
5 Para mí es necesario **plantar** árboles. **e**
6 Es necesario **reciclar** papel y vidrio. **h**
7 No es necesario **usar** el coche. **j**
8 Se debe **consumir** menos energía. **f**
9 No se debe **malgastar** agua. **b**
10 Se deben **comprar** productos ecológicos. **d**

2

Answers

1 Creo que/Pienso que/Opino que se debe proteger la naturaleza.
2 Es necesario usar más el transporte público.
3 Creo que/Pienso que/Opino que se debe plantar árboles.
4 Es necesario comprar productos ecológicos.

9 | 1 Piensa globalmente (Student Book pp. 158–159)

Main topics and objectives

- Discussing local solutions
- Using **para** + infinitive (in order to...)

Grammar

- **para** + infinitive (in order to...)

Key language

Me preocupa(n) más...
El mayor problema es...
El peor problema es...
la destrucción del ecosistema

la contaminación del aire
la basura
el calentamiento global
las especies amenazadas
la sequía

A ver...
Un momento...
Pues... no lo sé.
Espera...

Para ahorrar agua...
Para reducir la contaminación del aire...
Para consumir menos energía...
Para usar menos gasolina...

Para evitar la basura...
Para luchar contra el calentamiento global...
...es mejor...

Resources

CD 4, tracks 26–27
Cuaderno Verde, page 89

Starter 1

To review language for talking about environmental problems; to review *(no) se debe/es necesario*

Give students 3 minutes working in pairs to come up with as many sentences as they can offering a solution to environmental problems and featuring **se debe**, **no se debe** or **es necesario**.

Students swap answers with other pairs. Hear answers. The pair with the most correct responses wins.

1 Empareja las frases con las fotos. ¿Qué significan?

Reading. Students match the phrases on global problems to the correct pictures.

Answers
a 4 **b** 1 **c** 5 **d** 2 **e** 3

⭐ ResultsPlus

Tip box on listening for detail.

2 Listen. Which issue is each speaker most concerned about? Write a letter from exercise 1. (1–5)

Listening. Students listen to five people talking about global problems and identify the issue each speaker is most concerned about, using the phrases in exercise 1 (**a–e**). The tip box gives advice on exactly what to listen out for.

Audioscript *Track 26*

1 *Creo que el mayor problema es la destrucción del ecosistema.*
2 *La sequía no es un problema muy serio en mi región. Me preocupa más el calentamiento global porque afecta a todo el mundo.*
3 *Para mí la destrucción del ecosistema es un problema, pero el peor problema es la contaminación del aire y la basura.*
4 *Opino que la sequía es el mayor problema aunque las especies amenazadas me preocupan bastante.*
5 *La contaminación del aire no es un problema muy serio donde vivo, pero las especies amenazadas sí.*

Answers
1 a **2** c **3** b **4** e **5** d

3 Con tu compañero/a, haz este cuestionario.

Speaking. Students do the environment quiz, giving their answers as complete sentences and responding to their partner's answers. A sample exchange is given. Some vocabulary is glossed for support.

⭐ ResultsPlus

Tip box on thinking time expressions.

Starter 2

To review structures followed by the infinitive; to review *(no) se debe/es necesario*

Write up the following, jumbling the order of the words. Give students 3 minutes to write out each sentence in the correct order.

1 *Es importante pensar globalmente y actuar localmente.*
2 *Es necesario apagar las luces en casa.*
3 *Se debe usar el transporte público.*
4 *Se debe reciclar y reutilizar cosas.*

Check answers, asking students to translate the sentences into English. Ask students what form of the verb follows structures like **Es importante**....

4 Escucha y escribe las letras correctas del cuestionario (ejercicio 3). (1–6)

Listening. Students listen to and note the correct answers to the quiz in exercise 3.

Audioscript *Track 27*

1 *Para ahorrar agua, es mejor ducharse. No se debe malgastar agua.*
2 *Para reducir la contaminación del aire, es mejor andar o ir en bici, en vez de usar el coche.*
3 *Para consumir menos energía, es mejor apagar las luces.*
4 *Para usar menos gasolina, es mejor comprar productos locales.*
5 *Para evitar la basura, es mejor llevar una bolsa a la compra.*
6 *Para luchar contra el calentamiento global, es mejor hacerse miembro de un grupo ecologista.*

> **Answers**
>
> **1** a **2** a **3** b **4** a **5** a **6** b

G Grammar

Use the Grammar box to cover the **para +** infinitive structure.

5 Lee el texto y rellena los espacios en blanco con las palabras del cuadro.

Reading. Students read and complete the gap-fill text using the words supplied.

> **Answers**
>
> **1** proteger **2** consumir **3** ahorrar
> **4** reducir **5** evitar

6 Lee el texto. Contesta a las preguntas en inglés.

Reading. Students read the text, then answer the comprehension questions in English.

> **Answers**
>
> **1** global warming
> **2** the plants and the animals will die
> **3** tries to switch off lights when he leaves a room, goes to school by bike or walks to school
> **4** the price of petrol
> **5** less petrol is needed to transport them

7 Write a paragraph giving your opinions on global issues.

Writing. Students write a paragraph giving their own opinions on global issues. A model is supplied.

When students have finished, they could swap texts with a partner and check for accuracy. Ask them to identify but not correct errors, then do a second draft of their own text, correcting as necessary.

Suggest students look at the Spanish website of a voluntary organisation which is trying to tackle these issues, e.g. Oxfam, Greenpeace, Amnesty International. (Change the preferences in your search engine to Spanish only, and key in any of these to find the Spanish sites.) Ask students to summarise in English four facts on one particular issue.

Plenary

Ask students to identify in the exercise 6 texts at least four items of vocabulary to note down and learn for this topic. Which do they think are most useful to them and why?

Point out that it is always easier to learn and remember things you are interested in and that the speaking and writing parts of the exam give lots of opportunity to take advantage of this. Encourage students to develop a personal slant to their vocabulary lists, i.e. to think about which topics they are interested in writing and talking about and to use the Student Book and other resources to pull together information on these topics.

Remind students of the importance of noting, learning and reviewing vocabulary on an ongoing basis.

Cuaderno Verde, page 89

1

Answers

lacontaminacióndelaire/lasespeciesamenazadas/
lasequía/elcalentamientoglobal/labasura/
ladestruccióndelecosistema

1 las especies amenazadas
2 la contaminación del aire
3 la basura
4 el calentamiento global
5 la destrucción del ecosistema
6 la sequía

2

Answers

1 Para luchar contra *el calentamiento global*, no se
  debe malgastar energía.
2 Para proteger **las especies amenazadas** – las plantas
  y los animales – es necesario consumir menos
  energía.
3 Para evitar **la sequía**, se debe ahorrar agua y
  ducharse, en vez de bañarse.
4 Para reducir **la contaminación del aire**, se debe usar
  el transporte público o ir a pie.
5 Para evitar **la basura**, es necesario no tirar papeles
  al suelo.

3

Answers

(**c**) *En mi opinión, la destrucción del* (**f**) ecosistema es
el mayor (**a**) problema, así que es importante plantar (**e**)
árboles y proteger las especies (**h**) amenazadas. También,
para ayudar, se puede (**b**) usar menos energía, comprar
productos ecológicos y no (**g**) contaminar el aire. Se debe
gastar menos (**d**) gasolina y no se debe usar el coche.

2 Voluntarios (Student Book pp. 160–161)

Main topics and objectives
- Talking about global citizenship
- Using the future tense

Grammar
- The future tense
- Using **si** + present + future

Key language
Si me hago voluntario/a,...
Si doy dinero a Oxfam,...
Si apadrino a un niño,...
Si reciclo y reutilizo,...
Si compro productos de comercio justo,...
mejoraré la sociedad
daré al niño la posibilidad de sobrevivir
cuidaré el medio ambiente
ayudaré a otras personas
ayudaré a los trabajadores

los sin techo
la pobreza y el hambre

la discriminación y el racismo
el terrorismo

Resources
CD 4, tracks 28–29
Cuaderno Verde, pages 90–91
Gramática 202

Starter 1

To review verbs used to talk about global issues

Write up the following, omitting the words in bold. Give students 3 minutes to complete the table.

mejoro	mejorar	to improve
doy	**dar**	to give
hago	**hacer**	**to make**
cuido	cuidar	to look after
ayudo	**ayudar**	to help
me hago	hacerse	to become

Check answers. Ask students to identify the verb forms in each column (present tense, infinitive).

1 Lee las frases. ¿Qué significan?

Reading. Students translate the text in the speech bubbles.

Answers
1 *If I become a volunteer,...*
2 *If I give money to Oxfam,...*
3 *If I sponsor a child,...*
4 *If I recycle and reuse,...*
5 *If I buy Fairtrade products,...*

G Grammar
Use the Grammar box to introduce the future tense.

R Students translate the following into Spanish: I will give, you will go out, he will do, she will have, I will be, you will put.

(*Answers:* daré, saldrás, hará, tendrá, seré/estaré, pondrás)

2 Listen to the phrases from exercise 1, which are now finished off by the speakers. Write the letter of the phrase below that they use. What does it mean? (1-5)

Listening. Students listen to the complete statements made by the five people in exercise 1. They match each speech bubble (**1–5**) to the correct conclusion (from **a–e**). They then translate the conclusions into English. Some vocabulary is glossed for support.

Audioscript *Track 28*

1 Silvana
Si me hago voluntaria, mejoraré la sociedad.
2 Hasan
Si doy dinero a Oxfam, ayudaré a otras personas.
3 Gabriel
Si apadrino a un niño, daré al niño la posibilidad de sobrevivir.
4 Sabrina
Si reciclo y reutilizo, cuidaré el medio ambiente.
5 Juan Pablo
Si compro productos de comercio justo, ayudaré a los trabajadores.

Answers
1 a – I will improve society.
2 d – I will help other people.
3 b – I will give the child the opportunity to survive.
4 c – I will be looking after the environment.
5 e – I will help the workers.

3 Con tu compañero/a, haz estos diálogos.

Speaking. In pairs: students put together dialogues in which people put themselves forward for voluntary work. They take it in turn to ask and answer questions, using the sets of prompts supplied for Pablo and Esther. The questions and sample answer openings are also supplied.

G Grammar

Use the Grammar box to review **si** + present tense, + future tense.

✚ For further practice of the future tense, students give the correct verb forms for the following. They should use the verb tables at the back of the Student Book to look up any future stems they are not sure of.

trabajar – él
ir – ella
decidir – yo
estar – tú
ser – ella
escribir – yo
tener – él
hacer – tú
aprender – yo

Starter 2

To review sentences with *si* + present, + future

Write up the following. Give students 3 minutes to rewrite the sentences replacing the infinitives in brackets with the 'I' form of the verb in the correct tense.

1 *Si me (hacer) voluntaria, (mejorar) la sociedad.*
2 *Si (reciclar), (cuidar) el medio ambiente.*
3 *Si (comprar) productos de comercio justo, (ayudar) a los trabajadores.*

(*Answers:* **1** hago, mejoraré   **2** reciclo, cuidaré
3 compro, ayudaré)

4 Lee y empareja las frases con las fotos.

Reading. Students read the phrases and match them to the correct pictures.

Answers
1 d   **2** c   **3** a   **4** b

5 Escucha. Copia y completa la tabla en inglés. (1–4)

Listening. Students copy out the table. They listen to four people talking about what they can do to help resolve global problems, and complete the table with the details in English.

Audioscript *Track 29*

1 *Me preocupa mucho el hambre en África. Es una situación malísima en este momento. Si trabajo como voluntario, ayudaré a la gente en un país africano.*
2 *Me preocupa mucho el problema de los sin techo. Si compro la revista* Big Issue, *ayudaré un poco.*

3 *Creo que la discriminación y el racismo son problemas muy serios en la sociedad. Si me hago miembro de Amnistía Internacional, mejoraré la sociedad.*
4 *Para mí el peor problema es la pobreza. Si apadrino a un niño, daré al niño la posibilidad de sobrevivir.*

Answers

	problem	action
1	*famine in Africa*	work as a volunteer
2	homelessness	buy *The Big Issue*
3	discrimination and racism	join Amnesty International
4	poverty	sponsor a child

6 Read the texts and answer the questions below. Write K (Karim), S (Silvia) or K+S (Karim and Silvia).

Reading. Students read the two texts, then identify who is being described in the questions: Karim (K), Sylvia (S) or both of them (K + S).

Answers
1 S   **2** K   **3** K+S   **4** S   **5** K   **6** S

✚ Go round the class reading the texts in exercise 6. Students take it in turn to read a sentence aloud in Spanish and to translate it into English.

7 You are Luis. Write a paragraph about your ambitions. You can also add your own ideas. Try to include sentences with '*si* + present + future'.

Writing. Students read Luis's details, then write a paragraph about him. They should focus on what he wants to do, using the si + present, + future structure, but also include other details of his abilities and interests.

🗣 Ask students to research opportunities for young people to get involved in voluntary work in your area and to summarise this in Spanish. They could exchange emails on this topic with students in your Spanish partner school, if you have one.

Plenary

Ask students to summarise what tenses are used in the structure with **si** covered in this unit, giving you examples.

Practise the structure by prompting in Spanish with either the **si** clause or the clause featuring the future tense: students give the rest of the sentence. You could move on to prompting in English with either clause for students to produce the Spanish version.

Cuaderno Verde, pages 90–91

1

> **Answers**
>
> **1** *María* **2** Caterina **3** Luisa **4** Ana
> **5** Gustavo **6** Santiago **7** Marcos

2

> **Answers**
>
> **1** no hay mucho trabajo
> **2** trabajaré como voluntario
> **3** el año pasado conocí a mi novio
> **4** haré nuevos amigos
> **5** personas mayores
> **6** si me hago voluntaria
> **7** vi la pobreza
> **8** doy mi tiempo

3

Answers

1	I will help	*ayudaré*
2	you will give	darás
3	he will look after	cuidará
4	she will work	trabajará
5	I will do	haré
6	you will have	tendrás
7	he will put	pondrá
8	she will go out	saldrá

4

> **Answers**
>
> - ¿Cómo te llamas?
> - Me llamo José.
> - ¿Cuántos (**1**) ***años tienes***?
> - Tengo diecinueve años.
> - ¿Por qué (**2**) **quieres trabajar** como voluntario?
> - Odio la discriminación y el racismo. Si (**3**) **soy voluntario**, ayudaré a otras personas y (**4**) **mejoraré** la sociedad.
> - ¿En qué te gustaría trabajar?
> - Quiero trabajar con los (**5**) **niños sin techo** en la India. (**6**) **Si trabajo** como voluntario, (**7**) **tendré** unas (**8**) **experiencias** muy positivas y (**9**) **conoceré a** gente nueva.

3 Sin techo, sin derecho... (Student Book pp. 162–163)

Main topics and objectives

- Talking about homelessness
- Recognising different time frames

Grammar

- Recognising the preterite, present and future tenses

Key language

las personas sin casa/sin techo/
 sin hogar
¿Cómo te llamas?

¿Cuántos años tienes?
Te quedaste sin casa hace unos
 años, ¿verdad?
¿Cómo saliste de esta situación?
¿Cómo es un día típico?
¿Qué planes de futuro tienes?

Me llamo...
Tengo... años.
Sí, hace... años.
Un día conocí a...
Me ayudó mucho.
Encontré trabajo como...
Por lo general, estás...
Buscas...

En la calle hay problemas muy
 graves como...

En el futuro me gustaría...
viajar
conocer otros países
tener nuevas experiencias

Resources

CD 4, track 30
Cuaderno Verde, pages 92–93

Starter 1

To review big numbers

Write up the following, jumbling the order of the second column. Give students 3 minutes to match the numerals with the numbers in words.

2 000 000	dos millones
20 000	veinte mil
92%	noventa y dos por ciento
½	la mitad
29%	veintinueve por ciento
20 000 000	veinte millones
90 000	noventa mil

Check answers.

1 Read the text on homeless people and complete the sentences below.

Reading. Students read the text and complete the gap-fill sentences in English summarising it.

Answers

1 3 million **2** 30 000 **3** 82,7% **4** 29,9% **5** 50%

2 Listen and read. Match each numbered section of the text with one of the pictures.

Listening. Students listen to the interview with Arantxa, reading the text at the same time. They then match each section (**1–6**) with the appropriate picture (from **a–f**). Some vocabulary is glossed for support.

Point out to students that this activity focuses on listening for gist.

Audioscript *Track 30*

1 – ¿Cómo te llamas?
 – Me llamo Arantxa.
 – ¿Cuántos años tienes, Arantxa?
 – Tengo veinticuatro años.

2 – Y Arantxa, te quedaste sin techo hace unos años, ¿verdad?
 – Sí, hace cuatro años.
 – ¿Qué te pasó exactamente?
 – Pues, primero perdí a mi papá y luego a mi mamá. No tenía dinero ni familia.

3 – ¿Qué tal lo pasaste?
 – Lo pasé muy mal. En la calle hay problemas muy graves como el consumo de alcohol y de drogas y la violencia...

4 – ¿Cómo saliste de esta situación?
 – Un día conocí a un voluntario y este hombre me ayudó mucho. Ahora trabajo para su organización humanitaria. La organización se llama 'Café y bollos para los sin hogar'. Vivo en un piso en el centro.

5 – ¿Cómo es un día típico para una persona sin techo?
 – Difícil y triste. Por lo general, estás solo. Andas mucho. Buscas comida o dinero. Un día una señora me dio diez euros. Pasé el día entero en una cafetería. Bebí chocolate y leí el periódico. ¡Qué lujo!

6 – ¿Qué planes de futuro tienes?
 – A ver, en el futuro voy a viajar. Me encantaría conocer otros países. Me preocupa mucho el medio ambiente, sobre todo el calentamiento global. Si puedo ayudar, seré feliz...

Answers

1 a **2** f **3** d **4** e **5** b **6** c

Starter 2

To practise recognising different verb tenses

Write up the following. Give students 3 minutes to identify the tense used in each sentence.

1 Un día, un señor me dio veinte euros.
2 Ahora trabajo para una organización humanitaria.
3 En el futuro voy a viajar.
4 Si puedo ayudar, seré feliz.

Check answers (**1** preterite, **2** present, **3** near future, **4** future), asking students to translate the sentences into English.

3 Lee el diálogo otra vez y contesta a las preguntas en inglés.

Reading. Students reread the text in exercise 2 and answer the comprehension questions in English.

Answers

1 four years ago
2 none
3 alcohol abuse, drug abuse, violence
4 a volunteer
5 for the organisation that helped her
6 you are alone, you walk a lot, you look for food or money
7 a woman gave her 10€
8 global warming

✪ ResultsPlus

Tip box on how to answer questions in a reading task.

4 Match up the Spanish and English infinitives.

Reading. Students match the Spanish and English infinitives.

Answers

1 perder – *to lose*
2 salir – *to get out of*
3 conocer – *to get to know*
4 trabajar – *to work*
5 vivir – *to live*
6 leer – *to read*
7 beber – *to drink*
8 viajar – *to travel*
9 poder – *can/to be able to*
10 ser – *to be*

5 Copy and complete the grid with the colour-coded verbs from the exercise 2 text which refer to the past, present and future. Add the English.

Reading. Students copy out the grid. They reread the text in exercise 2 and complete the grid with the verbs from the text (all shown in colour), writing them in the past, present or future column as appropriate, and translating them into English.

past	present	future	English
perdí			I lost
(lo) pasé			I had
saliste			you went out
conocí			I got to know
bebí			I drank
leí			I read
	trabajo		I work
	vivo		I live
	puedo		I can
		voy a viajar	I am going to travel
		seré	I will be

6 Invent an interview with a homeless person. Use the *Vocabulario* section to help you.

Speaking. In pairs: students make up an interview with a homeless person, taking it in turn to ask and answer questions. The questions and sample answer openings are supplied.

Selected pairs could act out the interviews at the front of the class. Encourage the rest of the class to give constructive feedback on content, accuracy and acting ability.

🄡 Students write out their interviews.

Plenary

Ask students to imagine they are giving advice to students just about to start preparing for their GCSE in Spanish. Can they come up with six tips on how to do well in the exam? Write up suggestions and encourage students to copy the list and keep it as a final checklist to help them with revision.

Cuaderno Verde, page 92

1

Answers

1 ¿Cómo te llamas?
   Me llamo Santiago.
2 ¿Cuántos años tienes?
   Tengo veinte años.
3 ¿Te quedaste sin casa hace unos años?
   Sí, **perdí a mis padres en un accidente.**
4 ¿Cómo saliste de esta situación?
   Me **ayudó un voluntario de la Cruz Roja.** *Encontré*
   trabajo como camarero en un bar.
5 ¿Cómo es un día típico en la calle?
   Es muy peligroso porque hay mucha violencia.
6 ¿Qué planes de futuro tienes?
   En el futuro me gustaría viajar y conocer nuevos
   países/conocer nuevos países y viajar.

2

Answers

Answers

1 His name is Santiago.
2 He is twenty years old.
3 He lost his parents in an accident.
4 A volunteer from the Red Cross helped him.
5 He got a job as a waiter in a bar.
6 It is very dangerous because there is a lot of violence.
7 In the future he would like to travel and get to know
   new countries.

Cuaderno Verde, page 93

1

Answers

		Present (I)	Past (I)	Future (I)
1	to help (ayudar)	*ayudo*	**ayudé**	ayudaré
2	to drink (beber)	**bebo**	bebí	**beberé**
3	to live (vivir)	vivo	**viví**	**viviré**
4	to buy (comprar)	**compro**	compré	**compraré**
5	to use (usar)	uso	**usé**	usaré
6	to waste (malgastar)	**malgasto**	malgasté	malgastaré
7	to know (conocer)	conozco	**conocí**	**conoceré**
8	to recycle (reciclar)	reciclo	**reciclé**	reciclaré
9	to go (ir)	**voy**	fui	iré
10	to do/make (hacer)	hago	**hice**	**haré**
11	to have (tener)	**tengo**	tuve	**tendré**

2

Answers

1 *Se debe vivir…*
2 Es necesario usar…
3 No se debe comprar…
4 Para reciclar…
5 Se debe beber…
6 Se debe ayudar…
7 No es necesario malgastar…
8 Para hacer…

Topics revised

● Talking about the environment

Resources

CD 5, tracks 40–42

Overview

Read through the task box at the top of the page and outline for students how this section works. They will hear a Speaking controlled assessment model presentation in three parts and do exercises focused on the language used. These exercises, along with the advice/activities on how to improve speaking performance in Results Plus, will help them prepare to give a presentation of their own on the topic.

1 You are going to listen to Helen, an exam candidate, giving a presentation on the environment. Listen to part 1 and match up the two halves of Helen's sentences.

Listening. Explain to the students that they will hear a sample of the kind of presentation they are expected to have in the Speaking controlled assessment.

They listen to the first part of the presentation and match the sentence halves.

Audioscript *Track 40*

Part 1

Voy a hablar de los problemas con el medio ambiente en mi región. Vivo en una ciudad industrial y el mayor problema es que hay mucha contaminación porque hay demasiado tráfico y muchas fábricas. También hay muchos atascos y mucho ruido. Otro problema es que hay mucha basura. ¡Qué feo! Y opino que no tenemos muchos espacios verdes.

El año pasado en el colegio, no hice nada para proteger el medio ambiente. Pero ahora, tenemos contenedores. Por eso reciclo papel y vidrio por ejemplo. Nunca tiro basura al suelo. Y para consumir menos energía, apago las luces en el colegio y siempre desenchufo los ordenadores.

Answers

1 e **2** b **3** a **4** d **5** c **6** f

✚ Students listen again and identify all the instances of **mucho/a(s)** used, explaining the ending of the word in each case.

(*Answers:* mucha (FS – contaminación), muchas (FP – fábricas), muchos (MP – atascos), mucho (MS – ruido), mucha (FS – basura), muchos (MP – espacios verdes))

2 Listen to part 2 of Helen's presentation and note down the words that fill the gaps.

Listening. Students now listen to the second part of Helen's presentation and complete the gap-fill

version of the transcript. The answers are supplied in random order for support.

With a confident class you could ask students to read the text and try to work out plausible answers first, then use the recording to check.

Audioscript *Track 41*

Part 2

*En casa reutilizo lo más posible. Para ahorrar agua, **me ducho** en vez de bañarme. Cuando voy de compras **siempre** llevo una bolsa y compro productos locales. **Creo** que es muy importante. Ayer fui de compras pero no compré mucho y **cogí** el autobús en vez de usar el coche.*

*Por lo general, **para** proteger el medio ambiente, creo que primero se debe usar más el transporte **público** y reducir la contaminación. También se **debe** plantar más árboles y proteger la naturaleza. Eso es **importante**. Se debe mantener el agua limpia y no se debe consumir **demasiada** energía. No se debe encender todas las luces por **ejemplo**.*

Answers

Also in bold in the audioscript.
1 me ducho **2** siempre **3** Creo **4** cogí **5** para
6 público **7** debe **8** importante **9** demasiada
10 ejemplo

3 Now listen to part 3 of Helen's assessment. In which order does she use these phrases?

Listening. Students listen to the third and final part of Helen's presentation and answer the questions. These questions focus on linguistic detail. You may need to play the recording more than once.

Audioscript *Track 42*

Part 3

– *¿Qué vas a hacer en el futuro para proteger el medio ambiente?*
– *Creo que me voy a hacer miembro de un grupo ecologista. Me gustaría ser voluntaria con Greenpeace porque opino que es un grupo importante. Va a ser una experiencia muy positiva.*
– *¿Qué problemas te preocupan en el mundo?*
– *Bueno… para mí hay muchos problemas serios en el mundo. Me preocupan la discriminación y el racismo. También me preocupan mucho el calentamiento global y el precio de la gasolina. Opino que hay demasiada contaminación y la sequía es un problema. No se debe malgastar agua. Hay mucha pobreza y hambre en el mundo. Es triste.*

Answers

f, d, a, e, c, b

4 Here are the questions Helen was asked in part 3. What do the words mean?

Reading. Students read the two questions and say what the words in red mean.

> **Answers**
>
> para proteger el medio ambiente – *to protect the environment*
> te preocupan – *concern you*

⊛ ResultsPlus

The Results Plus support for speaking activities is differentiated, allowing students to identify and work towards their target level: covering the basics, Grade C, increasing their marks. Encourage students to adopt the techniques in these sections in all extended speaking activities.

Read through and discuss the Results Plus section together.

5 Now it's your turn! Prepare and give a presentation on the environment to your partner or your teacher.

Speaking. Students give a presentation on the environment in the style of a controlled assessment task. They should use all the support supplied, here and elsewhere on the spread:

- the Results Plus advice on the language to include
- Helen's responses, adapted to talk about themselves
- the English points in the task box, p. 164
- their answers to exercises 1–4.

Each student gives a presentation as the person answering the questions. If they are working with a partner, they will take turns asking and answering.

If possible, record the presentations or have the students record themselves. They can then swap recordings with a partner, listen to each other's version and offer comments on how it might be improved. A simple marking system is suggested (one/two/three stars for listed categories). Students should then identify two or three areas which they would like to improve next time they do an extended speaking task.

Topics revised

● Writing about the environment

1 Read the text and put these topics in the order of the text.

Reading. Students read Amy's text on the environment and reorder the topics (**a–e**) as they are mentioned.

Answers

d, c, e, b, a

2 Find these phrases in Spanish in the text.

Reading. Students reread the text in exercise 1 and find in it the Spanish versions of the ten English phrases listed.

Answers

1 …para mí el mayor problema es…
2 No hay muchos espacios verdes.
3 Yo creo que primero se debe plantar más árboles.
4 Otro problema en Manchester es que…
5 Para proteger el medio ambiente…
6 Para mí es importante ser…
7 Me preocupan mucho el medio ambiente y el calentamiento global.
8 Ahora me ducho en vez de bañarme.
9 …nunca utilizo bolsas de plástico.
10 Me voy a hacer voluntaria.

3 Read the text again. Make a list of the verbs in the preterite. There are seven of them. Which of them is in the 'we' form?

Reading. Students reread the text and identify the seven preterite verbs, identifying which of them is in the 'we' form.

Answers

fui, tuve, vi, trabajé, pasé, cenamos ('we' form), me hice

4 Read the text again and answer the questions in English.

Reading. Students reread the text in exercise 1 and answer the comprehension questions in English.

Answers

1 pollution
2 too much traffic/traffic jams
3 plant more trees, use public transport more
4 went to clean the streets (with a group of Scouts)
5 they had dinner together
6 she thinks it's important to be a responsible person
7 has a shower instead of a bath; turns off lights; never uses plastic bags; recycles glass, paper and plastic
8 do voluntary work, travel, get to know other cultures

5 You might be asked to write about the environment as a controlled assessment task. Use the Results Plus to help you prepare your account.

Students read through the language support material supplied in preparation for doing their own extended writing task in exercise 6.

⊛ ResultsPlus

The Results Plus section gives students the support they need to structure and improve their writing. The support is differentiated, allowing students to identify and work towards their target level: covering the basics, Grade C, increasing their marks. Encourage students to adopt the kind of approach taken in this section in all extended writing activities.

6 Now write a full account of your views on the environment.

Writing. Students write their own text on the environment in the style of a controlled assessment task (at least 100 words). As well as the Results Plus guidelines on the language to include, they should use all the support supplied here:

● Amy's text, adapted to refer to themselves
● relevant language from throughout the module
● the sample structure for the text.

7 Check carefully what you have written.

Writing. Students check their own work using the list of features supplied.

This section helps students develop their listening and reading skills in preparation for the exam.

Resources

CD 5, tracks 43–46

LEER

1 Read these pieces of advice on helping the environment and decide which part of our lives they will affect. Write the number followed by the correct letter. *(3 marks)*

Reading. Students read the three pieces of advice in Spanish and match them to the correct topic in English. There is one distractor.

These questions approximate to Grade D.

Answers
1 c **2** d **3** b

⭐ ResultsPlus

Tip box on looking for paraphrases.

2 Read these comments in a magazine by a homeless person and identify the four places he sometimes spends the night. Write the number followed by the correct letter. *(4 marks)*

Reading. Students read the text and identify the four places the speaker sometimes spends the night. There is one distractor.

All the places listed in the options are mentioned in the text. An accurate interpretation of the text eliminates the incorrect option. This question approximates to Grade C.

Answers
1 b **2** c **3** d **4** a

⭐ ResultsPlus

Tip box on looking at all the answer options and reading the text carefully.

3 Opinions on global issues. Answer the questions below. Write the person's name. *(4 marks)*

Reading. Students read the five texts, then identify who is being described in each of the questions. There is one distractor.

This question approximates to Grade C.

Answers
1 Beatriz **2** Ana **3** Noemí **4** Carlos

⭐ ResultsPlus

Tip box on tackling reading tasks in exams: reading the questions first, reading all text in detail, looking out for qualifiers and negatives.

ESCUCHAR

4 Listen to Roberto talking about the environment in his town and answer the questions in English. *(4 marks)*

Listening. Students listen to Roberto talking about the environment in his town and answer the comprehension questions in English.

The first two questions approximate to Grade G and the last two approximate to Grade F.

Audioscript *Track 43*

1 *Me gustan los jardines en mi ciudad.*
   [Repeated as above]
2 *Odio las tiendas en mi barrio.*
   [Repeated as above]
3 *En el futuro el transporte público va a ser muy bueno.*
   [Repeated as above]
4 *Para ayudar, yo reciclo todo tipo de cosas.*
   [Repeated as above]

Answers
1 the gardens **2** the shops **3** public transport
4 recycles (all sorts of things)

⭐ ResultsPlus

Tip box on listening for key words.

5 Listen to Alicia talking about recycling bins. Which bins do they have in (1) the shopping centre, (2) the restaurant and (3) the street? Write down the correct letter for each place. *(3 marks)*

Listening. Students listen to Alicia talking about recycling bins and identify what can be recycled (from **a–d**) in the three places mentioned. There is one distractor.

The vocabulary and structure here are quite straightforward but the level is raised by the stimulus text being longer. This question approximates to Grade E.

Audioscript *Track 44*

En el centro comercial hay un contenedor de latas. Es muy útil. En el restaurante hay un contenedor de botellas de vidrio. Es necesario. Y en la calle hay un contenedor de papel. Es muy práctico.
[Repeated as above]

Answers

1 a **2** b **3** c

 ResultsPlus

Tip box on keeping answers as simple as possible.

6 Improving the environment. Complete the sentences in English. *(3 marks)*

Listening. Students listen to three people talking about the environment and complete the sentence in English summarising what each of them thinks should be done.

This question contains some redundant language and approximates to Grade D.

Audioscript *Track 45*

1 – ¿Cómo podemos ayudar al medio ambiente, Beatriz?
*   – Tenemos espacios verdes, pero se debe plantar más árboles.*
[Repeated as above]
2 – ¿Qué piensas tú, Ricardo?
*   – Necesitamos electricidad y se debe apagar las luces.*
[Repeated as above]
3 – ¿Cuál es tu opinión, Manuela?
*   – Hay demasiados atascos, así que se debe andar al trabajo.*
[Repeated as above]

Answers

1 to plant more trees
2 switching/turning off lights/saving electricity
3 walk to work

7 Listen to this reporter interviewing a homeless person. Answer the questions below by writing down the letter which indicates the correct answer. *(4 marks)*

Listening. Students listen to an interview and answer the multiple-choice questions.

Each part contains more than one idea and so students need to identify and understand the correct language in order to select the right answer. This question approximates to Grade C.

Audioscript *Track 46*

1 – ¿Cómo será tu vida si sigues sin casa?
*   – Creo que me pondré muy enferma. Ya tengo tos y muchas veces tengo frío por la noche.*
[Repeated as above]
2 – ¿Y si no encuentras trabajo?
*   – Voy a pedir más dinero a la gente en la calle. No puedo volver a mi familia porque no tenemos buenas relaciones en este momento.*
[Repeated as above]
3 – ¿Cómo sobrevives en la calle, Marta?
*   – Algunas personas consumen alcohol para olvidar sus problemas. Yo prefiero hablar con voluntarios porque me ayudan mucho.*
[Repeated as above]
4 – ¿Y qué planes tienes para el futuro?
*   – Me gustaría ayudar a otros sin hogar en el futuro. Y quizás conseguir trabajo, por ejemplo en un bar o en un restaurante lavando platos.*
[Repeated as above]

Answers

1 c **2** a **3** b **4** b

 ResultsPlus

Tip box on identifying distractors.

● Self-access reading and writing

A Reinforcement

1 Write out these sentences correctly and then translate them into English.

Reading. Students write out the words snakes as sentences, then translate the sentences into English.

Answers

1 Si reciclo y reutilizo, cuidaré el medio ambiente.
2 Si compro productos de comercio justo, ayudaré a los trabajadores.
3 Si apadrino a un niño, daré al niño la posibilidad de sobrevivir.
4 Si me hago voluntaria, mejoraré la sociedad.
5 Si doy dinero a Oxfam, ayudaré a otras personas.

2 Match each object with the time you think it would take to decompose.

Reading. Students match the objects to the correct time.

Answers

1 e 2 d 3 b 4 g 5 a 6 f 7 c

3 Find the answers to these questions and write out the whole conversation in order.

Reading. Students work out (from the options supplied) the answers to the questions, then write out the conversation (questions plus appropriate responses) in full.

Answers

● ¿Cómo te llamas?
■ Me llamo Elena.
● ¿Cuántos años tienes ?
■ Tengo diecinueve años.
● Te quedaste sin casa hace unos años, ¿verdad?
■ Sí, hace dos años.
● ¿Cómo saliste de esta situación?
■ Un día conocí a una chica que me ayudó mucho.
● ¿Qué planes de futuro tienes?
■ A ver, en el futuro me gustaría viajar y conocer otros países. Me encanta tener nuevas experiencias.

B Extension

1 Complete these sentences in English.

Reading. Students read the text and complete the sentences summarising it in English

Answers

1 Finca Bellavista is located **in the mountains of the Pacific south coast**.
2 They use **hydroelectric** and **solar** energy.
3 They reuse **water**.
4 There is a **recycling centre** and a community garden.
5 Although you are immersed in nature, it is possible to **connect to the internet**.

2 Read the text and answer these questions in English.

Reading. Students read the text and answer the comprehension questions in English.

Answers

1 make notes/draw
2 they are cheaper and reduce waste
3 give them away to other children
4 give them to someone smaller than yourself
5 wood

3 Match up the Spanish and English slogans.

Reading. Students match the Spanish and English sentences.

Answers

1 d 2 f 3 a 4 b 5 e 6 c

Gramática (Student Book pp. 190–217: answers to exercises)

The present tense

1

1 Me llamo Mónica y **vivo** en Barcelona.
2 Todos los días **chateo** con mis amigos por Internet.
3 De vez en cuando **juego** con el ordenador o con la Wii.
4 **Descargo** música por las tardes.
5 No **leo** mucho.
6 A veces barro el suelo y siempre **preparo** la comida.

2

1 ¿Qué **estudias** en el cole?
2 Normalmente **limpiamos** el coche los sábados.
3 Mi madre no **cocina** mucho porque no le gusta.
4 Mi padre **juega** al fútbol conmigo.
5 A veces **comemos** chocolates y caramelos.
6 Siempre **viajan** en avión porque es fácil.

3

1 Mis clases **empiezan** a las ocho.
2 Mis amigos y yo **necesitamos** unos bolígrafos y una regla.
3 Mi amigo Carlos **bebe** un refresco de cola todos los días.
4 Yo **prefiero** ir en bici.
5 A veces, en el recreo, nosotros **jugamos** al tenis.
6 Mi amiga Silvia **prefiere** las asignaturas prácticas.

The present tense – irregular

1

1 *Por la mañana* **voy** *al instituto en bicicleta. In the morning I go to school by bike.*
2 **Salgo** *a las ocho y media. I go out at half past eight.*
3 *Si llueve, no voy en bicicleta,* **cojo** *el autobús. If it rains, I don't go by bike, I catch the bus.*
4 **Tengo** *geografía los martes. I have geography on Tuesdays.*
5 *Después del colegio* **voy** *al club de ajedrez. Me gusta mucho. After school I go to chess club. I like it a lot.*
6 *Los domingos* **hago** *natación. On Sundays I go swimming.*

2

1 **Hago** *mis deberes después del colegio. I do my homework after school.*
2 Me gusta la biología porque **es** divertida y también es fácil. *I like biology because it is interesting and easy too.*
3 Cuando nieva, ¿**haces** esquí? *When it snows, do you go skiing?*
4 Si llueve, ¿**vas** de compras o **vas** al cine? *If it rains, do you go shopping or to the cinema?*
5 ¿A qué hora sale el tren? **Sale** a las ocho diez. *At what time does the train leave? It leaves at ten past eight.*
6 Generalmente mi hermano **va** en moto porque es rápido. *Generally my brother goes by motorbike because it's fast.*

3

1 **Salgo** a las ocho.
2 Cada noche yo **hago** mis deberes.
3 Mis padres **salen** mucho.
4 Yo **voy** en autobús pero tú vas en tren.
5 Mis amigos y yo **hacemos** natación cada sábado.
6 Mis padres **tienen** una casa muy bonita.

4

1 Bilbao **está** en el norte de España.
2 **Es** delgado y alto.
3 El aseo no **está** limpio.
4 Normalmente cojo el autobús porque no **es** caro.
5 **Estoy** en Francia.
6 ¿Por dónde se va al supermercado? – **Está** muy cerca.

Reflexive verbs

1

1 **Me despierto** a las siete.
2 **Me levanto** a las siete y diez.
3 Luego **me ducho**.
4 Después **me visto**.
5 No **me afeito**.
6 **Me acuesto** a las once.

2

1 ¿*Os* ducháis a menudo? *Do you shower often?*
2 Mi hermana *se* despierta temprano.
   b *My sister wakes up early.*
3 Normalmente *se* levanta a las seis de la mañana.
   e *Normally she gets up at six in the morning.*
4 ¿A qué hora *te* vistes?
   a *What time do you get dressed?*
5 *Nos* acostamos a la una de la madrugada.
   d *We go to bed at one in the morning.*
6 Mis padres *se* levantan a las siete.
   c *My parents get up at seven.*

3

> Los fines de semana (**1**) *me* despierto tarde. Me (**2**) **levanto** a las diez, veo la televisión y escucho música. Luego me gusta chatear un poco con mis amigos. Mi mejor amigo, Javier, (**3**) **se** levanta a eso de las once, pero se (**4**) **viste** rápidamente y nos (**5**) **encontramos** en el parque donde jugamos al fútbol juntos. ¿Y tú? ¿Qué haces los fines de semana? ¿A qué hora (**6**) **te** levantas?

The preterite

1

> 1 La semana pasada *leí* un libro muy bueno.
> 2 Ayer **compré** un reloj y luego fui al cine.
> 3 La semana pasada **comí** paella.
> 4 **Tuve** una fiesta para celebrar mi cumpleaños.
> 5 Ayer no **hice** nada en casa.
> 6 **Estudié** ocho asignaturas en el colegio.

2

> 1 *Fui* a la bolera.
> 2 **Compramos** un perro grande.
> 3 **Limpió** su dormitorio.
> 4 **Jugó** con el ordenador.
> 5 **Bebimos** zumo de naranja.
> 6 **Nadé** en la piscina del colegio.

3

> 1 **Desayuno** a las diez.
> *Present – I have breakfast*
> 2 Primero **fuimos** al museo.
> Preterite – we went
> 3 **Hace** mucho sol aquí.
> Present – it is (sunny)
> 4 Mi amigo **compró** unos recuerdos.
> Preterite – he bought
> 5 **Practiqué** natación en el mar cerca de mi casa.
> Preterite – I did (swimming)
> 6 Siempre **hago** mis deberes.
> Present – I do
> 7 En el colegio **comemos** a las doce y media.
> Present – we eat
> 8 Anoche mis amigos **fueron** al cine.
> Preterite – they went

Other past tenses

1

> 1 Mi piso en Madrid *era* muy pequeño.
> 2 Antes **comía** mucha pizza.
> 3 Mi jefe **era** muy simpático.
> 4 El chico **estaba** en la plaza.
> 5 En el hotel, **había** una piscina grande.
> 6 **Tenía** un perro cuando era joven.

2

> 1 *He trabajado* como enfermera en un hospital.
> 2 **Ha servido** a los clientes.
> 3 **Hemos hablado** inglés y francés.
> 4 **He estudiado** ciencias y matemáticas.
> 5 **Ha vigilado** a la gente que nada en la piscina.
> 6 **He comido** una paella muy rica.

3

> 1 Mi profesor de inglés *era* genial.
> 2 En el colegio **había** una biblioteca pequeña.
> 3 Los profesores **eran** antipáticos.
> 4 El camping no **tenía** restaurante.
> 5 El hotel **estaba** muy limpio.
> 6 Mis amigos **comían** hamburguesas.

Talking about the future

1

> 1 Mañana voy a <u>comer</u> paella.
> 2 Voy a <u>sacar</u> muchas fotos en Sevilla.
> 3 No voy a <u>mandar</u> mensajes.
> 4 ¿Vas a <u>estudiar</u> comercio el año que viene?
> 5 La semana que viene voy a <u>ir</u> a la discoteca.
> 6 El fin de semana voy a <u>dormir</u> mucho.

2

> 1 Mañana **me gustaría/quiero** comer paella.
> 2 **Quiero/Me gustaría** sacar muchas fotos en Sevilla.
> 3 No **quiero/me gustaría** mandar mensajes.
> 4 **Me gustaría/Quiero** estudiar comercio el año que viene.
> 5 La semana que viene **me gustaría/quiero** ir a la discoteca.
> 6 El fin de semana **quiero/me gustaría** dormir mucho.

3

> En el futuro, el mundo <u>va a ser</u> muy diferente porque la tecnología <u>va a cambiar</u>.
> Por ejemplo, muchos coches <u>van a ser</u> eléctricos y <u>vamos a tener</u> un sistema de transporte público mejor.
> Los institutos <u>van a ser</u> muy diferentes. <u>Van a tener</u> más ordenadores y los profesores <u>van a dar</u> clase a través de los 'podcasts'. Creo que <u>voy a usar</u> mi ordenador mucho más en el futuro.

4

> 1 *Voy a comprar un piso.*
> 2 Mis amigos van a **ir** al cine.
> 3 Hoy mi padre **va** a cocinar.
> 4 Vamos a **visitar** museos
> 5 Maite va **a** estudiar para sus exámenes.
> 6 Van **a** ir en autobús.
> 7 Voy a **comprar** un collar.
> 8 Hoy vamos **a** jugar al fútbol.

The future tense

1

1 d In the future I will be a ski instructor.
2 b You will speak Spanish very well.
3 c He will help others.
4 f You will have very positive experiences.
5 a We will recycle more.
6 e In the future, we will have problems.

3

A: ¿Cuántos alumnos (1) *estudiarán* español el año que viene?
B: Pues, no lo sé pero el colegio (2) **tendrá** más de quinientos alumnos en total.
A: ¿(3) **Habrá** un club de fotografía?
B: Sí. El club de fotografía (4) **será** los lunes a la hora de comer.
A: Y tú, ¿(5) **harás** algún deporte?
B: Si tengo tiempo, yo (6) **jugaré** al béisbol los viernes o (7) **nadaré** los martes.

Poder, querer, deber + infinitive

1

1 *No se debe llevar maquillaje.*
2 No se debe correr en los pasillos.
3 Se debe hacer los deberes.
4 Se debe llevar uniforme.
5 No se debe comer chicle.
6 Se debe salir.

2

1 *Quiere* ir al cine. *He wants to go to the cinema.*
2 **Podemos** comer chicle. *We can eat chewing gum.*
3 ¿**Quieres** leer revistas? *Do you want to read magazines?*
4 **Puedo** escuchar música. *I can listen to music.*
5 **Queremos** salir con amigos. *We want to go out with friends.*
6 **Pueden** ver la tele. *They can watch TV.*

3

1 *Deberías comer más pescado.*
2 No deberías comer perritos calientes.
3 Deberías comer verduras.
4 Deberías ir al instituto en bici.
5 No deberías fumar.
6 Deberías beber agua o zumo.

Verbs for giving opinions

1

1 Me gusta *nadar* en la piscina.
2 Me encanta **estudiar** matemáticas.
3 Me interesa **jugar** al tenis.
4 Me gusta **tocar** el piano.
5 Me encanta **escuchar** música.
6 Me interesa **ver** documentales.

2

1 I like swimming/I like to swim in the pool.
2 I love studying maths.
3 I'm interested in playing tennis.
4 I like to play the piano.
5 I love listening to music.
6 I'm interested in watching documentaries.

3

1 *Me gusta tocar la guitarra.*
2 Le gusta nadar en la piscina.
3 Nos gusta estudiar español.
4 Les gusta hacer vela.
5 Os gusta ver telenovelas.
6 ¿Te gusta comer carne?

4

1 **Prefiero ver** la tele.
2 **Odia estudiar** ciencias.
3 **Nos encanta comer** peras y uvas.
4 **Preferimos jugar** al fútbol.
5 **Odia navegar** por Internet.
6 ¿**Te gusta trabajar** al aire libre?

Nouns and articles

1

1 *El francés es interesante.*
2 Me gustan **las** matemáticas, **el** español y **la** geografía.
3 Mi hermana va a **la** discoteca.
4 **El** piso es muy grande.
5 Me duele **la** mano.
6 **La** foto es bastante buena.

2

1 *Me gustan **las** manzanas pero prefiero **los** plátanos.*
2 Me encanta **la** geografía porque es informativa.
3 Me gustan mucho **las** películas románticas.
4 No me gusta nada **el** zumo de naranja.
5 Me encantan **las** bicis pero **los** coches son más prácticos.
6 Odio **los** programas de deporte porque son aburridos.

3

1 En mi piso tengo **una** lavadora y **una** ducha.
2 En mi instituto hay **una** biblioteca pero **las** aulas son muy pequeñas.
3 En mi casa tenemos dos dormitorios, **una** cocina, **un** cuarto de baño y **un** salón bonito.
4 **El** pescado, **la** carne roja y **los** huevos contienen proteínas.
5 Me interesa **la** historia porque me gustan los edificios antiguos.
6 En mi opinión, **los** cigarrillos son muy malos.

Adjectives

1

1 Vivo en una ciudad *pequeña*.
2 Mis padres están **divorciados**.
3 Mi profesor de inglés es muy **antipático**.
4 Mi mejor amiga es **galesa**.
5 Trabajo en una empresa **grande**.
6 Las chicas son **españolas**.

2

1 Llevo una gorra *azul*.
2 Llevamos una corbata **negra**.
3 Me gusta el jersey **rojo**.
4 Mi hermano tiene un móvil **blanco**.
5 La lámpara de mi dormitorio es **verde**.
6 En el hotel las cortinas son **naranja(s)**.

3

1 Mi amiga María es bastante *seria*.
2 Mis padres son muy **inteligentes**.
3 Mi tía es un poco **perezosa**.
4 Mi abuelo es muy **hablador**.
5 Nunca somos **severos**.
6 Siempre somos **optimistas**.

Comparatives and superlatives

1

1 *María es más alta que Julia.*
2 José es menos atractivo que Antonio.
3 Paulina es más antipática que Federico.
4 Mi hermano es más perezoso que mi hermana.
5 Mi madre es más delgada que mi padre.
6 Mi amiga es menos gorda que mi amigo.

2

1 *María is taller than Julia.*
2 José is less attractive than Antonio.
3 Paulina is more unpleasant than Federico.
4 My brother is lazier than my sister.
5 My mother is thinner than my father.
6 My (female) friend is less fat than my (male) friend.

3

1 *El centro comercial es más moderno que el cine.*
2 Los coches son más rápidos que las bicicletas.
3 El inglés es menos útil que las matemáticas.
4 El ordenador es más caro que el libro.
5 La natación es mejor que la equitación.
6 Los caramelos son peores que el chocolate.

4

1 *S – This restaurant is the best in the city.*
2 S – My house is the most modern.
3 C – Your car is faster than my moped.
4 C – My dog is less stupid than my cat.
5 S – My skirt is the prettiest.
6 S – My trousers are the ugliest.

Negatives

1

1 *No vivimos en el norte del país.*
2 No tienen muchos problemas.
3 Mi hermana no come mucha fruta y verduras.
4 Mis amigos de clase no juegan al baloncesto los viernes.
5 Jaime no se levanta a las ocho y media.
6 Mi madre no compró unas botas nuevas.

2

1 c Juan doesn't wear (a) uniform.
2 b María hasn't got an exercise book, nor a ballpoint pen or a ruler.
3 a Ana doesn't do anything to be fit.
4 d Manuel never does any exercise.
5 f Antonia never writes emails.
6 e Javier never travels by plane.
7 g Roberto doesn't speak Italian or German.

3

1 *Elena **nunca** come carne.*
2 No bebo **nada** por la mañana.
3 En el colegio no hay **ni** biblioteca **ni** piscina.
4 No come **nunca** huevos.
5 Mi madre no escucha a **nadie**.